THE GOVERNMENT'S SPEECH AND THE CONSTITUTION

Governments must speak in order to govern, and so governments have been speaking for as long as there have been governments. The government's speech is at times heroic, at other times banal, and at still other times despicable. Because the government's speech has changed the world for better and for worse, it deserves our attention, at times our appreciation, and at times our concern. When we discuss constitutional law, we usually focus on the constitutional rules that apply to what the government *does*. Far less clear are the constitutional rules that apply to what the government *says*. When does the speech of this unusually powerful speaker violate our constitutional rights and liberties? More specifically, when does the government's speech facilitate democratic self-governance and contribute to the marketplace of ideas – and when does the government's expression instead interfere with public discourse? Under what circumstances does the government's speech threaten liberty or equality? And when, if ever, does the Constitution prohibit our government from lying to us? This book considers these questions, and more.

Helen Norton holds the Ira C. Rothgerber Chair in Constitutional Law at the University of Colorado School of Law, where she teaches and writes about constitutional law and civil rights. Before entering academia, Professor Norton served as Deputy Assistant Attorney General for Civil Rights at the US Department of Justice.

Cambridge Studies on Civil Rights and Civil Liberties

This series is a platform for original scholarship on US civil rights and civil liberties. It produces books on the normative, historical, judicial, political, and sociological contexts for understanding contemporary legislative, jurisprudential, and presidential dilemmas. The aim is to provide experts, teachers, policymakers, students, social activists, and educated citizens with in-depth analyses of theories, existing and past conditions, and constructive ideas for legal advancements.

General Editor

Alexander Tsesis, Loyola University, Chicago

The Government's Speech and the Constitution

HELEN NORTON

University of Colorado School of Law

CAMBRIDGE
UNIVERSITY PRESS

University Printing House, Cambridge CB2 8BS, United Kingdom

One Liberty Plaza, 20th Floor, New York, NY 10006, USA

477 Williamstown Road, Port Melbourne, VIC 3207, Australia

314-321, 3rd Floor, Plot 3, Splendor Forum, Jasola District Centre, New Delhi - 110025, India

79 Anson Road, #06-04/06, Singapore 079906

Cambridge University Press is part of the University of Cambridge.

It furthers the University's mission by disseminating knowledge in the pursuit of education, learning and research at the highest international levels of excellence.

www.cambridge.org
Information on this title: www.cambridge.org/9781108405621
DOI: 10.1017/9781108278218

First published 2019
First paperback edition 2020

A catalogue record for this publication is available from the British Library

Library of Congress Cataloging in Publication data
NAMES: Norton, Helen L., 1963– author.
TITLE: The government's speech and the Constitution / Helen Norton, University of Colorado Boulder.
DESCRIPTION: Cambridge, United Kingdom ; New York, NY, USA : Cambridge University Press, 2019. | Includes bibliographical references and index.
IDENTIFIERS: LCCN 2019010667 | ISBN 9781108417723 (hardback : alk. paper) | ISBN 9781108405621 (pbk. : alk. paper)
SUBJECTS: LCSH: Freedom of speech–United States. | Communication in public administration–Law and legislation–United States. | United States–Official and employees–Civil rights. | Government information–Law and legislation–United States.
CLASSIFICATION: LCC KF4772 .N67 2019 | DDC 342.73/066–dc23
LC record available at https://lccn.loc.gov/2019010667

ISBN 978-1-108-41772-3 Hardback
ISBN 978-1-108-40562-1 Paperback

For Marianne Craft Norton and the memory of Bob Norton,

And for Kenny

Contents

Acknowledgments   *page* viii

Introduction: The Government's Speech and Why It Matters   1

1   **Determining Whether and When the Government Is
    Speaking (and Why That Matters)**   27

2   **The Government's Speech and Religion**   68

3   **The Government's Speech and Equality**   93

4   **The Government's Speech and Due Process**   127

5   **The Government's Speech, Free Speech, and a Free Press**   156

6   **The Government's Speech and Political Contests**   183

7   **Responding to the Government's Destructive Speech**   212

Conclusion   233

Index   235

Acknowledgments

Writing a book, like many worthy endeavors, is a team sport. A large number of people helped make this book possible – and helped make it better.

For those in our line of work, there may be no greater gift than an engaged, generous, challenging, and thoughtful read of one's work, especially at an early stage. The following friends and colleagues gave me that gift by reading draft chapters and offering their thoughtful comments and support: Rachel Arnow-Richman, Wayne Batchis, Brad Bernthal, Bill Briggs, Hal Bruff, Deb Cantrell, Alan Chen, Ming Chen, Danielle Keats Citron, Rick Collins, Roberto Corrada, Kristelia Garcia, Amy Griffin, Sean Helle, Sharon Jacobs, Marcia Johnson-Blanco, Beto Juarez, Margot Kaminski, Derek Kiernan-Johnson, Craig Konnoth, Sarah Krakoff, Ben Levin, Greg Magarian, John Davis Malloy, Amy Marshak, Toni Massaro, Scott Moss, Justin Pidot, Nantiya Ruan, Andrew Schwartz, Michael Scott, Joe Sellers, Scott Skinner-Thompson, Sloan Speck, Jane Thompson, Eric Van Vliet, Judy Winston, Claudia Withers, and that most remarkable book club: Kenny Johnson, Karen Schmidt, Susie Lee Stadnik, and Gina Maria Trinchero.

I've been writing about the government's speech for quite some time. Parts of this book build on, draw from, revise, and replace explanations and arguments that first appeared in earlier work (one coauthored with Danielle Keats Citron), including the following:

Not for Attribution: Government's Interest in Protecting the Integrity of Its Own Expression, 37 U.C. DAVIS. L. REV. 1317 (2004)

The Measure of Government Speech: Identifying Expression's Source, 88 BOSTON U. L. REV. 587 (2008)

Constraining Public Employee Speech: Government's Control of Its Workers' Speech to Protect Its Own Expression, 59 DUKE L.J. 1 (2009)

Government Speech 2.0., 87 Denv. U. L. Rev. 899 (2010) (with Danielle Keats Citron)

Campaign Speech Law with a Twist: When Government Is the Speaker, Not the Regulator, 61 Emory L.J. 209 (2011)

Imaginary Threats to Government's Expressive Interests, 61 Case Western L. Rev. 1265 (2011)

Government Speech in Transition, 57 S. Dak. L. Rev. 421 (2012)

The Equal Protection Implications of Government's Hateful Speech, 54 Wm. & Mary L. Rev. 159 (2012)

The Government's Lies and the Constitution, 91 Ind. L.J. 73 (2015)

Government Speech and Political Courage, 68 Stan. L. Rev. Online 61 (2015)

Government Speech and the War on Terror, 86 Fordham L. Rev. 543 (2017)

Remedies and the Government's Constitutionally Harmful Speech, 9 Con-LawNOW 49 (2018)

The Government's Lies and the Press Clause, 89 U. Colo. L. Rev. 453 (2018)

The Government's Manufacture of Doubt, 16 First Am. L. Rev. 342 (2018)

That earlier work was informed and improved not only by many of those listed above but also by many other friends and colleagues, including Joseph Blocher, Fred Boom, Anna Spain Bradley, Violeta Chapin, Caroline Mala Corbin, Aya Gruber, Melissa Hart, RonNell Andersen Jones, Heidi Kitrosser, Eva LaBarge, Eddie Renner, Pierre Schlag, Catherine Smith, Geof Stone, Tracy Thomas, Phil Weiser, Sonja West, and Ahmed White.

I am indebted to many wonderful research assistants. Hannah Armentrout and Shelby Morbach provided tireless and top-notch research, writing, and cite checking on draft chapters. The terrific students who helped me develop earlier, related work include Cassady Adams, Jordan Bunch, Katherine Decker, Mike Imdieke, Adam Kutniewski, Lydia Lulkin, Jessica Reed-Baum, Eddie Ramirez, and Katherine Struthers.

Heartfelt thanks to Jane Thompson, Matt Zafiratos, and the Wise Law Library faculty and staff for their cheerful excellence, and to the entire Colorado Law community for its support.

I'm also grateful to Alex Tsesis for the opportunity to participate in the Cambridge University Press series on constitutional rights and civil liberties, and for his longtime friendship.

Finally, my thanks and love to Kenny, quite possibly the world's greatest guy.

Introduction

The Government's Speech and Why It Matters

Governments must speak in order to govern, and so governments have been speaking for as long as there have been governments. The stone inscriptions on Nebuchadnezzar's Ishtar Gate, for instance, include sixth-century BC boasts of the King's reign and its many achievements.[1] Governments still boast today, just as they also speak in many other ways. Consider a few examples:

- The Surgeon General's report documenting the dangers of tobacco.
- A town council's prayers to open its meetings.
- The Johnson and Nixon administrations' lies about what the United States was doing, and why, in Vietnam.
- Exhortations from the Forest Service's Smokey Bear that "only *you* can prevent wildfires."
- The District of Columbia's motto of protest, "End Taxation Without Representation," displayed on its license plates.
- Apologies, decades after the fact, by Congress, the president, and the solicitor general for the federal government's World War II internment of Japanese Americans.
- President Trump's tweets attacking the press, the judiciary, and many other institutions and individuals.
- A school board's resolution opposing school voucher legislation, posted on its website.
- A Senate subcommittee report entitled "The Employment of Homosexuals and Other Sex Perverts in Government."

The government's expressive choices – and by this I mean the government's choices about whether and when to speak, what to say, how to say it, and to

---

[1]   *See* Brian Fagan, A Little History of Archaeology 9–10 (2018).

1

whom – are neither inevitably good nor evil, but instead vary widely in their effects as well as their motives. The government's expressive choices are at times heroic, at other times banal, and at still other times despicable. Through its speech, the government informs, challenges, teaches, and inspires. Through its speech, the government also threatens, deceives, distracts, and vilifies. Because the government's speech has changed the world for better and for worse, it deserves our attention, at times our appreciation, and at times our concern.

The government's speech can deliver great value. Through its expression, the government disseminates vital information to the public on a broad range of topics. Think again of the Surgeon General's groundbreaking 1964 report on the dangers of cigarettes, a report that challenged the tobacco industry's efforts to discount the mounting medical evidence linking its products to serious health conditions.[2] The government's speech also illuminates the workings of our democracy. Regardless of whether you love or hate the government's views, its expression generates important conversations and helps inform the public's political choices. The State of the Union address reveals the executive's values and policy priorities to the American public, as does a president's resort to the bully pulpit to advocate for everything from environmental conservation to free enterprise, immigration reform to child nutrition. The government's voice can assert moral and political leadership in ongoing battles for equality: consider President Lyndon Johnson's nationally televised promise that "We Shall Overcome" in the midst of 1960s civil rights battles,[3] and President George W. Bush's repudiation of anti-Muslim bigotry in a speech at a mosque immediately after the 9/11 attacks.[4]

But sometimes the government's speech instead wreaks grave harm. This can be the case of its lies told to resist legal and political accountability for its misconduct or to enable the exercise of its powers to imprison or to deploy lethal force. The government's speech can silence dissent: think of the FBI's efforts to muzzle antiwar protestors and other governmental critics during the 1950s and 1960s by spreading false information about them to their families, neighbors, and employers.[5] The government's speech can exclude and divide – and worse. In 1907, Mississippi Governor James Vardaman declared: "[I]f it is necessary every Negro in the state will be lynched; it will be done to

---

[2] *See* U.S. Dep't of Health, Education, & Welfare, Smoking and Health: Report of the Advisory Committee to the Surgeon General of the Public Health Service (1964).

[3] President Lyndon B. Johnson, Special Message to Congress (Mar. 15, 1965).

[4] President George W. Bush, Remarks by the President at Islamic Center of Washington, D.C. (Sept. 17, 2001).

[5] *See* Geoffrey R. Stone, Perilous Times: Free Speech in Wartime 490 (2004).

maintain white supremacy."[6] As of 2018, Alabama and Texas required their public schools' sex education curricula to include "[a]n emphasis, in a factual manner and from a public health perspective, that homosexuality is not a lifestyle acceptable to the general public."[7]

Because the government's speech holds the potential for great value as well as substantial harm, the constitutional rules that apply to it are important. When we discuss constitutional law, we usually focus on the constitutional rules that apply to what the government *does*. Far less clear are the constitutional rules that apply to what the government *says*. We need to empower our government to serve and protect us, even while we reasonably fear, and should take steps to protect ourselves from, its power to harm us. When does the speech of this unusually powerful speaker violate our constitutional rights and liberties? More specifically, when does the government's speech facilitate the public's democratic self-governance and contribute to the marketplace of ideas – and when does the government's expression instead interfere with public discourse? Under what circumstances does the government's speech threaten our liberty or our equality? And when, if ever, does the Constitution prohibit our government from lying to us? This book considers these questions, and more.

THE CONSTITUTIONAL IMPLICATIONS OF THE GOVERNMENT'S SPEECH

When we see or hear the terms "government" and "speech" in close proximity, we often think of the constitutional issues triggered when the government regulates *our* expression. This book focuses instead on the constitutional issues sparked by the government's own speech. When I refer to the *government's* speech, I mean the collective speech of a governmental body like an agency or a legislature. I also mean the speech of an individual who speaks for such a body (like the Secretary of Health and Human Services, or a congressional committee chair), as well as an individual who speaks when backed by the government's power (like a police officer interrogating a suspect). I put aside for now the speech of an individual government official or legislator when she expresses her own views in a personal, rather than governmental, capacity (although, as we'll see, the line between the two is not always bright).

---

[6] *See* CHRIS DANIELSON, THE COLOR OF POLITICS: RACISM IN THE AMERICAN POLITICAL ARENA TODAY 43 (2013).

[7] ALA. CODE § 16-40A-2(c)(8) (2017); TEX. HEALTH & SAFETY CODE ANN. § 85.007(b)(2) (West 2017) & 163.002(8) (West 2017).

The Constitution itself at times expressly commands the federal government's speech. Article I, for instance, requires Congress to speak in ways that make certain governmental actions transparent to the public. It directs that "a regular Statement and Account of the Receipts and Expenditures of all public Money shall be published from time to time,"[8] and that "[e]ach House shall keep a Journal of its Proceedings, and from time to time publish the same" (today this journal is called the *Congressional Record*).[9]

The Constitution sometimes requires the federal government to speak by consulting with other government actors. Article I charges a president who vetoes a bill to return it "with his Objections to that House in which it shall have originated."[10] Article II commands that the president "shall from time to time give to the Congress Information of the State of the Union, and recommend to their Consideration such Measures as he shall judge necessary and expedient."[11] (As we'll see, presidents remain free to choose when, where, and how to deliver their assessments of the State of the Union.) Article II also empowers, but does not compel, the president to "require the Opinion, in writing, of the principal Officer in each of the executive Departments upon any Subject relating to the Duties of their respective Offices."[12]

The Constitution also affirmatively *protects* government speech that takes the form of legislative debate, providing senators and representatives with immunity from criminal prosecution and civil liability for "any Speech or Debate in either House."[13] The Speech or Debate Clause thus prevents executive and judicial branch interference with the federal legislature's independence. "For Congress to compete effectively with the other branches in the public sphere, it must be able to communicate with the public," legal scholar Josh Chafetz observes. "This means that its members must be able to air their views publicly, without the threat of prosecution by the other branches."[14]

The Constitution also identifies, and sometimes requires, what some call "speech acts" or "performative utterances" – in other words, speech that, once uttered, accomplishes a change in legal status. Examples include Congress's Article I power to declare war; this declaration means that the United States is now a belligerent.[15] Article II requires that the president take an oath of office before undertaking service; once pronounced, this oath completes an individual's transition from private citizen to president.[16] And a written declaration of

[8] U.S. Const. art. I, § 9, cl. 7.   [9] U.S. Const. art. I, § 5, cl. 3.
[10] U.S. Const. art. I, § 7, cl. 2.   [11] U.S. Const. art. II, § 3.
[12] U.S. Const. art. II, § 2, cl. 1.   [13] U.S. Const. art. I, § 6, cl. 1.
[14] Josh Chafetz, Congress's Constitution 231 (2017).   [15] U.S. Const. art. I, § 8, cl. 11.
[16] U.S. Const. art. II, § 1, cl. 7.

a president's inability to discharge the duties of that office, as provided by the Twenty-Fifth Amendment, initiates the process through which a president may be replaced.[17]

And the Supreme Court has occasionally interpreted the Constitution to compel the government's speech to make specific constitutional protections meaningful. In the now-canonical *Miranda* v. *Arizona*, the Court required law enforcement officials to disclose available constitutional protections (like the right to remain silent and the right to counsel) to those in their custody.[18]

So the Constitution sometimes *requires* the government to speak. But for the most part, the government's speech reflects its *choice* of whether, when, and how to deploy its expressive power. What are the constitutional rules that govern those choices?

I propose a framework for thinking about this question that requires us to wrestle with what I will call "first-stage" and "second-stage" government speech problems. First-stage problems force us to untangle competing governmental and private claims to the same speech: this is important because the constitutional rules that apply to the government when it speaks itself are very different from those that apply to the government when it regulates others' speech. If we determine that the government itself is speaking (rather than regulating others' speech), we then turn to second-stage problems: these consider whether and when the government's speech infringes specific constitutional rights.[19]

First-Stage Government Speech Problems: Determining Whether and When the Government Is Speaking

The First Amendment's Free Speech Clause forbids the government from regulating nongovernmental parties' speech based on viewpoint. But the government itself must speak if it is to govern. For this reason, the Supreme Court's government speech doctrine (that is, its body of precedent considering these first-stage problems) generally shields the government's own expression from Free Speech Clause challenge by those who object to the government's views; the Court identifies political checks, rather than First Amendment litigation, as the appropriate recourse for those unhappy with their government's expressive choices. Because the constitutional standards that apply to the government as a speaker differ so dramatically from those that apply to the

---

[17] U.S. Const. amend. XXV.   [18] Miranda v. Arizona, 384 U.S. 436 (1966).

[19] This book focuses on the constitutional rights provided by the Establishment, Equal Protection, Due Process, Free Speech, and Press Clauses. Other constitutional provisions may also constrain the government's speech under certain circumstances, like the Take Care and Guarantee Clauses, but I set those possibilities aside for now.

government as a regulator of other parties' speech, the first step in our constitutional analysis is figuring out whether the government itself is speaking or instead regulating others' speech.

How do we decide whether contested speech is the government's or instead the speech of a nongovernmental party regulated by the government? As the key to solving first-stage government speech problems, I propose what I'll call the transparency principle. I focus on transparency because the government's speech is more valuable and less dangerous to the public when its governmental source is apparent. In other words, the government's expressive choices are valuable, and thus insulated from First Amendment scrutiny, because of what they offer the public: information that furthers democratic self-governance by enabling the public to identify and thus evaluate their government's priorities and performance. Because the public can hold the government politically accountable for its expressive choices only when it actually understands the contested expression as the government's, we should require the government's transparency as a condition of claiming the government speech defense. And when the governmental source of a message *is* clear, we should understand the Constitution to permit the government to control the content of that message – but not to restrict public comments on that message based on their viewpoint. The transparency principle also applies to the government's efforts to restrict the speech of its own workforce: in my view, we should understand the First Amendment to permit the government to control the speech of its employees as its own only when it has specifically commissioned or hired those employees to deliver a transparently governmental viewpoint.

Many courts and commentators think of the government speech doctrine as dealing only with these first-stage problems. But we still have work to do. Once we are convinced that the government itself is speaking, then the Free Speech Clause constraints on the government as a regulator – like those that forbid the government from regulating private parties based on their viewpoint – do not apply. But the second step in our constitutional analysis requires us to consider whether and when the government as a *speaker* runs afoul of specific constitutional protections. In other words, some constitutional limits still apply to the government as a speaker, even though they differ from those that apply to the government as a regulator.

Second-Stage Government Speech Problems: Determining When the Government's Speech, By Itself, Violates the Constitution

Second-stage government speech problems focus on whether and when specific constitutional provisions (like the Establishment Clause, the Equal

Protection Clause, the Due Process Clause, and more) restrain the government's speech. Second-stage problems present challenging constitutional questions in part because the government's speech involves an exercise of governmental power distinct from its lawmaking and other regulatory actions that control behavior through, for example, financial or criminal penalties; some describe this distinction as one between the government's "soft" and "hard" powers.[20] The Surgeon General's report on the dangers of tobacco exemplifies the government's speech, its soft power: the government informed but did not imprison, fine, or tax. Contrast, as an illustration of the government's hard power, Congress's later enactment of a law requiring tobacco manufacturers to publish the Surgeon General's warning on their packages and advertisements, with the failure to comply punishable by a $10,000 fine.[21] As another example, the original Pentagon Papers themselves – the series of reports commissioned by Defense Secretary Robert McNamara to study the history of the United States' involvement in Vietnam – represented the government's own speech, entirely apart from its lawmaking or other regulatory action. But the Nixon administration later exercised its hard powers when it sought – and for a few days, federal courts acquiesced in granting – an injunction to stop *The New York Times* and other newspapers from publishing the papers.[22] New Hampshire's choice of "Live Free or Die" as its motto represents the state's expressive choice, its speech, as does a school board's decision to start the day with the Pledge of Allegiance. But when the government compels private (that is, nongovernmental) parties on pain of punishment to display the state motto or repeat the Pledge, it exercises its traditional regulatory powers, which triggers the Free Speech Clause rules that apply to the government as regulator, rather than speaker.[23]

"Hard" and "soft" power are not legal terms of art, but instead metaphors that describe relative points on a continuum of government power. Even so, it's not always so easy to separate the two. And some things share both qualities at the same time depending on where you look, like an energetic kitten with the fur of an ermine and the teeth of a shark. Stroke it when it's at rest: it's soft. Receive its fangs with your flesh: it's hard (and sharp). The government's speech similarly comes in a variety of textures, some more flinty than others.

---

[20] *E.g.,* Josh Chafetz, *Congress's Constitution*, 160 U. PA. L. REV. 715, 721 (2012); Jacob E. Gerson & Eric A. Posner, *Soft Law: Lessons from Congressional Practice*, 61 STAN. L. REV. 573, 577 (2008).

[21] *See* Public Health Smoking Act of 1970, Pub. L. 91-222, 84 Stat. 87 (1970), http://uscode.house .gov/statutes/pl/91/222.pdf.

[22] *See* New York Times Co. v. United States, 403 U.S. 713 (1971).

[23] *See* Wooley v. Maynard, 430 U.S. 705 (1977).

To help us think about these second-stage government speech problems – that is, whether and when the government's speech, by itself, violates our constitutional rights – I suggest that we ask and answer a series of questions about the consequences of, and the motivations underlying, the government's speech. Some of these questions focus on the different types of harmful effects, or injuries, that the government's speech may inflict upon its listeners. When we look at the effects of the government's speech, we ask whether the targets of the government's speech suffered harm, whether we should hold the government responsible for causing that harm, and whether a specific constitutional provision bars the government from inflicting that particular harm. Some of these questions focus instead on the various purposes underlying the government's speech. When we look at the government's motives for speaking, we ask why the government chose to speak in a certain way, and whether the constitutional provision at issue denies the government the power to speak for that reason. Let's preview these questions in a bit more detail:

When does the government's speech change its targets' choices or opportunities to their disadvantage, and does the Constitution bar the government from causing those changes?

Here we consider whether and when the government's speech changes its listeners' choices or opportunities in ways that would violate a specific constitutional provision if the government accomplished those same changes through its lawmaking or other regulatory actions. Think, for example, of the government's threats that silence dissenters as effectively as jailing them, the government's lies that pressure its targets into relinquishing their constitutional rights as effectively as denying those rights outright, or the government's religious speech that coerces listeners' participation in prayer or other religious observance as effectively as fining or taxing those who fail to partake. This approach sometimes requires us to wrestle with difficult questions about the requisite causal connection between the government's speech and harm to its targets' choices and opportunities.

When does the government's speech inflict expressive, or dignitary, harm upon its targets, and does the Constitution bar the government from causing those harms?

Here we remain focused on the effects of the government's speech but consider instead whether it inflicts expressive, or dignitary, harm upon its targets. Rather than asking whether the government's speech has interfered with its targets' choices and opportunities, we query whether the government's speech has injured their dignity by treating them as outsiders to the political community, by failing to treat them with equal concern and respect because of who they are or what they believe. Think, for instance, of the government's speech that communicates hostility to or disrespect for its targets based on their religion (or nonreligion), or their race, gender, or sexual orientation. Under this approach, we grapple with difficult questions in determining when the government's speech delivers a message of denigration or disrespect, and whether the relevant constitutional provision protects us from those harms.

What are the purposes underlying the government's speech, and does the Constitution bar the government from seeking to accomplish those purposes?

Here we turn from the possible harmful consequences of the government's speech to consider instead the government's reasons for speaking. Sometimes the government speaks to accomplish objectives that some, perhaps many, of us find morally wrongful or constitutionally illegitimate. This can be the case, for example, of the government's speech intended to advance some religions at the expense of others, to harm members of unpopular groups, or to interfere with constitutionally protected rights. Under this approach, we must identify the government's reasons for speaking and determine whether the constitutional provision at issue denies the government the power to speak for those reasons.[24]

These questions reflect different approaches to the second-stage constitutional law problems triggered by the government's speech. As we'll see, our theory of a specific constitutional provision – in other words, our understanding of the values it protects – often drives our preferences among these approaches. And because different constitutional provisions often protect very different values, our preferences among the approaches may differ from provision to provision. By applying these approaches in different settings in the chapters that follow, I hope to illuminate their various strengths as well as their limitations in solving second-stage government speech problems. My point is not that any one of these approaches is necessarily better than another, nor to persuade you to answer these questions in any particular way; I hope instead to show that this series of questions gives us a helpful framework for thinking about these problems.

---

[24] In this book, I'll generally use the terms "intentions," "purposes," and "motivations" interchangeably. *See* Richard H. Fallon, Jr., *Constitutionally Forbidden Legislative Intent*, 130 HARV. L. REV. 523, 534–535 (2016) (observing that courts often use these terms synonymously). To be sure, we can, and in certain contexts should, recognize shades of distinction among these terms, but for now I put those subtleties aside.

The difficulties of these questions counsel that we proceed with care. We may wonder whether efforts to constrain the government's speech through constitutional litigation will deter government speakers from engaging in important expression. Indeed, a central thesis of this book is that the government's speech often delivers great value: the more the government speaks, often the better for the public. We may worry that the government's critics will exploit constitutional litigation to attack the government's speech for partisan, rather than principled, reasons. We may fear that efforts to identify constitutional limits on the government's speech will force courts to undertake difficult, even dangerous assessments of the political branches' expressive choices. We may query whether claims that the government's speech violates the Constitution are even justiciable – that is, whether the federal courts have the constitutional power to decide them. Difficult government speech problems force us to choose between holding our government constitutionally accountable for its destructive expressive choices and hamstringing the government's communication in counterproductive ways. This is no easy choice.

That constitutional litigation is a limited and imperfect tool for curbing abuses of the government's expressive powers, however, does not mean that it is without value. The ugliest of the government's expressive choices are often those least susceptible to political redress, as the government sometimes speaks in damaging ways precisely because those messages appeal to its preferred constituencies. This can be the case, for example, when the government targets vulnerable communities or unpopular dissenters. An independent judiciary offers a crucial check on the government's politically successful choices that undermine key constitutional values.[25]

As a constitutional scholar, teacher, and lawyer, I view these problems primarily through the lens of constitutional law. Even so, I acknowledge the great value offered by other disciplines in thinking about them. Philosophers and political scientists, for instance, can help us understand when the government's speech is good (or not) as a matter of moral or democratic theory, and behavioral experts can help us understand how speech shapes its targets' responses, for better and for worse. I hope that anyone interested in the uses and abuses of government power will engage these questions.

For these reasons, throughout this book I shine a spotlight on the many shapes and forms of the government's expression to help us recognize its

---

[25] *See* West Virginia State Bd. of Educ. v. Barnette, 319 U.S. 624, 637 (1943) (explaining that the Constitution "protects the citizen against the State itself and all of its creatures.... .[T]hese have, of course, important, delicate and highly discretionary functions, but none that they may not perform within the limits of the Bill of Rights.").

presence in, and assess its impact on, our daily lives. The more we notice the government's speech, the more clearly we can think about its constitutional implications. So before we begin to grapple with the hard and important constitutional problems raised by the government's speech, let's start to attune our ear to the government's voice – its timbre and pitch, its range and register.

THE ABUNDANCE AND DIVERSITY OF THE GOVERNMENT'S EXPRESSION

The government is unique among speakers because of its coercive power as sovereign, its considerable resources, its privileged access to key information, and its wide variety of speaking roles as policymaker, commander-in-chief, employer, educator, health care provider, property owner, and more.[26] Attending to the government's speech in its many manifestations helps us evaluate its potential for both value and harm. And once you start to listen for the government's voice, you'll hear it everywhere, sometimes in surprising places.

The Government's Many and Varied Audiences and Speakers

This book focuses on the speech of American governments to American audiences, but the targets of the government's speech also include our foreign allies, neutrals, and enemies. The government's audiences include other governmental actors too, as federalism (the vertical division of power among the federal, state, and local governments) and separation of powers principles (the horizontal division of power among the legislative, executive, and judicial branches) force different government actors to talk with each other. Sometimes the government's listeners are entirely internal, as can be the case when the government does not intend its speech to reach the public at large: recall the Defense Department's original Pentagon Papers, a series of reports and studies commissioned by then-Secretary of Defense Robert McNamara to

---

[26] *See* JOSEPH TUSSMAN, GOVERNMENT AND THE MIND 20 (1977) ("A Churchill is honored not only for his attempt to warn of things to come but for his capacity to make the country see itself as involved in a meaningful struggle, to lift its spirit in adversity, to sustain its awareness of its destined task. Apart from war, our great political heroes are often awakeners and summoners, creating the appropriate mood, expressing the necessary idea. And even routinely we expect government to direct attention to problems, to make us think about energy or pollution or population or crime. In various ways, legislators, executives, judges try to shape and reshape public awareness. Without claiming monopoly, government must, at least, enter the struggle for attention.").

document the history of the United States' involvement in Vietnam, or the government's diplomatic cables revealed by WikiLeaks.

The government itself is composed of sundry speakers, as "the government" can refer to any of many public entities and officials within the United States. When we think about the government's speech, we often focus on the president's expression, as the president is among the most visible of governmental speakers. But legislative and judicial branch speakers – as well as speakers from all levels of federal, state, and local governments – also demand our notice.[27]

Agencies' Speech

Federal, state, and local governmental agencies are now among the most prolific and significant of government speakers, bringing the government's speech into our everyday lives. The power of agencies' speech first became clear in the early twentieth century, when the federal Committee on Public Information (CPI) relied on expressive technologies then both old and new – posters, traveling exhibits, speeches, books, pamphlets, movies, and newsreels – to mobilize public support for the nation's World War I efforts. Writing in the Great War's immediate aftermath, reporter and political commentator Walter Lippmann portrayed the CPI as undertaking "the largest and most intensive effort to carry quickly a fairly uniform set of ideas to all the people of the nation,"[28] an effort that inspired some and alarmed others. More recently, historian Susan Brewer described the agency's "inner struggle between educating and inflaming the public," and how that struggle, in turn, led to damaging consequences: "The slogan, '100% American,' meant to be inclusive, was turned into a weapon against Americans suspected of being traitors because of their ethnic heritage."[29]

The expansion of the modern administrative state fueled enormous growth in agencies' expression. In the peace immediately following the Great War, for instance, agricultural extension agencies reached out to inform "farmers and

---

[27] As noted earlier, when I refer to the *government's* speech, I mean the collective speech of a governmental body like an agency or a legislature, or the speech of an individual empowered to speak for such a body – like a congressional committee chair, a police chief, or the Secretary of Health and Human Services. I do not include the speech of an individual government official or legislator when she speaks only for herself. To be sure, the line between the two is not always bright, as some of these examples show.

[28] WALTER LIPPMANN, PUBLIC OPINION 46–47 (1922).

[29] SUSAN A. BREWER, WHY AMERICA FIGHTS: PATRIOTIC AND WAR PROPAGANDA FROM THE PHILIPPINES TO IRAQ 57, 69 (2009).

farm women" about new farming practices through meetings and home visits, bulletins, exhibits, letters, and radio announcements; the agencies measured their success by "the extent to which improved practices have been adopted."[30] During the New Deal, federal agencies' speech celebrated the work of the Civilian Conservation Corps, educated the public about the spread of sexually transmissible diseases, and explained the terms and benefits of the newly enacted Social Security insurance program to its participants.[31]

Agencies' speech today is plentiful and pervasive. In "the country's longest-running public service announcement," the Forest Service's Smokey Bear implores us to take action to prevent wildfires.[32] Meanwhile the Department of State issues travel alerts, the Internal Revenue Service instructs us how to track the progress of our tax returns, the Federal Emergency Management Administration tells us how to prepare for natural disasters, and the Centers for Disease Control and Prevention advise us about the latest flu season. On the state and local level, city police departments post crime statistics, state transportation departments offer traffic reports available by phone and online, and much more.

Legislatures' Speech

Legislatures speak too. Through resolutions, for example, both chambers of Congress articulate their views on a dizzying array of topics both large and small, and state and local legislatures do the same. Virginia's House of Burgesses, for instance, passed a resolution objecting to the Stamp Act, and then watched its expressive campaign spread across colonial legislatures.[33] A few decades later, with the help of James Madison and Thomas Jefferson, the Virginia state legislature passed a resolution protesting the federal Alien and Sedition Acts as an affront to free speech rights.[34] More recently, Vermont's legislature resolved that the "State flavor shall be maple from the

---

[30] *See* U.S. Department of Agriculture, Technical Bulletins Nos. 101–125, Tech. Bull No. 106, February 1929, M.C. Wilson, Extension Methods and Their Relative Effectiveness 1–22.

[31] *See* JAMES C. McCAMY, GOVERNMENT PUBLICITY: ITS PRACTICE IN FEDERAL ADMINISTRATION 22–78 (1939).

[32] *See* ERIC RUTKOW, AMERICAN CANOPY: TREES, FORESTS, AND THE MAKING OF A NATION 267 (2013) (Smokey "remains an integral part of forest fire prevention in America. Various estimates have suggested that the character's impact in decreasing forest fires has saved the country tens of billions in forest damage.").

[33] *See* EDMUND S. MORGAN, BIRTH OF THE REPUBLIC 1763–1789 49 (3d ed. 1992).

[34] "Virginia Resolution – Alien and Sedition Acts," The Avalon Project, 2008 [https://perma.cc/B8XC-22VK].

Vermont sugar maple tree,"[35] Missouri declared the fiddle as the state's official musical instrument,[36] and California's legislature announced the saber-toothed cat as its official fossil.[37] More seriously, local governments debate whether to issue proclamations honoring "Gun Violence Awareness Day" or instead "Firearms Awareness and Safety Day,"[38] and in 2018 the Senate reaffirmed "that the press is not the enemy of the people,"[39] notwithstanding President Trump's assertions to the contrary.[40]

Legislative committees speak through their reports. The many examples include the 1970s work by the Senate Select Committee to Study Governmental Operations with Respect to Intelligence Activities (often known as the Church Committee, named after its chair, Senator Frank Church) that revealed the executive branch's widespread domestic surveillance of Americans.[41]

Legislatures' speech – like that of other governmental speakers – often takes the form of one-way communications like resolutions and reports. But sometimes the government's speech involves rebuttals, dialogue, conversations, and other forms of counterspeech. Consider the back-and-forth between President Andrew Jackson and the Congress.[42] Jackson's 1832 annual message on the state of the union (itself an example of government speech) included an attack on the Bank of the United States in which he disputed the Bank's ability to keep the government's deposits secure. The House of Representatives responded with governmental speech of its own: a resolution expressing the body's confidence in the Bank. In yet another exercise of government expression, the Senate then voted to censure Jackson, expressing its disapproval in what remains the only congressional censure of a president in American history. An angry Jackson retorted with still more speech through his "*solemn Protest* ... to be placed on the files of the executive department and to be

[35] 1 Vt. Stat. Ann. § 510 (1993).   [36] Mo. Ann. Stat. § 10.080 (West 1987).
[37] Cal. Gov't Code § 425.7 (West 2018).
[38] Sam Lounsberry, *Longmont Mayor Didn't Read Gun Rights Decree to Maintain "Cohesiveness,"* Boulder Daily Camera (Sept. 15, 2018, 04:55 PM) [https://perma.cc/P7Y3-YKGY].
[39] S. Res. 607 (115th Cong. (2018).
[40] Matea Gold & Jenna Johnson, *Trump Calls the Media 'the Enemy of the American People,'* Wash. Post. (Feb. 17, 2017), https://www.washingtonpost.com/news/postpolitics/wp/2017/02/17/trump-calls-the-media-the-enemy-of-the-american-people/ [https://perma.cc/7JVY-PXH6].
[41] *See* S. Rep. No. 94-755, bk. III, at 735–736 (1976).
[42] For a detailed discussion of these events, *see* Harold H. Bruff, Untrodden Ground: How Presidents Interpret the Constitution 99–105 (2015).

transmitted to the Senate."[43] Legislative oversight presents another example of government speech as a dialogue. As Josh Chafetz explains, "The aggressive questioning of an official, a nominee, or a private citizen, or the releasing of a critical (or supportive) report are mechanisms by which the congressional houses can make the public case for their own trustworthiness, and therefore for augmenting their own power."[44]

The Judiciary's Speech

In an important sense, the judiciary is defined by judges' speech. We often describe the judiciary's powers in terms of its expression: the judiciary holds the power of the pen, rather than that of the sword or purse. This includes not only its power to issue judgments, orders, and binding precedent backed by the state's coercive force, but also its softer power to write dicta, concurrences, and dissents. To illustrate, a federal appellate court recently added a footnote to one of its opinions to remonstrate a trial judge for sexist comments in the proceedings under review, comments that the appellate judges described as "demeaning, inappropriate, and beneath the dignity of a federal judge."[45]

Early judicial speech included grand jury charges directed not only to litigants but also to the American public, where federal judges weighed in on a wide range of contemporary issues through the equivalent of "informal advisory opinions."[46] These expressive efforts quickly met with outcry and opposition, as Supreme Court Justice and partisan Federalist Samuel Chase faced (and survived) impeachment proceedings for his use of grand jury charges to attack the Republican Party and its policies.[47] In the twentieth century, Chief Justice Charles Evan Hughes spoke for the Supreme Court with his letter to the Senate Judiciary Committee refuting President Roosevelt's claims that the nine-Justice Court was struggling to handle its workload; many considered his letter to be key in cohering opposition to

---

[43] President Jackson's Message of Protest to the Senate (April 15, 1834) (emphasis in original), *in* 3 A Compilation of the Messages and Papers of the Presidents 1288–1312 (James D. Richardson ed., 1897).

[44] JOSH CHAFETZ, CONGRESS'S CONSTITUTION 197–198 (2017).

[45] U.S. v. Swenson, 894 F.3d 677, 681 n.3 (5th Cir. 2018).

[46] *See* RICHARD DAVIS, JUSTICES AND JOURNALISTS: THE U.S. SUPREME COURT AND THE MEDIA 47 (2011).

[47] *See* Lynn H. Rambo, *When Should the First Amendment Protect Judges from Their Unethical Speech?*, 79 OHIO ST. L.J. 279, 285–286 (2018) ("Chase's impeachment (and near conviction) seems to have persuaded the judiciary that its grand jury charges, and other judicial appearances, should no longer include overtly political speeches.").

FDR's Court-packing proposal.[48] Today the Chief Justice and the Judicial
Conference regularly speak for the federal judiciary to Congress and other
audiences.[49]

The judiciary's expressive norms often vary from those of other government
speakers in their greater tendency toward formality and deliberation. Judges
(and government lawyers) are also unlike other government speakers in that
their speech is constrained by ethics codes that prohibit, among other things,
their false speech[50] and sometimes their campaign speech.[51] Even so, judicial
speakers increasingly join in a wide range of expressive efforts that include
educating the public about the judicial branch and debating competing
approaches to statutory and constitutional interpretation. As Judge Nancy
Gertner wrote, "[t]he issue is not whether judges should speak – we plainly
have to – but when and more importantly how."[52]

Presidents' Speech

Presidents, of course, also speak in many ways both mighty and slight. Examples
include their speeches and proclamations in which they offer their views on a
wide range of matters, as well as their signing or veto statements in which they
assess the merits and deficiencies of legislation passed by Congress. President
George W. Bush offers an illustration: his proclamations included his celebration of "National Character Counts Week,"[53] while his signing statements
included his view that the Detainee Treatment Act's bar on "cruel, inhuman,

---

[48] *See Reorganization of the Federal Judiciary: Hearings on S. 1392 before the Senate Comm. on
the Judiciary*, 75th Cong. 488–492 (1937) (statement of Senator Burton K. Wheeler) (reading
from Chief Justice Hughes's letter).

[49] *See* 28 U.S.C. § 331 (2012) (requiring the Chief Justice to submit the Judicial Conference's
annual report on the federal courts to Congress, along with any recommendations for
legislation).

[50] E.g., MODEL CODE OF JUDICIAL CONDUCT R. 4.1(A)(11) (2007) (prohibiting judges and judicial
candidates from "knowingly, or with reckless disregard for the truth, mak[ing] any false or
misleading statement"); MODEL RULES OF PROF'L CONDUCT R. 4.1(a) (2014) ("In the course of
representing a client a lawyer shall not knowingly[] make a false statement of material fact or
law to a third person[.]").

[51] E.g., *Williams-Yulee v. Fla. Bar*, 135 S. Ct. 1656, 1667 (2015) (upholding Florida's rule
prohibiting judges from engaging in speech soliciting campaign donations); *Myers
v. Thompson*, 192 F. Supp. 3d 1129, 1141–1142 (D. Mont. 2016) (upholding Montana's rule
prohibiting judges and judicial candidates from making knowing or reckless falsehoods).

[52] Nancy Gertner, *To Speak or Not to Speak: Musings on Judicial Silence*, 32 HOFSTRA L. REV.
1147, 1150 (2004).

[53] *See* Brandon Rottinghaus & Adam L. Warner, *Unilateral Orders as Constituency Outreach:
Executive Orders, Proclamations, and the Public Presidency*, 45 PRES. STUD. QTLY. 289, 290
(2015).

and degrading treatment of detainees" did "not interfere with his commander-in-chief authority, implying that Congress cannot prevent the president from ordering subordinates to engage in such treatment during wartime."[54]

Presidents have come to speak more boldly and directly over the years. Because the Framers so feared that charismatic speakers posed grave threats to a democratic state, they sought to limit those speakers' power and influence through norms (that is, customs and traditions) of discourse as well as structural constraints like separation of powers and federalism principles.[55] Starting with George Washington and continuing through most of the nineteenth century, presidents addressed policymakers and the public primarily through written communications that offered greater formality and opportunity for reflection. Thomas Jefferson started what would become a long-standing presidential tradition when he sent his assessment of the State of the Union to Congress in writing rather than through an oral address he felt more appropriate for a monarch.[56] For similar reasons, as legal scholar Harold Bruff explains, Andrew Jackson "made his arguments to the people in the form of official statements such as his annual messages and the Nullification Proclamation, rather than by giving speeches. This formalized process allowed presidential positions on the Constitution to be fully vetted with advisors and crafted for widespread consumption."[57]

An exemplar of thoughtful and restrained presidential rhetoric, Abraham Lincoln largely preferred to address the people through public letters published in the press without the intervention of journalists. Civil War historian Harold Holzer observes: "In an era in which presidential candidates did no public campaigning of their own – tradition forbade it, and the country was yet too vast and unconnected to permit it – the printed word became the chief weapon in battles for the presidency."[58] Communications scholar Mary Stuckey further explains that, during the presidency's early years, "[t]he president was above the public side of politics. For him to engage in public

---

[54] *See* Curtis A. Bradley & Eric A. Posner, *Presidential Signing Statements and Executive Power*, 23 CONST. COMMENT. 307, 357 (2006).

[55] *See* James W. Ceaser, *Demagoguery, Statesmanship, and Presidential Politics*, in THE CONSTITUTIONAL PRESIDENCY 251 (Joseph M. Bessette & Jeffrey K. Tulis eds., 2009) ("The Federalist is filled with grave warnings against flattery and against the 'artful misrepresentations of interested men' who encourage the people to indulge 'the tyranny of their own passions.'"); *id.* at 252 (explaining that the Framers sought to channel presidential communication "away from informal popular orations and towards more deliberative forms of rhetoric").

[56] *See* JEFFREY K. TULIS, THE RHETORICAL PRESIDENCY 56 (1987).

[57] HAROLD H. BRUFF, UNTRODDEN GROUND: HOW PRESIDENTS INTERPRET THE CONSTITUTION 105 (2015).

[58] HAROLD HOLZER, LINCOLN AND THE POWER OF THE PRESS 42 (2014).

politics would have been equivalent to demagoguery; rabble-rousing was not among the virtues that the founders ascribed to a successful president."[59]

Lincoln's successor, Andrew Johnson, provides the exception that demonstrates the pre-twentieth-century rule, as Johnson routinely engaged in direct and informal appeals to the public that his contemporaries found inappropriate, even outrageous. Articles of impeachment passed by the House of Representatives signal how his speech offended prevailing norms of presidential discourse. Ultimately unsuccessful in the Senate, those articles included allegations that President Johnson had made:

> with a loud voice certain intemperate, inflammatory, and scandalous harangues, and did therein utter loud threats and bitter menaces as well against Congress as the laws of the United States ... . Which said utterances, declarations, threats and harangues, highly censurable in any, are peculiarly indecent and unbecoming in the Chief Magistrate of the United States, by means whereof, ... Andrew Johnson has brought the high office of the President of the United States into contempt, ridicule, and disgrace, to the great scandal of all good citizens.[60]

(Just over a century later, another president would face impeachment for misconduct that included his speech, as the House Judiciary Committee's charges included allegations that Richard M. Nixon had made "false or misleading public statements for the purpose of deceiving the people of the United States."[61] Nixon would resign before the full House could vote on the Committee's recommendation.)

Presidents' expressive choices changed significantly in the twentieth century, beginning with Teddy Roosevelt's strategic decision to advocate for his policies directly to the people. Bruff describes Roosevelt's "[u]nprecedented bombardment of Congress with messages calling for legislation on this and funding of that.... . Eventually he learned to work his way indirectly, urging his views on the people until they were ready to pressure their legislators."[62] Woodrow Wilson built on this move, offering important policy statements directly to the citizenry through public speeches with visionary tones. In his Fourteen Points speech, for example, he identified the objectives to be achieved by the Great War, and thus his aspirations for the terms of treaty

---

[59] MARY E. STUCKEY, THE PRESIDENT AS INTERPRETER-IN-CHIEF 17 (1991).

[60] Cong. Globe, 40th Cong., 2d Sess. 1638–1639 (1868).

[61] *See Debate on Articles of Impeachment: Hearings on H. Res. 803 before the H. Comm. On the Judiciary*, 93d Cong., 2d Sess. 153 (1974).

[62] HAROLD H. BRUFF, UNTRODDEN GROUND: HOW PRESIDENTS INTERPRET THE CONSTITUTION 197 (2015).

negotiations. He also reclaimed a dramatic stage for presidential speech by delivering his assessment of the State of the Union to Congress in person, resuscitating the tradition dormant since Jefferson's time (and leaving the Senate "in a frenzy of puzzlement and excitement about the propriety of a presidential visit to their domain"[63]).

Newer communicative technologies further enabled and emboldened this turn in the norms of presidential discourse. Franklin D. Roosevelt "became the first master of the electronic media" with fireside chats broadcast directly to the public, and John F. Kennedy "began the practice of live televised press conferences [because he] wanted to control the news."[64] As political scientist Jeffrey Tulis summarizes this revolution:

> The rhetorical presidency and the understanding of American politics that it signifies are twentieth-century inventions and discoveries. Our pre-twentieth-century polity proscribed the rhetorical presidency as ardently as we prescribe it. . . . Today it is taken for granted that presidents have a *duty* constantly to defend themselves publicly, to promote policy initiatives nationwide, and to inspirit the population. And for many, this presidential "function" is not one duty among many, but rather the heart of the presidency – its essential task.[65]

The Government's Many and Varied Choices About What to Say and How to Say It

As we've seen, governmental speakers' choices about what to say and how to say it have varied dramatically over time, reflecting shifts in technology as well as politics. The earliest governments chiseled their speech onto stone tablets. And governments today still rely on visual displays like monuments, artwork, and architecture to express themselves. A government's display of statues honoring Confederate veterans in its parks or on its streets reflects the government's expressive choice, as does its decision to fly the Confederate flag above its capitol and courthouses. Just as expressive is a government's decision to take down these displays.

Newer technologies now empower government, along with the rest of us, to speak through social media platforms, webcasts, blogs, and more. During the Obama administration, for example, the White House's Office of Digital

---

[63] Carol Gelderman, All the President's Words: The Bully Pulpit and the Creation of the Virtual Presidency 5 (1997).

[64] Harold H. Bruff, Untrodden Ground: How Presidents Interpret the Constitution 231, 294 (2015).

[65] Jeffrey K. Tulis, The Rhetorical Presidency 4–7 (1987).

Services increasingly chose to break presidential news directly to the public through Obama's social media accounts rather than wait for traditional print media to do so. That office also relied on data analytics to "track what United States senators and the people who worked for them, and influenced them, were seeing online –and make sure that no potential negative comment passed without a tweet."[66]

Governmental speakers of all types and at all levels have seized these opportunities (so enthusiastically, in fact, that the Obama administration eventually undertook an effort called TooManyWebsites.Gov, charged with eliminating unnecessary federal websites[67]). The federal Government Accountability Office now tweets a fact a day from its reports (its first fact: "Over 65% of households in the U.S. relied solely or mostly on wireless phones to make and receive phone calls as of 2016.").[68] State and local governments use blogs and social media accounts to communicate with their citizens. Even as you read this, technological developments create new opportunities for the government's speech.

Changes in the means of delivering the government's speech can also lead to changes in the substance and tone of its expression. As Mary Stuckey observed more than a quarter-century ago, "Television does not simply mean that presidents talk more. It also means that they talk differently."[69] Today, Twitter requires brevity and rewards outrageousness – and President Trump often excels at both. Trump himself has celebrated his departures from traditional norms of presidential discourse, innovations that some find resonant and others repellent: "Trump argued over the weekend that his outsized Twitter presence was part of a calculated redefinition of the presidency: 'My use of social media is not Presidential—it's MODERN DAY PRESIDENTIAL'."[70] As just one of many examples, Trump is unusually combative and eager to engage conflict, rather than defuse it, with his speech – a choice that some attribute to his background in entertainment, media, and reality TV

---

[66] David Samuels, *The Storyteller and the President*, N.Y. Times Mag., May 8, 2016, at MM44.

[67] Macon Phillips, *TooManyWebsites.gov* (June 13, 2011), https://obamawhitehouse.archives.gov/blog/2011/06/13/toomanywebsitesgov [https://perma.cc/75ZG-9RC9].

[68] Eric Yoder, *Every Day, GAO to Tweet Just a Fact, Ma'am*, Wash. Post, (Aug. 13, 2018), [https://perma.cc/E8J5-GAJG].

[69] Mary E. Stuckey, The President as Interpreter-in-Chief 2 (1991).

[70] Jill Colvin, *Twitter Battle with Press May Come with a Price*, AP News (July 3, 2017) https://apnews.com/f3838ea7b4c645fb85b61303740cad86.

where the norms of discourse are very different from those of traditional politics – and especially effective in attracting public attention.[71]

The full range of the government's expressive choices includes not only its affirmative speech but also its secrets and its silences. Governmental secrets generally involve the government's decision not to disclose certain facts. Governmental silences, in contrast, reflect the government's decision not to express its views on a contested public policy issue or crisis.

Often these silences signal a failure of governmental nerve and at times its moral abdication. Think, for instance, of the congressional battle from 1835 to 1844 over efforts to enact, and later repeal, a series of parliamentary "gag rules" in which the House forbade its members to discuss – even for a moment – citizen petitions asking Congress to consider abolishing slavery in the District of Columbia. Although Congress assuredly had the constitutional power to consider the matter – even if it lacked the political will to do so – for years overwhelming majorities in Congress deemed the matter literally unspeakable on the House floor. To this end, they enacted rules that "No [such] petition shall be received by this House or entertained in any way whatever," which ensured that any such petition would be automatically laid on the table, without reading, debate, referral, or any of the legislative processes generally applied to citizen petitions. As historian William Lee Miller recounts in his wonderful book on this episode, the story includes the congressional effort to censure former president and then-Congressman John Quincy Adams for his persistence in fighting the gag rule, along with threats to prosecute and even assassinate Adams when he went so far as to present a petition on the floor of Congress signed by enslaved African Americans.[72]

Additional examples of the government's silences abound. During World War II, as Susan Brewer reminds us, "Bowing to the presence of anti-Semitic prejudice in American society, [federal government] officials did not want to reinforce Nazi allegations that the Allies fought on behalf of the Jews. When [they] did refer to German atrocities, [they] frequently avoided naming the victims as Jews."[73] Related silences include President Eisenhower's unwillingness to endorse the Supreme Court's decision and reasoning in *Brown*

---

[71] *See* Daniel W. Drezner, *Why Is Donald Trump so Bad at the Bully Pulpit?*, WASH. POST. (Aug. 14, 2017), http://wapo.st/2w4qic3 [https://perma.cc/6SZL-NBK2].

[72] *See* WILLIAM LEE MILLER, ARGUING ABOUT SLAVERY: THE GREAT BATTLE IN THE UNITED STATES CONGRESS (1996).

[73] SUSAN A. BREWER, WHY AMERICA FIGHTS: PATRIOTIC AND WAR PROPAGANDA FROM THE PHILIPPINES TO IRAQ 125 (2009).

v. *Board of Education.*[74] And the years-long failure of many city and state health departments, as well as the federal government, to speak about AIDS and its threats to public health.[75] And President Trump's reluctance to condemn white supremacists in the aftermath of violence in Charlottesville, Virginia.[76]

Sometimes the government chooses to speak while saying as little as possible: the Federal Reserve Board scrubs its statements to remove any signal of its plans that might trigger market reactions. And consider the following illustration of a governmental speaker's strategic silence for partisan advantage: Thomas Dewey, FDR's opponent during the 1944 presidential campaign, "bought time immediately after one of Roosevelt's radio talks in order to capitalize on Roosevelt's audience. Roosevelt finished his speech five minutes early, leaving dead time between his talk and Dewey's scheduled appearance. The audience turned en masse to other stations."[77] At times the government's expressive forbearance signals self-restraint or discretion. Think here of the Supreme Court Justices' decision not to issue any concurring opinions in *Brown* to bolster the strength and legitimacy of the Court's decision when announced through a single unanimous voice.[78]

As this sketch makes clear, the government's expressive choices – and again, by this I mean the government's choices about whether and when to speak, what to say, how to say it, and to whom – are abundant and diverse. Recognizing their nuances and complexities can help us understand why they deserve our attention and often our concern, as well as what's hard and important about the constitutional questions that they sometimes trigger.

---

[74] *See* NUMAN V. BARTLEY, THE RISE OF MASSIVE RESISTANCE 63 (1969) ("Eisenhower was later to state in his memoirs that the Supreme Court's judgment in the desegregation cases was unquestionably correct. During his years in office, however, the President failed to express publically his approval either of the principle enunciated in the *Brown* decision or of the ruling itself. Since the racial question was the dominant domestic issue of the period, he made many comments on the subject. Yet not once did he endorse the desegregation decision or offer support to those struggling to implement its provisions. 'I do not believe,' the President reiterated, 'it is the function or indeed it is desirable for a President to express his approval or disapproval of any Supreme Court decision.'").

[75] *See* RANDY SHILTS, AND THE BAND PLAYED ON: POLITICS, PEOPLE, AND THE AIDS EPIDEMIC (1987).

[76] Glenn Thrush & Maggie Haberman, *Trump Is Criticized for Not Calling Out White Supremacists*, N.Y. TIMES (Aug. 12, 2017), https://www.nytimes.com/2017/08/12/us/trump-charlottesville-protest-nationalist-riot.html.

[77] MARY E. STUCKEY, THE PRESIDENT AS INTERPRETER-IN-CHIEF 33 (1991).

[78] *See* RICHARD DAVIS, JUSTICES AND JOURNALISTS: THE U.S. SUPREME COURT AND THE MEDIA 148 (2011).

THE PLAN FOR THIS BOOK

This book's structure tracks the possible constitutional sources of constraint on the government's speech. To this end, Chapter 1 details the development of the Supreme Court's government speech doctrine in which the Court has considered Free Speech Clause challenges by private parties who seek to silence or alter what the government claims as its own speech. Because the Free Speech Clause protects private parties' speech from the government's interference while insulating the government's own speech from private parties' interference, these cases require the Court to determine when the government is speaking itself and when it instead regulates the speech of others (what I call first-stage government speech problems).

After looking back at this series of decisions, Chapter 1 then considers some challenging first-stage problems to come. We can't anticipate all the changes ahead, but we can develop a framework for thinking about them. As noted earlier, I urge what I call the transparency principle – that is, an insistence that the governmental source of a message be transparent to the public – as key to solving these first-stage government speech problems. Because the public can hold the government politically accountable for its expressive choices only when it actually understands the contested expression as the government's, we should require the government's transparency as a condition of claiming the government speech defense. After showing how the government can, as a practical matter, ensure its transparency, the chapter then revisits the Supreme Court's government speech canon – the series of cases described above that required the Court to consider first-stage government speech problems – to check their consistency with the transparency principle. Finally, it applies the transparency principle to emerging first-stage government speech problems that require courts to untangle competing expressive claims by private and governmental speakers using newer communications technologies; to determine when an individual government official speaks as the government or instead as a private citizen; and to ascertain whether an individual public employee's speech is actually the government's to control.

We then turn to second-stage problems that wrestle with whether and when the government's speech itself infringes specific constitutional rights. As explained earlier, I suggest a structure for thinking through these issues that involves a series of questions about the consequences of, and the motivations underlying, the government's expression. Chapter 2 embarks on these inquiries, starting with the Establishment Clause problems sometimes triggered by the government's religious speech. We begin here because courts and commentators to date have most often considered second-stage government speech problems in the Establishment Clause setting. Some find that the government's religious speech inflicts harmful, and constitutionally forbidden, consequences only when it coerces onlookers' participation in prayer or other religious practice. Some assert that the Establishment Clause prohibits the government from inflicting expressive as well as coercive harms, contending that the government's religious speech violates the Constitution when it sends a message that excludes its listeners based on their religion or nonreligion. Finally, some focus on the objectives underlying the government's speech instead of (or in addition to) its consequences, concluding that the Establishment Clause forbids the government's speech that abandons religious neutrality and seeks to advance religion (or nonreligion). As we'll see, our reactions to these various approaches turn largely on our preferences among the many values thought to underlie the Establishment Clause. We'll also see that these approaches illustrate available tools for thinking about whether and when the government's speech threatens equal protection, due process, free speech, and other constitutional protections. Chapter 2 also briefly considers whether and when constitutional challenges to the government's speech are justiciable – that is, whether the federal courts have the constitutional power to decide them. Later chapters will return to these questions.

Focusing on the Equal Protection Clause, Chapter 3 starts by surveying how the government's speech sometimes advances equality, and sometimes undercuts it. It then asks a series of familiar questions about the consequences of, as well as the motivations underlying, the government's speech. First, it explores how the government's speech can change its listeners' choices or opportunities in discriminatory ways – as can be the case, for example, when the government's expression commands, enables, or encourages discrimination by private parties; or when its speech deters its targets from exercising constitutional rights or pursuing important life opportunities. It then investigates whether we can understand the Equal Protection Clause to restrain the government's speech that inflicts expressive harm by disparaging its targets based on their race, gender, sexual orientation, or other class status. Moving from the effects of the government's speech to its purposes, this chapter then considers whether the government's speech offends the Equal Protection Clause when motivated by the government's discriminatory intent, including but not limited to its animus—that is, the government's bare desire to harm certain individuals or groups. These possibilities require that we ponder a number of tough questions, like the requisite causal connection between the government's speech and discriminatory consequences, and the dangers of deterring the government's laudable efforts to engage important conversations about discrimination and equality.

Chapter 4 interrogates whether and when the Due Process Clause restrains the government's speech, like its lies and other falsehoods, its disclosures of private information, and its humiliating or cruel expressive choices. It starts once again by looking at the effects of the government's speech, more specifically by studying the government's speech that interferes with its listeners' choices or opportunities in ways that would violate the Due Process Clause if the government accomplished those same changes through its lawmaking or other regulatory action. Think, for example, of law enforcement officers' lies that coerce their targets' waiver of constitutional liberties, or the government's lies that deny their targets the ability to exercise reproductive or voting rights. Next, it turns to the expressive, or dignitary, harms sometimes inflicted by the government's speech, investigating whether the government's speech that shames or humiliates its targets offends due process protections. Finally, it moves from the effects of the government's speech to its purposes, considering whether the Due Process Clause limits the government's speech motivated by its intent to interfere with protected liberties or to inflict cruelty. Judicial precedents here are rarer, but law enforcement officers crossed the line, according to one federal court, when they lied that they had a warrant to extract drugs involuntarily from a suspect's vagina such that she then extracted them herself.

Chapter 5 turns to the government's speech about others' speech, probing when, if ever, the government's expressive choices violate the First Amendment's Free Speech or Free Press Clauses. It starts yet again by considering the harmful consequences of the government's speech, more specifically how the government's speech can change, deter, or punish its targets' speech. This can be the case, for instance, of the government's threats, disclosures, and designations that silence its targets' speech, and its expressive attacks that incite or encourage third parties to punish its targets for their speech. It then considers the expressive, or dignitary, harms inflicted by the government's disparaging speech that targets disfavored speakers, and whether that speech infringes Free Speech or Free Press Clause protections apart from any effect on its targets' choices and opportunities. Finally, turning from the consequences of the government's speech about speech to its purposes, it considers whether the Free Speech and Press Clauses prohibit the government's expressive choices motivated by its intent to silence or punish speech to which it objects. Once again, these problems require us to wrestle with difficult questions of causation, intent, and unintended consequences.

Chapter 6 explores long-standing controversies over the government's speech to influence the public's views about ballot initiatives, referenda, and certain other political contests subject to vote by the people themselves or by their elected representatives. Those challenging the government's expressive efforts in these settings emphasize either or both of two sets of arguments. Invoking concerns about the consequences of the government's speech, one argument posits that the government's voice – with its advantages of resources and power – inevitably distorts public discourse and plays favorites in ways fundamentally unfair to those with other views. The other argument, steeped in concerns about the government's purposes for speaking, maintains that the government's role as sovereign requires it to refrain from taking sides in these contests. The chapter explains these arguments as applied to the government's persuasive speech in candidate campaigns, and then considers whether those objections still hold when applied to the government's persuasive speech in ballot and legislative campaigns. It closes by identifying certain conditions that exacerbate or diminish the constitutional dangers posed by that speech.

Finally, Chapter 7 identifies available responses to the government's speech that endangers constitutional values. It starts by outlining possibilities for, and barriers to, constitutional remedies that include injunctive relief, declaratory relief, and damages. It then turns to a range of legislative, structural, and political possibilities for constructively influencing the government's expressive choices apart from constitutional litigation.

*   *

The chapters that follow consider not only how courts, policymakers, and commentators to date have approached the constitutional questions sparked by the government's speech, but also how we might answer them going forward. By identifying and exploring relevant pockets of theory and doctrine that help us think about these questions – and noting their difficulties, gaps, and ambiguities – this book seeks to stitch together a coherent framework for understanding the relationship between the government's speech and our constitutional rights.

Because the constitutional standards that apply to the government as a speaker differ so dramatically from those that apply to the government as a regulator of other parties' speech, the first step in our constitutional analysis is figuring out whether the government itself is speaking or instead regulating. The next chapter embarks on that inquiry.

1

Determining Whether and When the Government
Is Speaking (and Why That Matters)

Even though governments have been speaking from their inception, only recently has the Supreme Court recognized "government speech" as an exercise of governmental power with constitutional implications of its own. In a handful of decisions over the last few decades, the Court has in fits and starts sketched out its emerging government speech doctrine, its body of law under which the constitutional standards for evaluating the government's own speech differ dramatically from those that apply to the government's regulation of other parties' speech.

First, some background. Bedrock First Amendment doctrine makes clear that the government may not restrict private parties' expression simply because the government, or the public, dislikes or disagrees with their speech. The First Amendment's Free Speech Clause thus provides nongovernmental speakers with a constitutional right to be free from the government's unjustified regulation of their expression. Meanwhile, the government itself does not have First Amendment rights of its own to use as a sword against nongovernmental parties,[1] as the Constitution protects us from the government and not vice versa.[2]

---

[1] The government is better understood as possessing not a right but a privilege to its own speech. *See* Wesley Hohfeld, *Some Fundamental Legal Concepts as Applied to Judicial Reasoning*, 23 YALE L.J. 16, 38–44 (1913) ("A right is one's affirmative claim against another, and a privilege is one's freedom from the right or claim of another."); Frederick Schauer, *Hohfeld's First Amendment*, 76 GEO. WASH. U.L. REV. 914, 914 (2008) ("Existing First Amendment doctrine takes a rather clear position with respect to the Hohfeldian: a First Amendment right is a right against the government and only against the government.").

[2] There may be reason to think about this differently when certain governments' expressive choices are not challenged by private parties but instead regulated by other governmental actors. For example, the Court has occasionally suggested that certain public institutions with unique communicative functions, like universities or broadcasters, may have First Amendment interests of their own. *See* Keyishian v. Bd. of Regents, 385 U.S. 589, 603 (1967) (observing that

Even so, the Supreme Court has recognized that we must permit government the power to control its own speech if we are to enable the government to govern:

> [I]mposing a requirement of viewpoint-neutrality on government speech would be paralyzing. When a government entity embarks on a course of action, it necessarily takes a particular viewpoint and rejects others. The Free Speech Clause does not require government to maintain viewpoint neutrality when its officers and employees speak about that venture.
>
> Here is a simple example. During the Second World War, the Federal Government produced and distributed millions of posters to promote the war effort. There were posters urging enlistment, the purchase of war bonds, and the conservation of scarce resources. These posters expressed a viewpoint, but the First Amendment did not demand that the Government balance the message of these posters by producing and distributing posters encouraging Americans to refrain from engaging in these activities.[3]

The Court's government speech doctrine thus provides the government with a defense, a shield, from Free Speech Clause challenges brought by private speakers who seek to shut down or change what is truly the government's own message: "[w]hen government speaks, it is not barred by the Free Speech Clause from determining the content of what it says."[4] This doctrine explains why tobacco companies don't have a First Amendment right to force the Surgeon General to deliver their views on the benefits of cigarettes, and why the administration's political critics don't have a First Amendment right to share the podium at the president's State of the Union address. What the First Amendment protects instead is those dissenting speakers' right to issue their own reports and hold their own press conferences.

Once the Court recognized the government's power to choose its own messages, it soon made clear that that power includes the power to hire or

---

universities' academic freedom is "a special concern of the First Amendment"); Arkansas Educational Television Comm'n v. Forbes, 523 U.S. 666, 673 (1998) (noting public and private broadcasters' First Amendment interests in journalistic freedom); United States v. American Library Association, 539 U.S. 194, 211 (2003) (declining to decide whether public libraries have First Amendment rights); *id.* at 225 (Stevens, J., dissenting) (urging the Court to recognize public libraries as First Amendment rightsholders). In a similar vein, some commentators urge that we recognize cities as having Free Speech Clause rights to be free from state or federal governments' unjustified regulation of their valuable expression. *E.g.,* Toni M. Massaro & Shefali Milczarek-Desai, *Constitutional Cities: Sanctuary Jurisdictions, Local Voice, and Individual Liberty,* 50 COLUM. HUM. RTS. L. REV. 1 (2018).

3   Matal v. Tam, 137 S. Ct. 1744, 1757–1758 (2017).
4   Walker v. Texas Div., Sons of Confederate Veterans, Inc., 135 S. Ct. 2239, 2245 (2015).

pay others to deliver the government's message, the power to tax others to fund the government's message (just like any other government activity), and the power to invite and accept input from nongovernmental parties when developing its own message while retaining control over that message.[5] These are substantial powers, the Court realized. Nevertheless, it reassured us, we need not fear them because they remain subject to political checks like voting, lobbying, petitioning, and protesting. In other words, if you don't like your government's expressive choices, you can try to persuade or pressure the government to make different choices. Or you can try to elect a different government.

This means that the constitutional consequences of identifying contested speech as the government's, or not, are enormous: the First Amendment protects private parties' speech from the government's interference while insulating the government's own speech from private parties' interference. This dichotomy gives rise to first-stage government speech problems that require us to untangle competing governmental and nongovernmental claims to the same speech.

Of course, the governmental source of a message is often obvious. Think again of the Surgeon General's report on the dangers of tobacco, which clearly identifies its governmental author. The same is true of much of the government's expression: its speeches, press releases, reports, resolutions, proclamations, websites, and much more.

More difficult first-stage government speech problems involve various forms of interaction or collaboration between governmental and private speakers that create doubt or controversy about a message's actual origin. These disputes require us to unravel rivalrous claims to contested speech: a private speaker maintains that an expressive opportunity reflects (or should be allowed to reflect) her own views free from the government's interference, while a governmental body characterizes that expression as its own, along with the ability to control its content. Related first-stage challenges arise when we must decide whether to characterize speech by an individual government official or employee as communicating the government's views,

---

[5] For additional illustrations, *see* Arkansas Educational Television Comm'n v. Forbes, 523 U.S. 666, 674 (1998) ("When a public broadcaster exercises editorial discretion in the selection and presentation of its programming, it engages in speech activity."); Legal Services Corp. v. Velazquez, 531 U.S. 533, 542 (2001) ("The attorney defending the decision to deny benefits will deliver the government's message in the litigation. The LSC lawyer, however, speaks on the behalf of his or her private, indigent, client."); Rumsfeld v. Forum for Academic and Institutional Rights, Inc., 547 U.S. 47, 62 at n.4 (2006) ("The military recruiters' speech is clearly Government speech.").

or instead those of the individual's as a citizen. Here too the consequences of this choice loom large: the constitutional rules that apply to the government's own speech as delivered by its agents and workers are again very different from those that apply to the personal speech of the individual citizens that it happens to employ.

This chapter takes a close look at the Court's government speech docket to date, which has largely focused on first-stage problems that require it to determine when the government itself is speaking or instead regulating others' speech. I show what the Court has resolved and what it has left open, spending some time looking back at this series of decisions because I hope to guide our thinking about how to go forward. I then offer a framework for approaching the challenging first-stage problems to come that will require us to unravel competing governmental and nongovernmental claims to the same speech, to determine whether an individual government official speaks as the government or instead as a private citizen, and to ascertain whether an individual public employee's speech is actually the government's to control. I propose what I call the transparency principle – that is, an insistence that the governmental source of a message be transparent to the public – as key to solving these first-stage government speech problems.[6] I emphasize transparency because, as a matter of democratic theory, the government's speech is most valuable and least dangerous to the public when its governmental source is apparent: only then is the government's speech open to the public's meaningful credibility and accountability checks. Under this transparency principle, the government is not free to claim the government speech defense to a First Amendment challenge unless it has made the contested message's governmental source clear to the public. When the governmental source of its message *is* transparent, we should understand the First Amendment to permit the government to control the content of its own messages, but not to permit it to regulate public reactions to those messages based on viewpoint. Finally, we should understand the First Amendment to permit the government to claim the constitutional power to control the speech of its employees as its own only when it has commissioned or hired those employees specifically to deliver a transparently governmental viewpoint, one that is thus open to meaningful accountability checks.

---

[6]   *See* Helen Norton, *The Measure of Government Speech: Identifying Expression's Source*, 88 BOSTON U. L. REV. 587 (2008) (proposing this test).

WHERE WE'VE BEEN SO FAR: THE SUPREME COURT'S
DEVELOPING GOVERNMENT SPEECH DOCTRINE

The series of cases in which the Court has dealt with first-stage problems reveals the Court's learning curve: we can watch the Court teach itself about government speech, solving one problem only to expose another yet to be solved. First, the Court determined that the constitutional rules for the government as regulator of others' speech must, as a matter of necessity, differ from those that apply to the government as speaker: when the government itself is speaking, then the Free Speech Clause constraints on the government *as regulator* do not apply.[7] Then the Court reassured us that we need not fear the government's speech because it remains subject to political checks – although it soon divided over how to ensure the meaningful availability of those checks. Later still the Court began to develop a framework for determining when contested speech is the government's; its efforts to do so remain a work in progress.

"[Else] the process of government as we know it [be] radically transformed"

Not until the decades bracketing the turn of the twenty-first century did the Supreme Court wrestle directly with the constitutional significance of the government's speech. Then it determined that in order to govern, the government must have the constitutional power to control its own expression exempt from Free Speech Clause challenges by private parties seeking to shut down or change the government's chosen message. Although relatively uncontroversial today, this conclusion took some time to develop.

In earlier cases, the Court had obliquely recognized the reality that the government does, and must, speak. As early as 1973, Justice Potter Stewart remarked in a footnote that "[g]overnment is not restrained by the First Amendment from controlling its own expression."[8] And in dictum (that is, in part of the Court's opinion not necessary to its ultimate decision and thus not part of the decision's precedent) in 1990, the Court observed that "If every citizen were to have a right to insist that no one paid by public funds express a view with which he disagreed, debate over issues of great concern to the public would be limited to those in the private sector, and the process of government as we know it radically transformed."[9]

---

[7] Chapter 5 considers possible Free Speech Clause constraints on the government as speaker.
[8] CBS v. Democratic National Committee, 412 U.S. 94, 140 n.7 (1973) (Stewart, J., concurring).
[9] Keller v. State Bar of California, 496 U.S. 1, 12–13 (1990).

The following year the Court decided *Rust* v. *Sullivan*,[10] a case that it would later describe as the beginning of its government speech doctrine even though *Rust* itself makes no mention of the term "government speech."[11] There the Court considered, and rejected, a First Amendment challenge to a Department of Health and Human Services' regulation that barred Planned Parenthood affiliates and other family planning clinics from discussing abortion in their federally funded counseling and referral services. Under this regulation, federally funded programs could not volunteer information about abortion services, and women who asked directly about them could be told that "the project does not consider abortion to be an appropriate method of family planning."[12]

Doctors and other clinic workers argued that the government had restricted their speech based on viewpoint in violation of the Free Speech Clause. A 5–4 Court disagreed, emphasizing the government's power to control the content of the programs and services it chooses to fund. To hold otherwise, the majority asserted, "would render numerous Government programs constitutionally suspect. When Congress established a National Endowment for Democracy to encourage other countries to adopt democratic principles, it was not constitutionally required to fund a program to encourage competing lines of political philosophy such as communism and fascism."[3] In the majority's view, the government's regulation did not discriminate against private speakers based on their viewpoint, but instead simply insisted "that public funds be spent for the purposes for which they were authorized."[4]

Foreshadowing tensions to come, Justice Harry Blackmun's dissent objected to the government's interference with a doctor's speech to her patient in a setting where that interference is not apparent to the patient. As he observed, a woman "has every reason to expect, as do we all, that her physician will not withhold relevant information regarding the very purpose of her visit."[5]

---

[10] 500 U.S. 173 (1991).

[11] E.g., Legal Services Corp. v. Velazquez, 531 U.S. 533, 541 (2001) ("The Court in *Rust* did not place explicit reliance on the rationale that the counseling activities of the doctors under Title X amounted to governmental speech; when interpreting the holding in later cases, however, we have explained *Rust* on this understanding. We have said that viewpoint-based funding decisions can be sustained in instances in which the government is itself the speaker, or instances, like *Rust*, in which the government used private speakers to transmit specific information pertaining to its own program.").

[12] *Rust*, 500 U.S. at 180.   [13] *Id.* at 194.   [14] *Id.* at 196.

[15] *Id.* at 212 n.3 (Blackmun, J., dissenting).

"[The government] may take legitimate and appropriate steps to ensure that its message is neither garbled nor distorted"

The Court's majority in *Rust* focused on the need to empower the government to control the content of the programs that it chooses to fund. In several opinions over the decade that followed, the Court further made clear that this power includes the power to control the speech with which those services are delivered.

To start, the Court invoked *Rust* to distinguish a public university's own speech from its financial support for others' speech. There the Court upheld a First Amendment challenge by student groups asserting that the University of Virginia had refused to fund their publications based on viewpoint. The Court made clear that the Free Speech Clause forbids the government from discriminating among private speakers based on their viewpoint when it funds a program intended to support a diversity of views. But the Court also took pains to emphasize that the university remains free to control the content of its own expression:

> [W]hen the State is the speaker, it may make content-based choices. When the University determines the content of the education it provides, it is the University speaking, and we have permitted the government to regulate the content of what is or is not expressed when it is the speaker or when it enlists private entities to convey its own message. In the same vein, in *Rust v. Sullivan* we upheld the government's prohibition on abortion-related advice applicable to recipients of federal funds for family planning counseling. There the government did not create a program to encourage private speech but instead used private speakers to transmit specific information pertaining to its own program. We recognized that when the government appropriates public funds to promote a particular policy of its own it is entitled to say what it wishes. When the government disburses public funds to private entities to convey a governmental message, it may take legitimate and appropriate steps to ensure that its message is neither garbled nor distorted by the grantee.[16]

Around the same time, in dictum that again invoked *Rust*, the Court identified political accountability – rather than Free Speech Clause litigation – as the appropriate check on the government's expressive choices: "When the government speaks, for instance to promote its own policies or to advance a particular idea, it is, in the end, accountable to the electorate and the political process for its advocacy. If the citizenry objects, newly elected officials later

---

[16] Rosenberger v. Rector and Visitors of the University of Virginia, 515 U.S. 819, 833–834 (1995).

could espouse some different or contrary position."[17] The Court would soon splinter over how to ensure that the government's expressive choices remain subject to meaningful political checks.

"Political safeguards more than adequate"

"Beef. It's What's for Dinner." Litigation over this slogan led the Court in *Johanns v. Livestock Marketing Ass'n* to reject a private party's Free Speech Clause claim – and for the first time expressly on the grounds that the contested speech was actually the government's.[18] *Johanns* is notable for its areas of consensus as well as disagreement. Recall the twin premises underlying the Court's emerging government speech doctrine. First, because the government must speak in order to govern, the Free Speech Clause poses no barrier to the government's ability to control its own messages free from interference by private parties who seek to stop or change those messages. Second, we need not fear the government's expressive power because its speech remains subject to political checks. In *Johanns*, all of the justices endorsed the first premise, but sharply divided over what it takes to make the second premise meaningful.

There the Court considered a First Amendment challenge to the US Department of Agriculture's (USDA's) requirement that beef producers fund a governmental advertising campaign that promoted generic beef products. Implemented through targeted taxes on beef producers, the USDA's advertisements bore only the attribution, "Funded by America's Beef Producers," and offered no indication of their governmental source. The challengers, a group of beef producers, argued that the Free Speech Clause barred the government from taxing them to support the government's expressive campaign that they felt undermined their efforts to promote their own specialty beef products.

The entire Court agreed that taxpayers *can* be compelled to pay for the government's speech to which they object, emphasizing that an effective government frequently requires taxpayers to fund the government's choices with which they quarrel. But the Court sharply divided over whether the First Amendment requires the government affirmatively to make clear its expression's governmental source as a condition of insulating that expression from Free Speech Clause challenge. A 5–4 majority held that the government's establishment and control of the advertisements' message, without more, was

---

[17] Board of Regents of the University of Wisconsin System v. Southworth, 529 U.S. 217, 235–236 (2000).
[18] 544 U.S. 550 (2005).

sufficient to enable the public to hold the government politically accountable for its expressive choices:

> [T]he beef advertisements are subject to political safeguards more than adequate to set them apart from private messages. The program is authorized and the basic message prescribed by federal statute, and specific requirements for the promotions' content are imposed by federal regulations promulgated after notice and comment. The Secretary of Agriculture, a politically accountable official, oversees the program, appoints and dismisses the key personnel, and retains absolute veto power over the advertisements' content, right down to the wording. And Congress, of course, retains oversight authority, not to mention the ability to reform the program at any time. No more is required.[19]

Justice David Souter's dissent, in contrast, argued that political accountability is but a fiction unless the government takes steps to ensure that the public understands the expression is the government's:

> It means nothing that Government officials control the message if that fact is never required to be made apparent to those who get the message, let alone if it is affirmatively concealed from them. The political accountability of the officials with control is insufficient, in other words, just because those officials are allowed to use their control (and in fact are deliberately using it) to conceal their role from the voters with the power to hold them accountable. Unless the putative government speech appears to be coming from the government, its governmental origin cannot possibly justify the burden on the First Amendment interests of the dissenters targeted to pay for it.[20]

As we'll see, this question continues to challenge the Court.

"[L]ittle chance that observers will fail to appreciate the identity of the speaker"

In *Johanns*, a closely divided Court concluded that contested speech was the government's, and thus that the government was free to control it. A unanimous Court so found in its 2009 decision in *City of Pleasant Grove* v. *Summum*.[21]

First, some background on the Court's public forum doctrine. In a series of decisions over many years, the Court developed the public forum doctrine to deal with situations where, as a functional matter, government has opened up its own property (or some other space under its control) for the public's speech. The doctrine is relatively easy to recite, albeit often hard to apply.

---

[19] *Id.* at 563–564.   [20] *Id.* at 578–579 (Souter, J., dissenting).   [21] 555 U.S. 460 (2009).

Courts first assess what type of forum the government has established, which then determines which test to apply to the government's control of private parties' speech within this forum. *Traditional* public forums, for instance, are those government properties that have been long been available for public expression: think parks, streets, and sidewalks. In contrast, the government opens up a *designated* public forum when it chooses to create a new opportunity for the public's speech on any and all matters. And it creates a *limited* public forum when it chooses to make space available for speech by certain speakers (as is the case, for example, when a public law school permits student organizations to use its classrooms when otherwise not in use) or certain topics (for example, when a school board invites the public's discussion of the items on its meeting agenda). The Court has developed different rules for the different types of forums, but – regardless of the type of forum at issue – the government may not restrict nongovernmental speakers' participation based on their viewpoint.[22]

Back to *City of Pleasant Grove* v. *Summum*. A public park in the city of Pleasant Grove, Utah featured a number of displays that included the city's first fire station, a September 11 monument, and a Ten Commandments monument donated by the Fraternal Order of Eagles. Summum, a religious organization, asked to donate a stone monument of its own for display in the park. Similar in size to the Ten Commandments monument, this monument featured the Seven Aphorisms of Summum, a series of statements that Summum adherents believe that God gave to Moses. The city rejected the offer, asserting that it had made the expressive choice to accept only monuments that either directly related to the town's history or that were donated by groups with long-standing ties to the community. Summum then filed a Free Speech Clause challenge, alleging that the City had impermissibly rejected its donation based on its viewpoint. (You might be wondering whether the City's acceptance of a Ten Commandments monument while rejecting Summum's donation suggests the government's religious discrimination in violation of the Establishment Clause, which directs that the government "shall make no law respecting an establishment of religion." Summum did not allege such a

---

[22] For example, speakers may be blocked from traditional or designated public forums only when necessary to serve a compelling government interest and the exclusion is narrowly drawn to achieve that interest. *See* Cornelius v. NAACP Legal Defense and Educational Fund, Inc., 473 U.S. 788, 800 (1985). But government may limit or deny access to a limited or nonpublic forum so long as its restrictions are reasonable and do not target speakers on the basis of their viewpoints. *See id.* The government's ability to regulate private speech thus often depends on how we characterize the forum, but one caveat remains constant: government may not regulate private parties' speech on the basis of viewpoint in any type of forum.

violation for strategic reasons: prevailing on an Establishment Clause claim might well have meant the removal of the Ten Commandments monument from the park, rather than the inclusion of its own.)

Summum required the Court to make a framing choice. Does a city's selective acceptance of private donations for display in its park involve the government's regulation of private parties' speech in a traditional public forum? If so, the government's choices as regulator are constrained by the Free Speech Clause, and it may not pick and choose among the donations based on their viewpoint. Or do a city's selections instead reflect its own expressive choices about the messages it decides to display on its own property? If that's the case, then the Free Speech Clause poses no bar to the government's ability, as speaker, to control those messages. A unanimous Court chose the latter.

The Court repeated its premise that the government must have the constitutional power to control the content of its own speech: "Indeed, it is not easy to see how government could function if it lacked this freedom."[23] And, as the Court further explained, that the government accepts donations from private parties in developing its message does not necessarily strip that message of its governmental character: "[a] government entity may exercise this same freedom to express its views when it receives assistance from private sources for the purpose of delivering a government-controlled message."[24] Just as the government may pay nongovernmental actors to deliver its own message (as in *Rust*) and tax nongovernmental actors to fund the delivery of its own message (as in *Johanns*), so too may it accept assistance of other kinds from nongovernmental actors in developing and delivering its own message.

All of the Justices agreed that the monuments "are meant to convey and have the effect of conveying a government message, and they thus constitute government speech."[25] In so holding, the Court considered multiple factors. These included not only that the government "established and controlled" the message, as emphasized in *Johanns*, but also that observers would likely attribute the expression to the city based on the park's history, governments' long-standing practice of using monuments for their own expressive purposes, and the monuments' location on the city's own property. All served as cues that signaled the expression's governmental source to the public.

A strong dose of pragmatism also contributed to the unanimous result, given the dramatic results of a ruling to the contrary. If Summum's claim were to prevail, the Court predicted, governments must either "brace themselves for

---

[23] *Summum*, 555 U.S. at 468.   [24] *Id.*   [25] *Id.* at 472.

an influx of clutter" on their public property or remove long-standing and cherished monuments.[26] To illustrate the point, consider the efforts by opponents of gay rights to donate a monument to the city of Laramie, Wyoming. Their proposed display would have declared that Matthew Shepard, a gay man murdered in Laramie in a homophobic hate crime, "entered hell October 12, 1998 in defiance of God's warning."[27] If the government did not have the constitutional power to select the monuments displayed on its property, Laramie would have been put to the choice between displaying this hateful monument or instead ridding its public places of all donated displays.

At the same time, members of the Court took pains to identify meaningful checks on the government's speech for cases to come. Justice Souter repeated his interest in ensuring that the government remains politically accountable to the public for its expressive choices:

> [T]he best approach that occurs to me is to ask whether a reasonable and fully informed observer would understand the expression to be government speech, as distinct from private speech the government chooses to oblige by allowing the monument to be placed on public land. . . . [T]he government should lose when the character of the speech is at issue and its governmental nature has not been made clear.[28]

Justice Stevens separately emphasized the availability and importance of additional constitutional, as well as political, checks on the government's objectionable speech:

> [E]ven if the Free Speech Clause neither restricts nor protects government speech, government speakers are bound by the Constitution's other proscriptions, including those supplied by the Establishment and Equal Protection Clauses. Together with the checks imposed by our democratic processes, these constitutional safeguards ensure that the effect of today's decision will be limited.[29]

Finally, the Justices acknowledged the possibility of danger in other cases, noting "the legitimate concern that the government speech doctrine not be used as a subterfuge for favoring certain private speakers over others based on

---

[26] *See id.* at 479–480 (citation omitted).

[27] *See* Mary Jean Dolan, *Why Donated Monuments are Government Speech: The Hard Case of Pleasant Grove v. Summum*, 58 Cath. U. L. Rev. 7, 10 (2008).

[28] *Summum*, 555 U.S. at 485 (Souter, J., concurring).   [29] *Id.* at 482 (Stevens, J., concurring).

viewpoint."[30] Some saw those dangers lurking in the next government speech dispute to confront the Court.

"Were the Free Speech Clause interpreted otherwise, government would not work"

The dispute in *Walker* v. *Texas Div., Sons of Confederate Veterans, Inc.* invited the Court to further develop its framework for identifying the source of contested expression when disentangling competing claims to the same speech.[31] After Texas denied the Sons of Confederate Veterans' (SCV's) request that the state issue a specialty license plate that would, among other things, emblazon the Confederate flag alongside the state's name, the SCV challenged the state's decision on Free Speech Clause grounds. By a 5–4 vote, the Court agreed with Texas that the words and images displayed on its specialty license plates reflected the state's own expression that it remained free to control without running afoul of the First Amendment. In concluding that the specialty license plates reflected the government's own speech, the Court focused on three factors drawn from *Summum* and *Johanns* (without asserting that the three comprised an exhaustive list of relevant factors): whether the government had historically used the contested speech for its own expressive purposes, whether the contested speech was closely identified in the public mind with the government, and whether the government had established and maintained control over the message. Based on these factors, the majority found that "[t]he governmental nature of the plates is clear from their faces: The State places the name "TEXAS" in large letters at the top of every plate.... Texas license plates are, essentially, government IDs."[32]

The Court split over the significance of the many and diverse messages displayed on the 350 plates Texas had approved at the time, plates that celebrated, among other things, not only the University of Texas but (as the dissent noted) also many of the Longhorns' rival universities. The dissent doubted that Texas really adopted all of those messages as its own, asserting instead that the state had instead created a forum for private parties' speech from which it had impermissibly excluded the SCV because it disliked the organization's views. The majority was not so troubled, concluding that Texas was free "to choose how to present itself and its constituency. Thus, Texas offers plates celebrating the many educational institutions attended by its citizens. But it need not issue plates deriding schooling."[33]

[30] *Id.* at 473 (majority opinion).   [31] 135 S. Ct. 2239 (2015).   [32] *Id.* at 2248–2249.
[33] *Id.* at 2249.

In so holding, the Court again emphasized the value and often the inevitability of the government's speech, such that "[w]hen government speaks, it is not barred by the Free Speech Clause from determining the content of what it says.... . Were the Free Speech Clause interpreted otherwise, government would not work."[34] At the same time it acknowledged other constraints, both legal and political, on the government's expressive choices:

> That is not to say that a government's ability to express itself is without restriction. Constitutional and statutory provisions outside of the Free Speech Clause may limit government speech. And the Free Speech Clause itself may constrain the government's speech if, for example, the government seeks to compel private persons to convey the government's speech. But, as a general matter, when the government speaks it is entitled to promote a program, to espouse a policy, or to take a position. In doing so, it represents its citizens and it carries out its duties on their behalf.[35]

"[A] doctrine that is susceptible to dangerous misuse"

Two years later, in *Matal v. Tam*,[36] the Supreme Court finally rejected a governmental claim to contested speech, and it did so unanimously. There the federal Patent and Trademark Office had denied a trademark application by the Asian American rock band "The Slants," relying on a statute prohibiting the federal registration of trademarks that may "disparage ... or bring ... into contemp[t] or disrepute" any "persons, living or dead."[37] The band's lead singer, Simon Tam, brought a First Amendment challenge alleging that the government's decision constituted impermissible viewpoint discrimination – in other words, that the government had punished a private party's speech with which it disagreed.

The government offered a potpourri of defenses, none of which impressed the Court. These defenses included the government's claim that trademark registration reflected its own expression. In response, the Court repeated its now-familiar refrain that "the First Amendment does not say that Congress

---

[34] *Id.* at 2245–2246.
[35] *Id.* at 2246. Note how the Court's discussion of its doctrine became more nuanced over time. In *Johanns*, for example, the majority characterized the government's own speech as "exempt" from Free Speech Clause scrutiny. *Johanns*, 544 U.S. at 553. But by the time of *Walker*, the Court recognized that the government's own speech is still subject to some Free Speech Clause constraints. *Walker*, 135 S. Ct. at 2246. The more accurate description is that the government's own expressive choices are exempt from the Free Speech Clause constraints that apply to the government as *regulator*, but there may be different Free Speech Clause constraints that apply to the government as *speaker*. Chapter 5 examines those possibilities.
[36] 137 S. Ct. 1744 (2017).   [37] 15 U.S.C. § 1052(a).

and other government entities must abridge their own ability to speak freely,"[38] but then underscored the need to limit the government's ability to claim and control speech as its own:

> But while the government-speech doctrine is important – indeed, essential – it is a doctrine that is susceptible to dangerous misuse. If private speech could be passed off as government speech by simply affixing a government seal of approval, government could silence or muffle the expression of disfavored viewpoints. For this reason, we must exercise great caution before extending our government-speech precedents.[39]

The Court distinguished its decisions in past cases that identified contested speech as the government's, describing those decisions as based on "many factors."[40] These factors included whether the speech has the intent and effect of delivering the government's message, whether the contested speech is closely identified with the government by the public, whether the government had historically used the speech in question for its own expressive purposes, and the practical implications of denying the government the power to control the contested speech. The Court then found that the government's trademark registration exhibited none of these characteristics.

Where Does This Leave Us?

Return to the justifications, both practical and theoretical, that underlie the Court's government speech doctrine. As a practical matter, the government must speak if it is to govern. And as a matter of democratic theory, we need not fear the government's expressive power so long as it remains meaningfully accountable to political checks. In describing its approach to first-stage government speech problems, the Court started by emphasizing the importance of the government's power to control its own speech. Only later in this series of cases did it recognize the need to identify limiting principles; at that point it started to search for indicia distinguishing governmental from private speech, and eventually offered its illustrative list of "many factors" to add rigor and predictability to its analysis.

In developing its government speech doctrine, the Court provided a helpful and important vocabulary for recognizing both the inevitability and the value of government speech. In so doing, it also solved a problem faced by a number of lower courts that up until that time had no language for dealing with what we now understand as government speech. Before the emergence of the

---

[38] *Matal*, 137 S. Ct. at 1757.   [39] *Id.* at 1757–1758.   [40] *Id.* at 1759.

government speech doctrine, lower courts often struggled mightily by seeking to apply some sort of forum doctrine to what were really the government's own expressive choices. In other words, lower courts sometimes simply tried to pound the square peg of what we now understand as government speech into the round hole of public forum doctrine – with confusing and unsettling results.

An example illustrates the point. In *Griffin v. Department of Veterans Affairs*[41] – a decision that predates *Johanns* – a federal appellate court purported to apply forum analysis when rejecting a Free Speech Clause challenge to the Veterans Administration's (VA's) refusal to fly the Confederate flag over one of its cemeteries. Even though the court concluded that "[r]equiring the VA to allow the Confederate flag to fly daily over Point Lookout certainly 'garbles [and] distorts'" the agency's chosen message,[42] it had little government speech precedent from which to draw. It thus strained to characterize the government program at issue as a nonpublic forum, in which the government remains free to regulate private parties' speech so long as its actions are reasonable and viewpoint-neutral. Yet an honest assessment of the facts would acknowledge that the VA's decision to fly the American, and not the Confederate, flag over a Civil War cemetery is actually viewpoint-based, rather than viewpoint-neutral – and thus forum analysis, if properly applied, would have led the court to strike down the agency's actions. But once the government speech doctrine enables us to understand the VA's choice about which flag to fly over its property as the government's own expression, this becomes a much easier and more intellectually coherent decision: this was not a case in which the government regulated private parties' speech in some type of forum, but instead a situation in which government itself was speaking, and was thus free to control its own message.

Yet by solving some problems, the Court's government speech doctrine exposed others, like the need to identify limits to the government speech defense. The government's increasing use of new technologies that vary in their interactivity and transparency presents us with fresh first-stage government speech problems. We need a doctrine that preserves the government's important, often necessary, control over its own expression. But we also need a doctrine that prevents the government from concealing itself as a message's source to escape political accountability for its choices, and from overstating its expressive interests to muffle others' voices. As we'll see, government bodies sometimes assert government speech interests to claim – and some courts permit them to exercise – the power to punish private parties' speech that does

---

[41] 274 F.3d 818 (4th Cir. 2001), *cert. denied*, 537 U.S. 947 (2002).
[42] *See id.* at 822 (citation omitted).

not threaten the government's ability to express its own views. We must recognize the value of the government's speech while remaining appropriately skeptical of the government's expressive claims.

In the next section, I'll first make the case for transparency as the key to first-stage government speech problems. Under the transparency principle that I propose, expression constitutes government speech exempt from the Free Speech Clause scrutiny that applies to the government as regulator only when its governmental source is apparent to the public, thus enhancing the public's ability to evaluate their government. Then I'll show how the government can, as a practical matter, ensure this transparency. Next, I'll revisit the Supreme Court's government speech canon – the series of cases described above that required the Court to consider first-stage government speech problems – to check their consistency with the transparency principle. Finally, I'll apply the transparency principle to the first-stage problems that arise when the government uses newer expressive technologies that permit interaction with and comment by the public, as well as the first-stage problems that arise when governmental employers claim their employees' speech as their own, along with the power to control it.

WHERE WE SHOULD BE GOING: TRANSPARENCY AS THE KEY TO FIRST-STAGE GOVERNMENT SPEECH PROBLEMS

As the Court has repeatedly reminded us, those unhappy with their government's views remain free to try to change them through political efforts like lobbying, campaigning, and voting. But because the public can take such action only when it actually understands the contested expression as the government's, we should require the government's transparency – that is, we should require the government to ensure that the governmental source of its message is clear to the public – as a condition of claiming the government speech defense to Free Speech Clause challenges.

Why Does Transparency Matter?

An insistence on transparency recognizes that the value of the government's speech springs primarily from its capacity to inform the public about its government's principles and priorities: the government's expression gives the public more information with which to evaluate their government. This is true even – and perhaps especially – when the government's speech unsettles, even infuriates, us. As is true of speech more generally, that expression is "valuable" for these purposes does not necessarily mean that it is good, wise, or accurate; instead "constitutionally valuable" speech is that which furthers specific constitutional values – here, democratic accountability. But the government's speech offers this value only when the public recognizes the speech as the government's. This requires the government to make its expressive choices visible to its public. In other words, the government should pay for its ability to invoke the government speech defense by transparently taking political responsibility for its expressive choices.

An insistence on transparency also helps address the Court's "legitimate concern that the government speech doctrine not be used as a subterfuge for favoring certain private speakers over others based on viewpoint."[43] Although the government has a substantial interest in protecting its ability to communicate its own views, some government litigants and courts are all too willing to imagine threats to that governmental interest where none exist. By insisting that the governmental source of a message is clear to the public at the time of its delivery, we guard against this danger.

An insistence on transparency also prevents the public from being misled about the source of a message in ways that change the effectiveness of the message and thus distort public discourse. As a large body of cognitive psychology research makes clear, listeners often use a message's source as a mental shortcut, or heuristic, for evaluating its quality.[44] The more credible a speaker, the more likely his message will be effective. Of course, a message's source can have positive or negative effects on its persuasiveness, depending on listeners' assessments of the source's credibility. And because public attitudes toward government vary so widely – depending on the government, the audience, and the issue – the public's assessments of the government's credibility differ too. For these reasons, as legal scholar Lawrence Lessig explains, the government will sometimes try to boost the persuasiveness of its message by attributing it to other, more credible speakers:

> Call this the Orwell effect: when people see that the government or some relatively powerful group is attempting to manipulate social meaning, they react strongly to resist any such manipulation. What the Orwell effect means is that efforts by the government to regulate social meaning that are seen as efforts by the government to change social meaning will be less effective than efforts that are not so viewed. . . . What the Orwell effect will mean is that government will have an incentive to minimize the extent to which its

---

[43] *See* City of Pleasant Grove v. Summum, 555 U.S. 460, 473 (2009).
[44] For additional discussion, *see* Helen Norton, *The Measure of Government Speech: Identifying Expression's Source*, 88 Boston U. L. Rev. 587 (2008).

messages seeking change seem to be messages from it, by tying its messages to independent authorities (for example, doctors) or authority (science).[45]

For these reasons, the government sometimes deliberately obscures its identity as a message's source to manipulate the public's attitudes toward its views. This skews public debate and inhibits informed self-governance by leading listeners to evaluate ideas differently than they would if those views were accurately assigned to the message's actual source.

And just as dangers lurk when the government masks its role as a message's source to boost its success, related concerns arise when nongovernmental speakers seek the government's perceived imprimatur. Views mistakenly perceived as the government's not only mislead the public about its government's actual values, but those views may carry greater persuasive force than they would otherwise enjoy. Consider, for example, the differing effects of the statement that "The Confederate flag is a symbol of heritage not hate" if delivered by the state of Texas as opposed to the SCV. Or the view that "Human behavior does not significantly contribute to climate change" if attributed to the National Oceanic and Atmospheric Administration as opposed to an oil company executive. In short, sometimes private parties want the public to (mis)understand the government as endorsing their views, and sometimes the government wants the public to (mis)attribute its views to other more credible speakers. Either way, when speakers mislead their listeners about a message's true source, they can change the message's reception and distort the public discourse. Again, requiring the government to make the governmental source of its messages clear to the public helps guard against these dangers.

Transparency provides these benefits while posing little or no cost to the government – especially but not only because the government, unlike private parties with First Amendment rights of their own, has no constitutionally protected autonomy interests in anonymity. Why *not* require federally funded family planning programs to make clear that the government has instructed them not to talk about abortion? Why *not* label the "Beef. It's What's for Dinner" ads as "A Message from the U.S. Department of Agriculture" rather than "Funded by America's Beef Producers"? Only if one worries that the message will be less effective if the public accurately understands it as the government's. Or if one seeks to insulate the government from political accountability for its expressive choices. Neither is a good answer. Transparency costs the government nothing but increased accountability – which is exactly the point.

---

[45] Lawrence Lessig, *The Regulation of Social Meaning*, 62 U. CHI. L. REV. 943, 1017 (1995).

Achieving Transparency: Cues for Determining a Message's Governmental or Private Source

So far I've proposed the transparency principle as the key to first-stage government speech problems – that is, that the government should identify itself as the source of its message in exchange for insulating its chosen message from Free Speech Clause challenge. But what does it mean, in practice, to require the government to ensure that the public understands its message's source as governmental?

We can draw from relevant experience in other areas to examine a variety of characteristics, or "source cues," that reveal or obscure a message's origin as governmental or private. These include not only explicit signals of a message's origin, but also less direct signals like a message's physical location or onlookers' expectations based on past practice.

A message often expressly signals its genesis at the time of its delivery. Straightforward examples include government press conferences where the government's position is communicated by a public official; press statements appearing on government letterhead and attributed to a government source; or the government's reports and websites. Because they are so clear, these express cues are most helpful to the public in exposing a message's governmental origins and thus facilitating meaningful accountability. As a matter of both constitutional law and sound public policy, governments should design their communications to enhance, rather than obscure, transparency by employing express cues whenever possible. As a doctrinal incentive for governments to do so, courts could treat express cues as triggering a presumption that a contested message is governmental in origin and thus exempt from Free Speech Clause scrutiny, while presuming the absence of express cues to signal the message's nongovernmental source. By insisting that the government be clear about when it is speaking, on the one hand, and when it intends instead to create an opportunity for private parties' speech on the other, courts can generate a doctrinally principled and technologically workable solution to first-stage government speech problems.

A message's location also serves as a cue to its source. Absent strong indications to the contrary, onlookers often attribute signs, displays, and other visual messages to the owner of the property where they appear.[46] For this reason, a state's expressive choice to display the United States, Confederate, or

---

[46] *See Summum*, 555 U.S. at 470–480 (explaining how the messages communicated by public park monuments are generally attributed to the government as property owner); City of Ladue v. Gilleo, 512 U.S. 43 (1994) (striking down a city ban on homeowners' posting of signs on Free

some other flag on its property remains transparently governmental in source, as does a mayor's decision to display in City Hall only patriotic art for the city's Fourth of July celebration, or art advocating racial equality for its observance of Black History Month.

The Court has considered related first-stage problems in the Establishment Clause context, in which it must distinguish between "*government* speech endorsing religion, which the Establishment Clause forbids, and *private* speech endorsing religion, which the Free Speech and Free Exercise Clauses protect."[47] In other words, determining the applicable constitutional rule requires the Court to characterize contested speech either as the government's or that of private parties. (Chapter 2 explores in detail the second-stage question of when what is clearly *the government's* speech promotes religion in violation of the Establishment Clause). Often the Court finds this determination a simple one based on the expression's setting. For example, it concluded that a public school's graduation prayer, even though delivered by nongovernmental clergy, "bore the imprint of the State" because the government not only invited the clergy's prayer but also hosted and supervised the entire ceremony.[48] In another case, a religious display's prominent location on government property clearly signaled its governmental source: "[T]he crèche sits on the Grand Staircase, the 'main' and 'most beautiful part' of the building that is the seat of county government. No viewer could reasonably think that it occupies this location without the support and approval of the government."[49] And in yet another case, the Court again relied on functional considerations to find that student-read prayers at a public high school's football games reflected the government's own expression: "The delivery of such a message—over the school's public address system, by a speaker representing the student body, under the supervision of school faculty, and pursuant to a school policy that explicitly and implicitly encourages public prayer— is not properly characterized as 'private' speech."[50]

Harder first-stage problems arise where the available cues send mixed or ambiguous signals about a message's author. Let's consider some confounding factors, factors that obscure expression's source as private or governmental.

Speech Clause grounds and observing that the city had foreclosed a common and helpful means of signaling a message's source).

[47] Bd. of Ed. of Westside Comm'y Sch. v. Mergens, 496 U.S. 226, 250 (1990) (plurality); *see also* Santa Fe Indep. Sch. Dist. v. Doe, 530 U.S. 290, 302 (2000).

[48] Lee v. Weisman, 505 U.S. 577, 590 (1992).

[49] County of Allegheny v. ACLU, 492 U.S. 573, 600 (1989).

[50] Santa Fe Indep. Sch. Dist., 530 U.S. at 310.

First, as we've seen, that a message originates with or is uttered by a private party does not necessarily defeat the government's claim to that speech – although, to be sure, it complicates it. Speakers often rely on suggestions from others when developing their own messages, and the decision to encourage and select from a variety of contributions can be an expressive choice of its own, one that provides valuable information to the electorate. The government's reliance on the input of private parties to bolster its own message is both commonplace and valuable: like many other speakers, governments often draw upon third-party sources to illustrate, explain, and support their positions. Consider, for example, a governor who approvingly quotes the Chamber of Commerce but not the Sierra Club in an op-ed opposing additional oil and gas regulation. The governor's expressive choices remain transparently governmental, providing citizens with valuable information about her priorities and enabling them to hold her accountable for those positions if they wish.

As another illustration, the United States Postal Service's Citizens' Stamp Advisory Committee invites contributions from the public as to who or what the government might honor with a postage stamp, but the Postal Service expressly maintains control over the ultimate decision. Just because the government makes the expressive choice to honor Dr. Martin Luther King, Jr. with a commemorative stamp based in part on the public's urging, for instance, does not deprive that decision of its transparently governmental source, nor would it compel the government to comply with public requests to issue a stamp honoring longtime segregationist George Wallace. So long as the government makes clear that it invites input into what it claims, and intends to control, as its own speech – thus encouraging public participation but preserving political accountability as the remedy for those displeased with its choices – that invitation does not strip the expression of its governmental character. (Along these lines, the United Kingdom invited the public's input, through Twitter, into the naming of its new polar research vessel, but retained control over the final decision. It thus declined to adopt the public's clear favorite, "Boaty McBoatFace."[51])

The presence of a variety of messages within a particular setting also complicates the conclusion that government is the source of all of them.

---

[51] *See* Genevieve B. Tung & Ruth Ann Robbins, *Beyond #TheNew10–The Case for a Citizens Currency Advisory Committee*, 69 RUTGERS L. REV. 195, 223–224 (2016) ("[T]his left the chief executive of the council, who had the final say, in the unpopular position of having to choose between public good will and the scientific gravitas desired by the United Kingdom's science ministry"— with gravitas the ultimate winner); *see also id.* at 224 n.168 ("The boat was eventually named the Royal Research Ship Sir David Attenborough.").

But governments, like other speakers, may have a great deal to say on a large number of issues, and thus may choose to express a host of views. Prospects for meaningful accountability are not necessarily thwarted by a variety of messages so long as express or other strong source cues – like the state's name prominently displayed on a license plate – signal a message's governmental source. The Postal Service's annual slate of commemorative U.S. stamps again illustrates this point: in 2018 it celebrated Lena Horne, John Lennon, Sally Ride, and STEM (Science, Technology, Education, and Mathematics) education, along with magic, Meyer lemons, and, of course, bioluminescent creatures and frozen treats.[52] The diversity of the government's choices itself communicates a message, maybe of the government's whimsy. And the government remains the transparent source of these multiple messages, as the Postal Service made clear its intent to speak for itself in choosing who and what to feature on postage stamps even while it invited public input, and the signifier "USA" on the stamps themselves is an express cue that ensures that onlookers understand the message's source as governmental. But when the government fails to identify itself as the message's source, it should lose the privilege of asserting the government speech defense.

Reconsidering the Supreme Court's Government Speech Canon

So far I've suggested that we return to the foundational premises underlying the government speech doctrine, which remind us that the government's speech is more valuable and less dangerous when its governmental source is apparent to the public. For this reason, we should require the government to ensure that the governmental source of its message is clear to the public if it wants to claim the government speech defense to private parties' Free Speech Clause challenges. Applying this transparency principle to the Court's government speech canon confirms some of its conclusions while revealing that others – especially those early in its learning curve – should come out differently.

Recall, for example, *Rust v. Sullivan*, where the Court upheld federal regulations that barred federally funded family planning programs – including those operated by Planned Parenthood affiliates and other nonprofits – from discussing abortion. Health care providers in those programs were "expressly prohibited from referring a pregnant woman to an abortion provider, even upon specific request. One permissible response to such an inquiry is that 'the

---

[52] U.S. Postal Service, *U.S. Postal Service Provides a Sneak Peek at Select 2018 Stamps* (Dec. 12, 2017), https://about.usps.com/news/national-releases/2017/pr17_079.pdf.

project does not consider abortion an appropriate method of family planning and therefore does not counsel or refer for abortion.'"[53] In rejecting the providers' First Amendment challenge to the regulations, the Court's majority emphasized the government's power to control the content of the programs that it chooses to fund.

But the governmental source of the speech and its restrictions were not apparent to listeners – that is, patients – at the time of the message's delivery. Doctors, nurses, and other health care providers uttered the counseling and referral speech at issue, and those private parties' role as the literal speakers of the message obscured its governmental origins. Women seeking help from the clinics might well misunderstand the clinic's health care professionals to be offering their own independent counsel rather than speaking as the government's agents bound to a governmental script that precluded the discussion of abortion. And because patients might well perceive health care professionals as more expert and objective than the government, those women may have been misled into evaluating the counseling differently than they would have if the government had made clear the message's actual source.

To be sure, the First Amendment permits the government to choose to transparently advocate a pro-life or a pro-choice view (or neither), as these choices provide the public with valuable information about its government's priorities and values. As a practical matter, this means too that the First Amendment permits the government to pay employees or other agents to help it deliver its chosen message. But if the expression is to be characterized as the government's and thus exempt from Free Speech Clause challenge, the expression should be delivered in a way that enables the public to understand it as their government's viewpoint. Only then can the message's recipients accurately assess its credibility and voters hold the government accountable for that viewpoint. The constitutional injury inflicted by the government's expressive choice here lies not in the content of its message but instead in the government's failure to own up to the message.

Return too to *Johanns* v. *Livestock Marketing Ass'n*,[54] where again the government did not make its message's governmental source apparent to onlookers, as the beef advertisements bore only the attribution "Funded by America's Beef Producers." That politically accountable bodies (Congress and

---

[53] Rust v. Sullivan, 500 U.S. 173, 180 (1991). The regulations did not require that the government be identified as the message's source, although the majority observed that "[n]othing in [the Title X regulations] requires a doctor to represent as his own any opinion that he does not in fact hold." *Id.* at 200.

[54] 544 U.S. 550 (2005).

the Department of Agriculture) had authorized and implemented the program, the Court's majority claimed, was enough to put the public on notice of its governmental source and seek political redress if they so chose. But that's an insider's view of accountability, a judicial choice to privilege form over function. Most of those watching the ads while sitting at home in their living rooms, like the women seeking help at the family planning clinics, were far from the halls of power in Washington, D.C. in both time and space. They were thus unlikely to realize the expression's governmental source unless the government made that affirmatively clear at the time it delivered the message. Yet the government declined to do so, even though this transparency would have cost the government nothing while providing value to the public.

The transparency principle also shows why *Walker* v. *Texas Div., Sons of Confederate Veterans, Inc.*[55] was a hard case even if (as I believe) correctly decided. Although specialty license plates are far from the most important exercise of the government's expressive power,[56] this dispute illustrates how entanglements and interactions between governmental and nongovernmental speakers complicate first-stage government speech problems on an everyday basis. On one hand, the specialty license plates are manufactured, issued, and sometimes even owned by the state, and prominently feature the state's name. On the other hand, private parties choose to display them on their own property–their cars. Onlookers often rely on a message's location as a cue to its source, concluding that it reflects the view of the property owner. Think, for instance, of the political campaign signs in your neighbor's yard.

I suggest that we understand specialty license plates as reflecting the government's message that private parties are free to buy and endorse, or not. This permits the government to control the content of its own expression but not to compel others to join it. In other words, sometimes we can most accurately describe speech as simultaneously reflecting the views of governmental and private speakers who have chosen to share a message. Examples include situations where a public actor offers private speakers a voluntary opportunity to join and display the government's own speech – an opportunity that may be especially attractive because it appears to carry some indication of government endorsement or imprimatur (otherwise why didn't the SCV just print up their own bumper stickers?). Recognizing this reality values both speakers' expressive interests: those who agree with the government's view may

---

[55] 135 S. Ct. 2239 (2015).
[56] Sometimes the government speaks to raise revenue through direct appeals (for example, by imploring the public to buy war bonds) and sometimes by selling entertaining or attractive products like commemorative stamps and specialty license plates.

choose to buy and display those messages, but government may not compel anyone to do so, nor prevent anyone from producing and displaying their own counter-messages.

West Virginia State Bd. of Ed. v. *Barnette* reflects this approach, where the Court did not question the state's expressive choice to start its school day with the Pledge of Allegiance even while it held that the First Amendment forbids the government from forcing dissenting students to endorse its expression by saluting the flag.[57] Similarly, in *Wooley* v. *Maynard*, the Court raised no quarrel with New Hampshire's expressive choice of "Live Free or Die" as its motto nor its choice to display that message on the state's license plates. But the Court denied the state the power to fine an objecting private speaker who covered up the motto on his car's plates.[58] In other words, the Free Speech Clause protects a private party's right to be free from the government's efforts to compel her to join or utter its message, but it does not empower her to force the government to join or utter hers. Recognizing this reality accommodates individuals' autonomy interests as well as the government's expressive interests.

FIRST-STAGE GOVERNMENT SPEECH PROBLEMS TO COME

Next we apply the transparency principle to emerging first-stage government speech problems. These problems require courts to untangle competing expressive claims by private and governmental speakers using newer communications technologies; to determine when an individual government official speaks as the government or instead as a private citizen; and to ascertain whether an individual public employee's speech is actually the government's to control.

First-Stage Complications Created by Newer Expressive Technologies

Despite substantial shifts over time in how the government and other parties actually communicate, the Supreme Court to date has developed its government speech doctrine only in the context of disputes involving long-standing forms of expression: the spoken and written word, advertisements in print and electronic form, and visual displays like license plates and public monuments.

---

[57] 319 U.S. 624 (1943).   [58] 430 U.S. 705 (1977).

The Court's doctrine – already slow to develop – has yet to grapple with the constitutional significance of major changes in how the government speaks.[59]

New first-stage government speech problems will emerge as technological changes, along with our imaginations, create new opportunities for expressive partnerships and interactions between the government and the public. Courts will continue to struggle with how to characterize increasingly complicated associations, alliances, and entanglements between governmental and private speakers through blogs, social media platforms, and more. We can't anticipate all the changes to come and the novel first-stage problems they'll bring, but we can develop a framework for thinking about them. The transparency principle again provides the starting point, regardless of the communicative technology involved.

The government's reliance on emerging digital technologies can facilitate democratic accountability, free expression, and related constitutional interests by expanding public access to government information and enabling citizens' participation in governmental processes. Through its digital expression, the government provides the public with valuable data and opinions. Not only can members of the public find these materials helpful in developing their own positions, but they also learn much more about their elected officials' values and priorities, which helps inform the public's views on whether those officials should be reelected or instead replaced.

Some digital expression involves noninteractive technologies in which the government exclusively controls the content of the expression and makes clear that it is doing the talking. Much like old-school television ads or op-ed columns, governmental websites often provide the public with information without providing any means for the public to insert their own expression. Certain governmental blogs and microblogging services do the same, where governmental bloggers provide information to interested readers without offering those readers the opportunity to respond or comment on the government's posts. Think, for example, of a government website that informs the public about an agency's programs and priorities. It may provide hyperlinks to other websites and permit readers to subscribe to news feeds and to receive e-mail updates to the site. But as a matter of design, the government may choose not to enable the public to comment on its posts or to interact with agency officials through the website. Here the speech is one-way, and is clearly the government's, along with the constitutional power to control its content.

---

[59] Danielle Keats Citron and I explored related issues in *Government Speech 2.0*, 87 Denv. U. L. Rev. 899 (2010).

Consider the following illustration: The board of a local public school district in South Carolina passed a resolution expressing its opposition to pending school voucher legislation that would have required the state to make public funds available for parents to pay their children's private school tuition. The resolution itself reflected the government's speech: the board's views on a contested public policy issue. The school board also directed the delivery of those views to the public through posts on the district's website, as well as through e-mails and letters to parents and school employees. These posts, letters, and e-mails also constituted the government's speech.

A supporter of the legislation then asked that he be allowed to post or link his pro-voucher materials on the district's website. When the district declined, he filed a First Amendment lawsuit. Noting that the district's website linked to those of other organizations that shared the district's views on the voucher legislation, he argued that the school district had opened up its website as a type of forum for the expression of private parties' views, and thus that the district could not exclude him based on his viewpoint.

A federal appellate court rejected the challenger's claim, recognizing that the government speech doctrine permits the school board to communicate its own viewpoint on its website (and elsewhere) without any obligation to allow others to change, stop, or interfere with the delivery of its own views.[60] There the design and context of the board's website made clear not only its viewpoint but also its role as source of that particular message. The board's links to other speakers' websites helped elaborate and support its own position, just like a speaker's citation to a supportive reference in a hard-copy policy paper. So long as the government speaker makes clear that it is referencing or linking to third-party speech to bolster its explanation of its own position, the government's inclusion of those links in support of its own views does not strip those views of their governmental character.

This dispute again illustrates how and why the government's speech can be valuable to the public. The board publicly took a position on pending legislation, and communicated that position on a website that clearly identified its governmental origins. The school board thus informed the public about the opinions of a public education body on proposed public education policy. That's important for members of the public to know. They may find those views helpful in informing their own views. And if they disagree with the board's position, they now know where their elected officials stand, and can try

---

[60] *See* Page v. Lexington County School District One, 531 F.3d 275 (4th Cir. 2008).

to persuade them otherwise or to elect new board members. The expressive technology involved should not confuse the issue.

Contrast a public school board's choice to create some type of public forum for the ventilation of individual views on the pending legislation, or any other topic. The board might do so, for example, at its public meetings by devoting time for members of the public to offer their views or ask questions. Or the board could do so online by enabling a comment function on its website, or by choosing to communicate through a social media platform that permits public commentary. The government's posts reflect its own speech, which it remains free to control. And nothing in the Constitution compels the government to communicate its views through platforms that enable the public to weigh in. But once the government chooses a platform that permits public comment, it has created a type of forum for nongovernmental parties' speech, and it is now bound by traditional First Amendment principles when regulating the speech of the commenters on that platform. The most important of those principles is that the government may not restrict private parties' speech based on viewpoint.

So far these examples involved the school board's speech on websites or social media platforms where the governmental origin of that expression was transparent to the public. As a matter of both constitutional law and good public policy, the government should identify itself affirmatively as the source of expression when it speaks – regardless of the type of technology involved. And many government actors already do this.

But a commitment to transparency should preclude the government's use of opaque technologies that conceal the governmental source of speech.[61] These include those that foster a deceptive dynamic known as sock puppetry, where speakers create a "fake online identity to praise, defend, or create the illusion of support for one's self, allies, or company."[62] Consider too "deep fake" technologies, in which machine-learning algorithms "enable the

---

[61] You may be wondering whether some governmental actors' masking of their identity, like undercover law enforcement officers' lies about their identity to uncover wrongdoing, run afoul of the transparency principle. Keep in mind that the transparency principle applies to first-stage government speech problems. In other words, when the governmental source of the speech is transparent to the public, then the government can claim the government speech defense to Free Speech Clause challenges by private parties who claim that the government is instead regulating their speech. Undercover police officers' deception does not trigger Free Speech Clause claims of this sort, so the transparency principle is not in play. Chapter 4 considers the very different second-stage question of whether and when the government's deceptive speech violates the Due Process Clause when the governmental source of the speech is uncontested.

[62] Brad Stone & Matt Richtel, *The Hand that Controls the Sock Puppet Could Get Slapped*, N.Y. TIMES, July 16, 2007.

creation of realistic impersonations out of digital whole-cloth," such that audio or video speech can be made to look like it comes from someone, anyone, other than the actual speaker.[63]

Determining Whether a Government Official Speaks in His Governmental or Personal Capacity

So far we've considered the first-stage government speech problems that arise when multiple speakers – both governmental and nongovernmental – simultaneously claim contested expression as their own. Next we turn to related but distinct problems involving the expression of a single government official in settings where we must determine whether he is speaking as the government or instead as an individual citizen. Here too, the answer to this question drives the choice between very different constitutional rules. When an official speaks as the government, then he has the constitutional power (not a constitutional right) to control that governmental message, but as the government he is constrained by the Free Speech Clause if he seeks to restrict nongovernmental parties' speech. On the other hand, when he speaks as a private citizen with First Amendment rights of his own, his choices are protected, rather than restrained, by the Constitution.

Take President Trump and Twitter. President Trump has regularly used his @realDonaldTrump Twitter account to speak to the world about a wide range of issues of public concern. The Twitter platform enables members of the public to follow, view, and reply to his posts. But Trump blocked some of his critics from access to his account, which means that they can no longer view his tweets and the resulting comment threads, nor can they reply to his tweets, from those blocked accounts.[64]

If Trump's tweets reflect his own speech in his personal capacity as a private citizen, then his choice to speak or block, or not, is protected, not restricted, by the First Amendment. And if Trump is speaking in his governmental capacity, then he has the power to control the content of his tweets as government speech exempt from Free Speech Clause challenges by those who would try to stop or change his messages. But once he chooses to engage in governmental speech through a platform that permits the public to comment on his posts, then he has enabled a forum for nongovernmental parties' expression in which he may not restrict their expression based on viewpoint.

---

[63] Bobby Chesney & Danielle Keats Citron, *Deep Fakes: A Looming Challenge for Privacy, Democracy, and National Security*, 107 Cal. L. Rev. (forthcoming 2019).

[64] *See* Knight First Am. Inst. v. Trump, 302 F. Supp. 3d 541 (S.D.N.Y. 2018).

The analysis remains the same regardless of the expressive technology or the identity of the government speaker. Take the brick-and-mortar example of a school board meeting where the board provides time for public input on the matters identified in its agenda. Here the government has created a limited public forum for discussion of those topics. Note that the government's control, rather than its ownership, of the forum is key. The government's choice to make time for public comments at a school board meeting creates a public forum regardless of whether it owns the building in which it meets, whether it rents it from a commercial source, or whether it borrows it gratis from the local YWCA. So long as the government controls the space at the time in question and chooses to make it available for the ventilation of nongovernmental parties' views, it has created a forum for the public's speech. Under the constitutional rules that apply to the government's administration of a limited public forum, the board can cut folks off who want to speak on other topics – like the World Series or the stock market. It can also cut folks off for other reasons unrelated to viewpoint – for example, if they exceed a reasonable time limit, or if they rattle off obscenities. But the First Amendment most assuredly bars the school board from cutting off speakers because they disagree with the board's views.

Of course, President Trump is not the only government official who relies on social media and related platforms to communicate to and interact with the public. Nor is he the only government official to have blocked his critics from those platforms.[65] Again, the applicable constitutional rules depend on whether the contested speech is that of the officials speaking as the government or instead as private individuals. The choice between the two requires a fact-specific inquiry; the nature, scope, and power of the speaker's governmental position should help guide this analysis, along with the expression's topic and its audience. A government official speaking to the public about matters within the purview of his governmental position generally speaks as the government, which means that the Constitution protects his expression of governmental views from interference by private parties, and that the Constitution protects private parties' comments on those views from his interference. To be sure, even high-ranking officials can escape their governmental role when speaking on matters unrelated to their jobs or in private settings; think, for example, of a government official's social media platform devoted to her thoughts about soccer or her summer reading list. But the greater the speaker's governmental power, the harder for him to deny his governmental association

---

[65] E.g., Davison v. Randall, 912 F.3d 666 (4th Cir. 2019).

when speaking to the public about matters related to that power. This is especially the case when the official expressly or implicitly threatens the exercise of governmental power. Indeed, some government officials serve as the voice or the face of the government. This is almost always true of the president, at least when speaking to the public on matters of public concern. He's not just another guy; he's The Man.

Does Trump speak as president when he tweets? All signs point in that direction. His account is registered to "Donald J. Trump, 45th President of the United States of America, Washington, D.C." White House officials support its administration and acknowledged that the tweets reflect official White House statements. As a federal judge summarized (in litigation that remains ongoing as I write this),

> President Trump uses @realDonaldTrump, often multiple times a day, to announce, describe, and defend his policies; to promote his Administration's legislative agenda; to announce official decisions; to engage with foreign political leaders; to publicize state visits; to challenge media organizations whose coverage of his Administration he believes to be unfair; and for other statements, including on occasion statements unrelated to official government business. President Trump sometimes uses the account to announce matters related to official government business before those matters are announced to the public through other official channels – like nominations.[66]

As a functional matter, when Trump tweets to the public on matters of public concern he does so as the government. This means that his critics don't have a First Amendment right to stop him from tweeting, to change his tweets to their liking, or even to correct his typos – just as they have no First Amendment right to snatch his microphone or to rejigger his remarks at a public speech. Nor do they have a First Amendment right to force him to use a platform like Twitter that enables public commentary. But when Trump chooses to engage in government speech on a platform that permits the public to weigh in on his speech, he has enabled a forum for the public's comment. And when he blocks those who disagree with him, he does so as the government – and thus the First Amendment forbids him, as the government, from doing so on the basis of these private parties' views.

Some might misunderstand this conclusion to mean that we should treat Twitter itself as a government actor subject to First Amendment constraints – meaning, among other things, that the First Amendment limits Twitter's

---

[66] Knight First Amendment Institute v. Trump, 302 F.Supp.3d 541, 552–553 (S.D.N.Y. 2018).

ability to discipline users who violate its terms of service. No. This conclusion simply applies the First Amendment to the *government's* choice to participate in a platform that permits public interaction. When the government makes that expressive choice, the Constitution permits it to control the content of its own posts but not to regulate the public's participation based on their viewpoint. But the Constitution constrains only the government and its choices, and Twitter – despite its considerable power – is a private party and not the government.[67]

Properly applied, the government speech doctrine empowers the government to speak to us, including through new expressive technologies, while denying it the power to throttle dissent. The importance of this principle becomes even more apparent when we see how, a few years earlier, another president, along with two federal courts, confused the government's power to control its own speech with the power to shut down opposing views.

In *Weise v. Casper*, federal courts invoked the government speech doctrine to justify the government's ejection of nondisruptive private citizens from a public event based solely on their viewpoint. That case involved a First Amendment challenge by a couple forcibly removed by government agents from a speech by then-President George W. Bush. Their offense? They arrived at the event's parking lot in a car that displayed a "No Blood for Oil" bumper sticker. The two didn't say anything. They didn't do anything. They just had a bumper sticker on their car.

Dramatically overstating the government's speech interests, the federal district court found that the couple's ejection did not violate the First Amendment: "President Bush had the right, at his own speech, to ensure that only his message was conveyed. When the President speaks, he may choose his own words."[68] The federal appellate court affirmed, concluding that the law was not clearly established as to "how to treat the ejection of a silent attendee from an official speech based on the attendee's protected expression outside the speech area."[69] Justice Ruth Bader Ginsburg (joined by Justice Sonia Sotomayor) wrote an astonished dissent from the Supreme Court's refusal to consider the case: "I cannot see how reasonable public officials, or any staff or

---

[67] This "state action" principle – that is, the principle that the Constitution limits actions by the government and not those by nongovernmental parties – explains why you have no First Amendment claim if your nongovernmental employer fires you because of your speech. You may or may not have statutory or common law claims against your nongovernmental employer (depending on your jurisdiction), but the Constitution does not protect you from private parties' actions that are independent of the government.

[68] Weise v. Casper, No. 05-cv-02355-WYD-CBS, 2008 WL 4838682 (D. Colo. Nov. 6, 2008).

[69] Weise v. Casper, 593 F.3d 1163, 1165 (10th Cir. 2010), *cert. denied*, 562 U.S. 976 (2010).

volunteers under their direction, could have viewed the bumper sticker as a permissible reason for depriving [the couple] of access to the event."[70]

Justice Ginsburg got it right. The government speech doctrine permits the president (or any other government speaker) to control the content of his own speech and to refuse to share the event's podium and microphone with anyone, friend or critic alike. But the mere presence of parties who may disagree with the government's views, silently or otherwise, in no way threatens the president's ability to express his own views. We must remain wary of courts and other government actors that misunderstand the government speech defense as a sword with which the government may pierce others' free speech rights, when it instead simply offers the government a shield from certain Free Speech Clause challenges by private parties who seek to interfere with what is really the government's own expression.[71]

Ascertaining When Public Employees' Speech Is the Government's to Control

Finally, we turn to related yet distinct first-stage controversies involving the public workforce. When do public employees speak for themselves, and when do they speak for their governmental employer such that their speech is the government's to control without running afoul of the Free Speech Clause? It's hard but important to get this right. Federal, state, and local governments employ more than 20 million workers, and the government has legitimate expressive and managerial interests of its own as an employer. But public employees' speech is often important not only to the employees themselves but also to the general public. If we are too quick to characterize public employees' speech as the government's to restrict, we lose speech of great value to the public, speech that helps ensure that the government and its officials are not above the law.

---

[70] Weise v. Casper, 562 U.S. 976 (2010) (Ginsburg, J., dissenting from the denial of ceriorari).

[71] Other examples include public entities' efforts to invoke government speech interests to justify the punishment of student expression in public schools *E.g.*, Doe v. Silsbee Ind. Sch. Dist., 402 Fed. Appx. 852, 855 (5th Cir. 2010), *cert. denied*, 563 U.S. 974 (2011) (rejecting a public high school student's First Amendment challenge to her dismissal from the cheerleading squad when she failed to cheer for a basketball player whom she alleged had sexually assaulted her: "In her capacity as a cheerleader, H.S. served as a mouthpiece through which [the school] could disseminate speech – namely, support for its athletic teams. Insofar as the First Amendment does not require schools to promote particular student speech, [the school] had no duty to promote H.S.'s message by allowing her to cheer or not cheer, as she saw fit."). For an example of a government's unsuccessful effort to assert the government speech defense to justify the exclusion of peaceful dissenters from a public event, see Liberty & Prosperity 1776, Inc. v. Corzine, 720 F. Supp. 2d 622 (D. N.J. 2010).

In *Garcetti v. Ceballos*, the Supreme Court dramatically expanded the government's ability to claim, and thus control, its workers' speech as its own.[72] There the majority created a bright-line rule that treats public employees' speech delivered pursuant to their official duties as speech for which the government has paid with a salary, and thus speech that the government may restrain and punish without running afoul of the First Amendment.

The dispute began when Richard Ceballos, a prosecutor in the Los Angeles District Attorney's office, wrote an internal office memo that criticized a police department affidavit that he felt included serious misrepresentations. When his employer disciplined him for his memo, he brought a First Amendment challenge. Citing *Rust* v. *Sullivan* and other decisions that emphasized the government's power to control its own speech, a 5–4 Court held that public employees' speech made pursuant to their official duties receives no First Amendment protection. "Restricting speech that owes its existence to a public employee's professional responsibilities does not infringe any liberties the employee might have enjoyed as a private citizen," the Court asserted. "It simply reflects the exercise of employer control over what the employer itself has commissioned or created."[73]

Justice Souter again led a vigorous dissent, acknowledging the government's managerial interests as an employer yet underscoring the value that government workers' speech can deliver to the public. "[R]esist[ing] the demand for winner-take-all," he instead proposed a balancing test in which the First Amendment protects public employees' speech when "private and public interests in addressing official wrongdoing and threats to health and safety [] outweigh the government's stake in the efficient implementation of policy."[74]

The *Garcetti* rule permits the government to control public employees' expression by characterizing such speech as the government's own for which it has paid with a salary – regardless of that expression's value to the public interest. But a thoughtful application of this principle requires us to delve more deeply into what exactly the government employer has "bought." Mr. Ceballos, the prosecutor disciplined in *Garcetti*, was not hired to deliver a specific governmental viewpoint that the police are infallible. He was hired instead to provide sound legal advice and competent prosecution. And, as far as we know, that's exactly what his employer, the Los Angeles District Attorney's Office, got. The public interest in what Mr. Ceballos had to say did not diminish because he uttered his views about the veracity of police affidavits

---

[72] 547 U.S. 410 (2006).   [73] *Id.* at 421–422.   [74] *Id.* at 428 (Souter, J., dissenting).

pursuant to his official duties as a prosecutor – if anything, his job responsibilities likely enhanced the value of his speech.

Lower courts now routinely apply *Garcetti's* expedited review to dispose
of government workers' First Amendment claims at great cost to the
public's interest in government transparency, precisely the value that the
government speech doctrine supposedly protects. Although public entities
frequently hire workers specifically to flag dangerous or illegal conditions,
Garcetti now empowers the government to punish them for doing just that.
The many examples include police officers terminated after reporting
public officials' illegal or improper behavior, health care workers disciplined after conveying concerns about patient care, primary and secondary
school educators punished after describing concerns about student treatment, financial managers fired after reporting fiscal improprieties, and a
wide variety of public employees discharged after detailing health and
safety violations.[75]

More specifically, one federal court applied *Garcetti* to hold that a prison
guard's internal reports of a possible breach of prison security were unprotected because those reports were among her official responsibilities to keep
the prison secure.[76] Another held that the First Amendment did not protect a
university employee fired after reporting improprieties in the university's
federal financial aid awards because her duties as a financial aid manager
required her to flag such problems.[77] And another applied *Garcetti* to conclude that the First Amendment does not protect internal reports by state
troopers and firearms instructors of health and safety hazards, including
elevated heavy metals levels, at the state's shooting range because such reports
were made pursuant to their official duty to report operational problems and to
maintain a safe worksite.[78] Still another concluded that the First Amendment
does not protect a special education counselor who complained about the lack
of proper classes for special education students because her official duties
required her to monitor her students' needs and progress.[79] And as a federal
appellate judge explained in yet another case: "Detective Kolatski was performing his job admirably at the time of these events, and although his

---

[75] For a sampling of these decisions, *see* Helen Norton, *Constraining Public Employee Speech: Government's Control of Its Workers' Speech to Protect Its Own Expression*, 59 DUKE L.J. 1 (2009).

[76] Spiegla v. Hull, 481 F.3d 961, 965–966 (7th Cir. 2007), *cert. denied*, 552 U.S. 975 (2007).

[77] Battle v. Board of Regents, 468 F.3d 755, 761–762 (11th Cir. 2006).

[78] Foraker v. Chaffinch, 501 F.3d 231, 247 (3rd Cir. 2007).

[79] Woodlock v. Orange Ulster B.O.C.E.S., 281 Fed. Appx. 66 (2nd Cir. 2008).

demotion for truthfully reporting allegations of misconduct may be morally repugnant, after *Garcetti*, it does not offend the First Amendment."[80]

For a time, some lower courts even understood *Garcetti* to mean that the First Amendment offers no protection to public employees punished for testifying truthfully about their on-the-job observations of government wrong-doing. One federal appellate court, for example, applied *Garcetti* to conclude that the Constitution posed no obstacle to the government's firing of a state employee who accurately testified under oath about his discovery that a state legislator on a state agency payroll had not been reporting for work.[81] Fortunately, in *Lane v. Franks* the Supreme Court unanimously reversed the lower court, holding that *Garcetti* did not apply because the challenger's job respon-sibilities did not ordinarily include testimony.[82] But under this reasoning, the First Amendment protected his testimony not because it was valuable to the public but instead because it was not pursuant to his official job duties; the Court took pains to note that it did "not address in this case whether truthful sworn testimony would constitute citizen speech under *Garcetti* when given as part of a public employee's ordinary job duties."[83] Incredibly, the Court has yet to tell us whether the First Amendment protects law enforcement officers, government lawyers, and others who testify truthfully about public corruption when it is their job to do so.

Garcetti imposes a wooden bright-line rule to avoid the often challenging but entirely commonplace task of balancing constitutional interests, and it does so to the public's detriment. It treats a wide swath of public employee speech as entirely unprotected without any showing of an adverse effect on government operations. This frustrates a meaningful commitment to repub-lican government by allowing government officials to punish, and thus deter, whistleblowing and other valuable work-related speech that would otherwise facilitate the government's accountability for its performance.

The *Garcetti* majority defended its formalistic rule as posing relatively little cost to the public's interest, arguing that statutory and common law remedies protect whistleblowing and similar speech even if the Constitution does not.[84] In short, the majority trusted the government itself to provide meaningful nonconstitutional protections for public employees' valuable speech about their jobs. But reality betrays this confidence: those protections are incom-plete, patchwork, and of decidedly limited utility. In the great majority of

---

[80] Morales v. Jones, 494 F.3d 590, 599 (7th Cir. 2007) (Rovner, J., concurring in part and dissenting in part), *cert. denied*, 552 U.S. 1099 (2008).
[81] Lane v. Cent. Ala. Comm. College, 523 Fed. Appx. 709 (11th Cir. 2013).
[82] 573 U.S. 228 (2014).   [83] *Id.* at 238 n.4.   [84] *Garcetti*, 547 U.S. at 425–426.

cases, lower courts' application of *Garcetti* to reject employees' First Amendment claims meant the end of the case, as no other legal claims remained available.[85]

Some judges alert to these threats limit *Garcetti*'s reach by interrogating whether a public employee's speech actually occurred pursuant to her official job duties, and thus whether her government employer should have the power to control it. Federal appellate Judge J. Harvie Wilkinson identified the high stakes: "[A]s the state grows more layered and impacts lives more profoundly, it seems inimical to First Amendment principles to treat too summarily those who bring, often at some personal risk, its operations into public view. It is vital to the health of our polity that the functioning of the ever more complex and powerful machinery of government not become democracy's dark lagoon."[86]

There's yet another way to approach these problems, one expressly tethered to the foundational premises underlying the government speech doctrine, and thus to the transparency principle. Recall that the government's expressive choices are valuable, and thus generally insulated from First Amendment scrutiny, because of what they offer the public: information that furthers democratic self-governance by enabling the public to identify and thus evaluate their government's priorities and performance. The democracy-enhancing value of the government's speech should also guide our approach to determining when the First Amendment permits the government to control its employees' speech as its own. As the transparency principle makes clear, the government's speech is more valuable and less dangerous when the governmental source of the specific message is apparent to the public.

A rule that better accommodates the weighty interests at stake here would permit the government to claim the power to control the speech of its employees as its own only when it has specifically commissioned or hired those employees to deliver a transparently governmental viewpoint for which the public can hold it accountable. This is the case, for example, when a school board hires a press secretary or lobbyist to promote its anti-voucher position, a health department hires an employee to promote teen abstinence to prevent pregnancy and sexually transmissible diseases, an agriculture department hires a marketer to extol the benefits of beef, or a mayor commissions a muralist to create patriotic art for the Fourth of July or art promoting equality to celebrate Dr. King's birthday. Each of these exemplifies government speech that is valuable to its listeners because it clearly reveals to the

---

[85] *See* Helen Norton, *Constraining Public Employee Speech: Government's Control of Its Workers' Speech to Protect Its Own Expression*, 59 DUKE L.J. 1, 40 n.155 (2009).

[86] Andrew v. Clark, 561 F.3d 261, 273 (4th Cir. 2009) (Wilkinson, J., concurring).

public the expressive choices of its government, enabling voters to evaluate the message's credibility and take accountability measures as appropriate. And we should understand the First Amendment to permit the government to protect that viewpoint from being garbled, for example, by disciplining an employee who was hired to deliver the government's views, only to speak in a way that undermines that viewpoint. But this approach describes a much smaller slice of public employee speech than does *Garcetti*'s "pursuant to official duties" test, as it insists on more careful attention to what it is that government seeks to communicate and whether that message is actually impaired by its workers' speech.

This less deferential approach to the government's expressive claims, itself an application of the transparency principle, still leaves room to safeguard the government's significant interests in effectively managing its workforce. That the government cannot claim the speech of an employee as its own in a particular situation under the test I propose does not mean that that worker's First Amendment claim will necessarily prevail. Far from it.

In my view, public employee expression that does not meet this demanding transparency-based test for government speech should continue on to the long-standing balancing test that the Court applied to public employees' First Amendment claims for decades prior to *Garcetti*.[87] Under this framework, courts assess whether the public employee's speech addresses a matter of public concern. The Court has defined speech on a matter of public concern as speech that addresses "a subject of legitimate news interest – that is, a subject of general interest and of value and concern to the public at the time of publication."[88] If a court concludes that the speech in question does *not* touch upon a subject of public concern – for example, a public employee's personal grievance about her own working conditions that is primarily of value to the employee as opposed to the listening public – it upholds the government's decision to discipline such private-concern speech, without any additional analysis. If, however, the challenger's speech concerns a matter of public concern, then the dispute proceeds to a balancing inquiry. There the court weighs the value of the employee's speech against any detrimental impact on the government's efficient workplace operations, like any adverse effect on the employer's ability to maintain discipline and harmony among coworkers. Public employees' First Amendment claims that involve speech on matters of public concern should fail under this balancing inquiry when their

---

[87] *See* Connick v. Myers, 461 U.S. 138, 143 (1983); Pickering v. Board of Education, 391 U.S. 563, 568 (1968).

[88] City of San Diego v. Roe, 543 U.S. 77, 83–84 (2004) (per curiam).

speech is intemperate or inaccurate or when it distracts the employee from performing her job.[89] And this is sometimes the case: public employees' speech even on matters of public concern holds the potential to undermine governmental efficiency when, for example, its boorish tone or factual inaccuracy disrupts workplace operations.[90]

A return to balancing means that we cannot forecast the outcomes with certainty, to the dismay of government. But uncertainty is greatly preferable, in my view, to workers' all-too-certain defeat under *Garcetti*. Before *Garcetti*, the Court's balancing test meant that government employers were free to ignore internal whistleblowing, but had to think twice before punishing, and thus deterring, it. After *Garcetti*, supervisors generally discipline such speech with impunity, chilling valuable expression to the public's detriment. Permitting a greater number of public employees' First Amendment claims to proceed to a balancing inquiry encourages transparency while still attending to the government's legitimate efficiency concerns.[91]

To be sure, the more contextual inquiry I suggest here demands more of courts and of the government than simply applying *Garcetti*'s bright-line rule. Advocates of the *Garcetti* rule underscore the efficiencies created when courts simply defer to government employers' personnel decisions. But *Garcetti*'s categorical approach reduces litigation and its attendant costs while imposing substantial costs of its own to workers' free speech rights and the public's interest in transparent government. Although efficiency is a significant government interest, some values are even more important.

As legal scholar Heidi Kitrosser reminds us, "government employees are crucial safety valves for protecting the people from abuse and incompetence, given their unique access to information and to a range of avenues for

---

[89] Before *Garceti's* bright-line rule, courts generally characterized government workers' allegations of unsafe, illegal, or improper behavior as matters of public concern, but reached mixed results when determining whether the value of that speech outweighed any detrimental impact on the government employer's operations, depending on its accuracy or tone. *See* Stephen Allred, *From Connick to Confusion: The Struggle to Define Speech on Matters of Public Concern*, 64 IND. L.J. 43, 62–63 (1988).

[90] *See Garcetti*, 547 U.S. at 427 (Stevens, J., dissenting) (explaining that the *Pickering/Connick* balancing test allows employers to discipline employee speech that is inflammatory or misguided).

[91] Note too that the employee must ultimately prove, as an additional element of her First Amendment claim, that her expression was a substantial or motivating factor in her punishment by her governmental employer. If she establishes such causation, the government defendant may still escape liability by establishing the affirmative defense that it would have taken the same action against the plaintiff even absent her speech. Mount Healthy City Sch. Dist. v. Doyle, 429 U.S. 274, 287 (1977).

transmitting the same."[92] We lose this essential check when the Court interprets the Constitution to permit the government to fire its workers for telling the truth about their jobs – particularly when that truth includes their reports of government mismanagement, deceit, or corruption.

*   *

The government's own speech – once we're convinced that in fact the government is speaking itself rather than regulating others' speech – remains exempt from the Free Speech Clause rules that apply to the government as a regulator. Next we turn to second-stage government speech problems that consider the constitutional rules that apply to the government as a speaker.

---

[92] Heidi Kitrosser, *The Special Value of Public Employee Speech*, 2015 Sup. Ct. Rev. 301, 330 (2016).

2

The Government's Speech and Religion

Suppose that you're sitting in the audience at your city council's weekly meeting, where you plan to comment on a proposal to build a homeless shelter in your neighborhood. At the meeting's start, the mayor – as he does every week – asks all to stand and bow their heads and offers a prayer, closing with "thanks to our Lord and Savior, Jesus Christ." Do you stand and bow your head; do you join the prayer; do you wait silently; do you object or leave? Do you feel valued and appreciated? Excluded? Does how you act, and how you feel, depend on whether you're Christian or instead agnostic, atheist, Jewish, Muslim, or some other faith? Does the government's prayer violate the Establishment Clause, which commands that the government "shall make no law respecting an establishment of religion"?

The government speaks, and has spoken, about religion in many ways, some more controversial than others. Frequently the government's religious speech involves prayer. Presidents routinely issue Thanksgiving Proclamations in which they "give thanks to Almighty God for our abundant blessing" and "encourage all Americans to gather, in homes and places of worship, to offer a prayer of thanks to God for our many blessings."[1] Congress and many state legislatures begin their legislative sessions with prayer, and some city councils open their meetings with prayer.[2] Congress has designated the first Thursday in May as a National Day of Prayer, and asks us on that date to "turn to God in prayer and meditation."[3] At times public schools offered prayers to start their school day, their graduation ceremonies, and even their football games.[4]

---

[1]   Proclamation No. 9678, 82 Fed. Reg. 55,721 (Nov. 17, 2017).
[2]   *See* Marsh v. Chambers, 463 U.S. 783 (1983); Town of Greece v. Galloway, 572 U.S. 565 (2014).
[3]   36 U.S.C. § 119 (2012).
[4]   *See* Engel v. Vitale, 370 U.S. 421 (1962); Lee v. Weisman, 505 U.S. 577 (1992); Santa Fe Indep. Sch. Dist. v. Doe, 530 U.S. 290 (2000).

The government's speech on matters religious also includes public schools' curricular choices, which communicate the values that the government as educator seeks to impart. At times public schools have refused for religious reasons to teach evolution, or required the teaching of creation science as a counterweight to any teaching of evolution.[5]

The government's displays and mottos also sometimes include religious references. Public entities' holiday displays sometimes showcase Nativity scenes and menorahs; their courthouses, capitols, schools, and parks sometimes display the Ten Commandments.[6] Governments' official seals and monuments occasionally feature crosses, and at one point South Carolina offered a specialty license plate depicting a cross and the statement "I Believe."[7] An Arizona town declared "Bible Week in Gilbert, Arizona" and urged its citizens to read the Bible.[8] The federal government adopted "In God We Trust" as its official motto, and displays that motto on its coins and currency. Ohio chose as its motto "With God, All Things Are Possible."[9] Congress added the phrase "under God" to the Pledge of Allegiance in the 1950s, and President Eisenhower's signing statement asserted that "[f]rom this day forward, the millions of our school children will daily proclaim in every city and town, every village and rural schoolhouse, the dedication of our Nation and our people to the Almighty."[10] And in a courtroom with a frieze that features the Ten Commandments, the Supreme Court opens its sessions with an entreaty that "God save the United States and this Honorable Court."[11]

WHEN, IF EVER, DOES THE GOVERNMENT'S SPEECH "ESTABLISH" RELIGION?

We begin our exploration of second-stage government speech problems with the First Amendment's Establishment Clause, the area in which courts and commentators to date have most often wrestled with whether and when the

---

[5] *See* Epperson v. Arkansas, 393 U.S. 97 (1968); Edwards v. Aguillard, 482 U.S. 578 (1987).
[6] *See* Lynch v. Donnelly, 465 U.S. 668 (1984); Wallace v. Jaffree, 472 U.S. 38 (1985); Cnty. of Allegheny v. ACLU, 492 U.S. 573 (1989); McCreary Cnty. v. ACLU, 545 U.S. 844 (2005).
[7] Summers v. Adams, 669 F. Supp. 2d 637 (D.S.C. 2009).
[8] Ariz. Civil Liberties Union v. Dunham, 112 F. Supp. 2d 927 (D. Ariz. 2000).
[9] ACLU v. Capitol Square Review and Advisory Bd., 243 F.3d 289 (6th Cir. 2001).
[10] Statement by the President Upon Signing Bill to Include the Words "Under God" in the Pledge to the Flag, PUB. PAPERS 563 (June 14, 1954), *available at* http://tinyurl.com/PubPapersUnderGod, *reprinted in* 100 CONG. REC. 8618 (1954).
[11] *See* Cnty. of Allegheny v. ACLU, 492 U.S. 573, 672 (1989) (Kennedy, J., concurring in the judgment in part and dissenting in part).

government's speech, by itself, violates the Constitution. The Establishment Clause requires some amount of separation between church and state. Just how wide the Constitution requires that gap to be, however, remains deeply contested. Wrestling with the meaning of the Establishment Clause requires that we struggle with even more fundamental matters. Are we a religious nation? A Christian nation? A secular political community in which faith is irrelevant? Something else entirely? These are important and challenging questions, questions that I don't claim to answer here. Instead, I explore how our different answers to those queries shape our different opinions on when, if ever, the government's religious speech violates the Constitution.

More specifically, our views on whether the government's speech runs afoul of the Establishment Clause generally turn on our theory of the Clause and the values it protects – in other words, on our answers to questions like "Why does the Constitution include an Establishment Clause? What harms does the Clause strive to prevent? What goals does it seek to achieve?" The many possible responses to those questions include protecting individuals' religious choices from the government's interference, restraining the government from trampling religious minorities, promoting equality and inclusion for all regardless of their religion or nonreligion, protecting religious institutions from the government's corrupting influence, and quelling religious divisiveness.

Almost everyone agrees that, at a minimum, the Establishment Clause forbids the government from creating an official church and from compelling religious oaths or observances of its citizens.[12] After that, there's plenty of disagreement. Some feel that so long as the government does not coerce its citizens' religious beliefs or practices, it is free not only to prefer religion over nonreligion but also to favor some religions, like Christianity, over others. Others understand the Clause to permit the government to favor religion over nonreligion so long as it does not prefer some religions over others. Still others understand the Clause to require the government's neutrality not only among religions, but also between religion and nonreligion.

Courts and commentators considering whether the government's religious speech runs afoul of the Establishment Clause have identified at least three different approaches to solving this second-stage government speech problem. Under the noncoercion principle, we focus on the *effects* of the government's religious speech on its listeners, asking whether it coerces listeners' religious

---

[12] Justice Clarence Thomas is an exception, characterizing the Establishment Clause as a federalism provision that bars only the federal government, and not the states, from establishing an official religion. E.g., Town of Greece v. Galloway, 572 U.S. 565, 604 (2014) (Thomas, J., concurring).

practice or other behavior. Under the nonendorsement principle, we remain attentive to the *effects* of the government's expression on its listeners but ask instead whether the government's speech endorses religion in ways that communicate a message of exclusion to nonbelievers or other religious minorities. Finally, under the neutrality principle, we turn to the *purposes* underlying the government's expressive choices, asking whether the government seeks to advance religion through its speech.

These different approaches reflect different answers to the query "What does the Establishment Clause forbid?" The government's coercion of our religious belief or practice? The government's messages of exclusion based on our religion or nonreligion? The government's taking sides on religious matters? Our choice among these approaches largely turns on our view of the values underlying the Establishment Clause. Those who think that the Establishment Clause ensures the government's neutrality on all matters religious will be relatively quick to find that the government's religious speech violates the Clause. Those who instead believe that the Clause seeks simply to stop the government from affirmatively interfering with our religious choices will be relatively slow to find Establishment Clause violations.

The Supreme Court's decisions in this area do not reflect a consistent approach to the Establishment Clause problems triggered by the government's religious speech. Far from it. And whether any of these three approaches currently commands a majority of the Court remains uncertain; indeed, in recent years the Court has been increasingly reluctant to find Establishment Clause violations of any kind. What's important for our discussion here is that each of the three approaches demonstrates a different way to think about whether and when the government's speech, by itself, violates the Constitution. As explained in the Introduction, in thinking about second-stage government speech problems, I suggest that we ask and answer a series of questions about the consequences of, and the motivations underlying, the government's speech. As we'll see in the chapters to come, this series of questions can also help us think about whether and when the government's speech infringes constitutional protections other than those provided by the Establishment Clause.

FOCUSING ON GOVERNMENT EXPRESSION'S EFFECTS: THE NONCOERCION PRINCIPLE

Those who adopt the noncoercion principle understand the Establishment Clause to protect an individual's religious autonomy – in other words, an individual's liberty to believe and worship as she chooses, free from the government's interference. The noncoercion principle thus focuses on the effects of the government's religious speech on its listeners (or, in the case of a visual display, on its observers). Under this view, the government's speech offends the Establishment Clause when it inflicts the harm of coercing its listeners' religious practice, as would be the case if the government's speech compelled listeners to participate in a religious activity through its commands or threats. But so long as the government's religious speech does not cause this forbidden effect, the noncoercion principle does not require the government's speech to remain neutral on religious matters.

What does it mean to coerce another? This question has challenged philosophers, legal scholars, and courts for centuries.[13] Most would agree that to coerce is to force, to insist, to compel, to muscle another to choose "x" when he would otherwise choose "y." To coerce another is to overcome his will, to override his free or voluntary choice. A speaker coerces her listeners when she exerts pressure that her listeners can't reasonably be expected to resist. Coercive speech is distinct, at least in theory, from persuasive speech. The former overrides the listener's free choice, while the latter does not. The line between the two is sometimes hard to see.

When does the government's speech coerce its listeners' religious belief and practice? Certainly when it threatens physical force, legal punishment, or some other retaliation against listeners who resist its message. Beyond this, those who advocate the noncoercion principle occasionally clash over whether and when the government's voice, by itself, achieves this forbidden effect, this constitutionally prohibited harm, by coercing its targets.[14] Justices Anthony Kennedy and Antonin Scalia, for instance, agreed that the government's coercion – and only the government's coercion – violates the Establishment Clause. But Scalia was considerably slower than Kennedy to treat the government's religious speech as coercive; he applied an historical approach to characterize the government's religious speech as impermissibly coercive only when it threatened the government's punishment of those who resist its

---

[13] *See* J. Roland Pennock, *Coercion: An Overview, in* COERCION 1 (J. Roland Pennock & John W. Chapman eds., 1972) (describing philosophers' debates over the definition of coercion).

[14] *See* Michael W. McConnell, *Coercion: The Lost Element of Establishment*, 27 WM. & MARY L. REV. 933, 941 (1987) ("A noncoercion standard, of course, would not answer all questions. For example, it obviously would not answer the question, 'What is coercion?' Enormous variance exists between the persecutions of old and the many subtle ways in which government action can distort religious choice today.").

religious commands.[15] Under this view of coercion, the government's religious speech almost never offends the Establishment Clause.

While also attentive to historical tradition, Justice Kennedy added a functional gloss: "a fact-sensitive [inquiry] that considers both the setting [of the government's prayer or other religious speech] and the audience to whom it is directed."[16] More specifically, Kennedy considered impermissible "coercion" to include the government's speech that shapes listeners' behavior through peer pressure and other social dynamics. Under this more expansive view of coercion, a government speaker can coerce its listeners by badgering them when they are "captive" – when they are unable to escape or resist the government's speech – until they abandon their opposition. In particular, Kennedy consistently treated the government's prayer and other religious speech in public elementary and secondary schools – "where the line between voluntary and coerced participation may be difficult to draw"[17] – as coercive. In *Lee* v. *Weisman*, for instance, he found this to be true of a public school's choice to open its graduation ceremony with prayer:

> The undeniable fact is that the school district's supervision and control of a high school graduation ceremony places public pressure, as well as peer pressure, on attending students to stand as a group or, at least, maintain respectful silence during the invocation and benediction. This pressure, though subtle and indirect, can be as real as any overt compulsion.... The prayer exercises in this case are especially improper because the State has in every practical sense compelled attendance and participation in an explicit

---

[15] For more on the Court's historical approach to the government's legislative prayer, *see* Marsh v. Chambers, 463 U.S. 783, 790 (1983) ("Standing alone, historical patterns cannot justify contemporary violations of constitutional guarantees, but there is far more here than simply historical patterns. In this context, historical evidence sheds light not only on what the draftsmen intended the Establishment Clause to mean, but also on how they thought that Clause applied to the practice authorized by the First Congress—their actions reveal their intent."); Town of Greece v. Galloway, 572 U.S. 565, 576–577 (2014) ("Yet *Marsh* must not be understood as permitting a practice that would amount to a constitutional violation if not for its historical foundation. The case teaches instead that the Establishment Clause must be interpreted 'by reference to historical practices and understandings . . . .' *Marsh* stands for the proposition that it is not necessary to define the precise boundary of the Establishment Clause where history shows that the specific practice is permitted. Any test the Court adopts must acknowledge a practice that was accepted by the Framers and has withstood the critical scrutiny of time and political change.").

[16] Town of Greece v. Galloway, 572 U.S. 565, 587 (2014).

[17] Westside Community Board of Education v. Mergens, 496 U.S. 226, 262 (1990) (Kennedy, J., concurring).

religious exercise at an event of singular importance to every student, one the objecting student had no real alternative to avoid."[18]

Justice Scalia dissented, arguing that we should bind ourselves to a much narrower understanding of coercion: "[t]he coercion that was a hallmark of historical establishments of religion was coercion of religious orthodoxy and of financial support by force of law and threat of penalty."[19] Peer pressure, under his historical approach, does not assert force akin to coercion.

When we turn to the government's prayer in adult settings, we see less disagreement among the noncoercion principle's adherents on the Supreme Court, as Kennedy felt that adults are considerably less vulnerable to peer pressure than children and teenagers. For this reason, in *Town of Greece v. Galloway* he declined to describe as coercive a town council's choice to open its meetings with prayers by local pastors invited from local congregations (almost all of the local congregations were Christian and so almost all of the prayers were Christian too).[20] Justice Scalia, even slower to see coercion, agreed.[21]

Kennedy went on to suggest that the government's prayers might violate the Establishment Clause even in adult settings if, over the course of time they "denigrate nonbelievers or religious minorities, threaten damnation or preach conversion" or if the government "directed the public to participate in the prayers, singled out dissidents for opprobrium or indicated that their decisions might be influenced by a person's acquiescence in the prayer opportunity."[22] We can also imagine that some settings involving adults threaten more coercion than others: think of the government's speech in its jails and prisons where listeners are obviously not free to leave, or in its public workplaces where its workers depend on their jobs for their families' livelihood.

Lower courts have since divided over whether prayers that open a local government's meetings coerce their listeners' participation when offered by the government officials themselves, rather than by invited clergy. Return to the hypothetical that opened this chapter, where a mayor opens a city council meeting by asking all to stand, bow their heads, and join a prayer that includes "thanks to our Lord and Savior, Jesus Christ." Some judges conclude that the relatively intimate setting of such a meeting increases the social pressure on those in attendance to comply with the government official's request, especially since some of those listeners are in attendance because they hope to

---

[18] 505 U.S. 577, 598 (1992).   [19] *Id.* at 640 (Scalia, J., dissenting).
[20] *Town of Greece*, 572 U.S. at 565.   [21] *Id.* at 587.   [22] *Id.* at 583, 588.

persuade that official to take some action.[23] Others instead see these practices as consistent with a long-standing tradition of legislative prayer, in which adults are free to join, or not, as they choose.[24]

How does the noncoercion principle apply to the government's religious displays? Think of nativity scenes, crosses, or menorahs in the government's holiday displays, or the Ten Commandments in a government courthouse or on its capitol lawn. The noncoercion principle's adherents generally conclude that the government's religious displays in these public settings threaten no coercive effect because they require no response from their onlookers. For the same reason, those advocates see no coercion threatened by a governmental motto like "In God We Trust" or "With God, All Things are Possible," or the government's insertion of "under God" in the Pledge of Allegiance – so long as the government does not force anyone to recite the motto or the Pledge on pain of punishment.

Even so, Justice Kennedy (joined at the time by Justice Scalia) again suggested that in rare circumstances the government's religious displays, without more, might rise to the level of impermissible "proselytization" that violates the noncoercion principle:

> Coercion need not be a direct tax in aid of religion or a test oath. Symbolic recognition or accommodation of religious faith may violate the Clause in an extreme case. I doubt not, for example, that the Clause forbids a city to permit the permanent erection of a large Latin cross on the roof of city hall. This is not because government speech about religion is *per se* suspect, as the majority would have it, but because such an obtrusive year-round religious display would place the government's weight behind an obvious effort to proselytize.[25]

So those who adopt the noncoercion principle find that the government's religious speech offends the Establishment Clause only when it coerces listeners' religious beliefs or practices, even as they sometimes disagree about when the government's speech in fact coerces. The noncoercion principle

---

[23] *See* Lund v. Rowan County, 863 F.3d 268 (4th Cir. 2017), *cert. denied*, 138 S. Ct. 2564 (2018) ("Relative to sessions of Congress and state legislatures, the intimate setting of a municipal board meeting presents a heightened potential for coercion. Local governments possess the power to directly influence both individual and community interests .... The decision to attend local government meetings may not be wholly voluntary in the same way as the choice to participate in other civic or community functions.").

[24] *See* Bormuth v. County of Jackson, 870 F.3d 494 (6th Cir. 2017) (en banc).

[25] Cnty. of Allegheny v. ACLU, 492 U.S. 573, 661 (1989) (Kennedy, J., concurring in the judgment in part and dissenting in part).

thus seeks to protect individuals' autonomy, their liberty to believe and worship as they choose, from the government's interference.

But the principle's critics contend that it is incomplete because it fails to recognize the equality and inclusiveness values they believe that the Establishment Clause also protects. These critics fear that a focus only on the coercive effects of the government's religious speech does not "adequately protect the religious liberty or respect the religious diversity of the members of our pluralistic political community."[26] This brings us to the nonendorsement principle, which finds that, even absent any coercive effects, the government's speech violates the Establishment Clause when it sends a message of exclusion or disrespect based on religion or nonreligion.

FOCUSING ON GOVERNMENT EXPRESSION'S EFFECTS: THE NONENDORSEMENT PRINCIPLE

Most everyone agrees that the government's coercive religious speech violates the Establishment Clause. But advocates of the nonendorsement principle contend that the Establishment Clause also forbids the government's religious speech that inflicts expressive, or dignitary, harm regardless of whether it coerces its listener. Under this approach, as legal scholar Caroline Mala Corbin explains, "the government violates the Establishment Clause's equality component if its religious speech fails to treat believers and nonbelievers with equal concern. Again, the injury turns not on intent or on material harms, but on the state's message of unequal worth."[27]

Identifying equality and inclusiveness as key values underlying the Establishment Clause, the nonendorsement principle's adherents conclude that the government violates the Clause when it delivers a message that citizens' status as insiders or outsiders depends on their religion or nonreligion. As Justice O'Connor, a champion of the nonendorsement principle during her tenure on the Court, explained:

> As a theoretical matter, the endorsement test captures the essential command of the Establishment Clause, namely, that government must not make a person's religious beliefs relevant to his or her standing in the political community by conveying a message "that religion or a particular religious belief is favored or preferred." . . . [G]overnment cannot endorse the religious practices and beliefs of some citizens without sending a clear message to nonadherents that they are outsiders or less than full members of the political

---

[26] *Id.* at 627–628 (O'Connor, J., concurring in part and concurring in the judgment).

[27] Caroline Mala Corbin, *Nonbelievers and Government Speech*, 97 IOWA L. REV. 347, 381 (2011).

community and an accompanying message to adherents that they are insiders, favored members of the political community.[28]

In other words, the nonendorsement principle seeks to protect individuals' dignity, their standing as full and equal members of the community regardless of religion or nonreligion, from the government's messages of disrespect or exclusion.

How do we determine whether the government's speech violates the non-endorsement principle? Under Justice O'Connor's approach, we ask whether a reasonable observer, aware of the history and context of the community and forum in which the government's expression takes place, would understand the government's message as endorsing or disapproving religion or nonreligion.[29] (Although courts and commentators often use "nonendorsement" as shorthand for this approach, the test prohibits the government's disapproval, as well as its endorsement, of religion or nonreligion.[30]) And just as Kennedy underscored the importance of context in determining when the government's religious speech coerces its targets' behavior, O'Connor urged a fact-sensitive inquiry for determining whether the government's speech sends a message that some are insiders or outsiders based on their religion or nonreligion.

Let's look at how the nonendorsement principle applies to the government's prayer. Advocates of the nonendorsement approach generally find that a public school's "sponsorship of religious speech," including its prayer at graduation ceremonies as well as at football games, sends an impermissible message that nonadherents are religious outsiders.[31] Whether the government's prayer in adult settings offends the nonendorsement principle depends on the facts. Return to *Town of Greece* v. *Galloway*, involving an Establishment Clause challenge to a town's practice of asking clergy selected from local

---

[28] Cnty. of Allegheny v. ACLU, 492 U.S. 573, 627 (1989) (O'Connor, J., concurring in part and concurring in the judgment) (citations omitted).

[29] *See* Capitol Square Review and Advisory Bd. v. Pinette, 515 U.S. 753, 779–780 (O'Connor, J., concurring in part and concurring in the judgment) ("[B]ecause our concern is with the political community writ large, the endorsement inquiry is not about the perceptions of particular individuals or saving isolated nonadherents from … discomfort … . It is for this reason that the reasonable observer in the endorsement inquiry must be deemed aware of the history and context of the community and forum in which the religious [speech takes place].").

[30] Lynch v. Donnelly, 465 U.S. 668, 692 (1984) (O'Connor, J., concurring) ("What is crucial is that a government practice not have the effect of communicating a message of government endorsement or disapproval of religion. It is only practices having that effect, whether intentionally or unintentionally, that make religion relevant, in reality or public perception, to status in the political community.").

[31] Santa Fe Indep. Sch. Dist. v. Doe, 530 U.S. 290 (2000).

congregations to offer a prayer to open the town council's monthly meetings.[32] And because almost all of the local congregations were Christian, almost all of the prayers were Christian too. Recall that the Court's majority applied the noncoercion principle to uphold the town's practice, underscoring the nation's long historical tradition of legislative prayer and finding that the prayer in this particular setting did not coerce its adult listeners, whom the majority characterized as free to respond as they chose. Dissenting Justice Elena Kagan instead urged the nonendorsement principle, contending that the town's predominantly Christian prayers did not "square with the First Amendment's promise that every citizen, irrespective of her religion, owns an equal share in her government."[33] Underscoring equality and inclusiveness as among the Establishment Clause's core values, she found that the town, through its prayers, impermissibly aligned "itself with, and placed its imprimatur on, a particular religious creed."[34]

Next let's consider how the nonendorsement principle applies to the government's religious displays. Although the nonendorsement principle's advocates are quicker to find that the government's religious displays violate the Establishment Clause than are adherents of the noncoercion principle, the nonendorsement principle still permits the government to acknowledge or celebrate religion through its speech so long as it does not communicate that onlookers' insider or outsider status depends on their religion.

Consider the Establishment Clause challenges brought against two different governmental holiday displays in downtown Pittsburgh. One of the displays featured an 18-foot Chanukah menorah placed outside the City-County Building, next to the city's 45-foot decorated Christmas tree. The other display featured a crèche – a depiction of the Christian Nativity scene – placed on the county courthouse's Grand Staircase, the courthouse's "main," "most beautiful," and "most public" area; the scene included a banner proclaiming "Gloria in Excelsis Deo," which means "Glory to God in the Highest."[35] Justice O'Connor's vote, rooted in the nonendorsement principle, helped secure a majority that upheld the first display while putting a stop to the second. She found that the government's inclusion of the menorah as part of a broader and more varied holiday display signaled the government's message of pluralism, of respect for and welcome to all.[36] But she found that the government's prominent display of a crèche in a county courthouse by itself, without any

---

[32] Town of Greece v. Galloway, 572 U.S. 565, 587 (2014).   [33] *Id.* at 616 (Kagan, J., dissenting).
[34] *Id.* at 619.   [35] *See Cnty. of Allegheny*, 492 U.S. at 579–580.
[36] *Id.* at 635–636 (O'Connor, J., concurring in part and concurring in the judgment).

broader context that gestured towards inclusion, communicated the government's religious endorsement.[37]

Just as some advocates of the noncoercion principle are quicker than others to find that the government's speech coerces its listeners, so too are some advocates of the nonendorsement principle quicker than others to find that the government has communicated an impermissible message of inclusion or exclusion based on religion or nonreligion. For example, some of the nonendorsement principle's advocates conclude that the long-standing historical tradition underlying certain religious references, like the governmental motto "In God We Trust" or the government's insertion of "Under God" in the Pledge of Allegiance, strips those expressive choices of a religious character as understood by today's reasonable observers.[38] Others disagree, maintaining that the nonendorsement principle, properly applied, requires that we adopt the perspective of nonbelievers or other religious minorities who may be more likely to perceive the government's long-standing religious references as endorsing religion.[39]

To be sure, the nonendorsement principle's critics contest the premise that the Establishment Clause requires the government's inclusiveness on religious matters. These critics identify the Clause as instead protecting individuals' religious autonomy from the government's interference, and thus contend that "the endorsement test wrongly elevates mere offense, alienation, or symbolic harm to judicially redressable injury."[40] Some even charge that the nonendorsement principle itself reflects religious hostility when it fails to recognize that religion has played, and continues to play, a role in American life worthy of the government's support:

> Government policies of accommodation, acknowledgment, and support for religion are an accepted part of our political and cultural heritage, and the Establishment Clause permits government some latitude in recognizing the central role of religion in society. Any approach less sensitive to our heritage would border on latent hostility to religion, as it would require government in

---

[37] *Id.* at 626–627 (O'Connor, J., concurring in part and concurring in the judgment).

[38] *See* Elk Grove Unified Sch. Dist. v. Newdow. 542 U.S. 1, 36 (2004) (O'Connor, J., concurring in the judgment) ("The reasonable observer discussed above, fully aware of our national history and the origins of such practices, would not perceive these acknowledgments as signifying a government endorsement of any specific religion, or even of religion over nonreligion.").

[39] *See* Caroline Mala Corbin, *Nonbelievers and Government Speech*, 97 IOWA L. REV. 347 (2011).

[40] Jay Wexler, *The Endorsement Test*, 21 WASH. U. J.L. & POL'Y 263, 274–275 (2006) (canvassing critiques of the nonendorsement principle).

all its multifaceted roles to acknowledge only the secular, to the exclusion and so to the detriment of the religious.[41]

So while the nonendorsement principle's advocates feel that the government's religious messages can contribute to religious divisions, the principle's detractors sometimes feel that the government's *failure* to communicate religious messages itself fuels religious hostility. The principle's critics also consider it unmanageable as a practical matter, objecting that it is "inherently incoherent and incapable of consistent application."[42] Determining whether and when the government impermissibly communicates religious endorsement or disapproval, in their view, is unavoidably subjective, leading to unpredictable and unprincipled results.

Both the noncoercion and the nonendorsement principles focus on the effects of the government's religious speech on its listeners as the key to an Establishment Clause violation. Both agree that the government's religious speech sometimes produces constitutionally forbidden effects, although they disagree about the range of effects from which the Establishment Clause protects us. Next we turn to the neutrality principle, which focuses not on the effects of the government's religious expression, but instead on the purposes underlying the government's expressive choices.

FOCUSING ON THE GOVERNMENT'S PURPOSES WHEN SPEAKING:
THE NEUTRALITY PRINCIPLE

The neutrality principle's advocates understand the Establishment Clause to bar the government's words, as well as its deeds, when inspired by what they understand to be a constitutionally impermissible purpose: the government's objective to take sides on religious matters. As Justice Souter explained, "[W]hen the government acts with the ostensible and predominant purpose of advancing religion, it violates that central Establishment Clause value of official religious neutrality, there being no neutrality when the government's ostensible object is to take sides."[43] The neutrality principle identifies the government's evenhandedness as the value at the heart of the Establishment Clause, concluding that the government's neutrality on all matters religious prevents religious divisiveness, and simultaneously protects both the government from religion and religion from the government. Contending that

---

[41] Cnty. of Allegheny v. ACLU, 492 U.S. 573, 664 (1989) (Kennedy, J., concurring in the judgment in part and dissenting in part).
[42] Jay Wexler, *supra* note 40.   [43] McCreary Cnty. v. ACLU, 545 U.S. 844, 860 (2005).

religious freedom is at least as long-standing and important an American tradition as religion itself, the neutrality principle's advocates maintain that the government's speech that seeks to advance religion over nonreligion threatens this principle as much as its speech that seeks to advance one religion over another.[44]

To identify the purposes underlying the government's religious speech, courts commonly rely on a number of factors drawn from other areas of law that require judges and juries to determine the motivations of governmental (and nongovernmental) actors. These include governmental decisionmakers' descriptions of their own motives, the historical background and specific series of events leading up to the government's expressive choice, and the availability of other explanations for the government's choice. The Supreme Court first applied the neutrality principle to the government's religious speech in the 1960s. *Engel* v. *Vitale* involved an Establishment Clause challenge brought by parents who objected to their local school board's choice to start the school day with a prayer composed by the New York State Board of Regents: "Almighty God, we acknowledge our dependence upon Thee, and we beg Thy blessings upon us, our parents, our teachers and our Country."[45] The Court found that the board sought to advance religion with its expressive choice, and thus held that it violated the Clause apart from any coercive effect (the school board's policy permitted students who objected to the prayer to remain silent or be excused):

> When the power, prestige and financial support of government is placed behind a particular religious belief, the indirect coercive pressure upon religious minorities to conform to the prevailing official approved religion is plain. But the purposes underlying the Establishment Clause go much further than that. Its first and most immediate purpose rested on the belief that a union of government and religion tends to destroy government and to degrade religion.[46]

---

[44] Note that both the nonendorsement principle and the neutrality principle might be understood as parts of, or refinements to, the test for Establishment Clause violations more generally announced in Lemon v. Kurtzman, 403 U.S. 602 (1971). There the Supreme Court held that a challenger proves a violation of the Establishment Clause when she shows any one of three things: that the government's contested action was not motivated by a secular purpose; that the action's principal or primary effect was to advance or inhibit religion; or that its action fostered an excessive government entanglement with religion. Although the *Lemon* test has generated plenty of criticism, lower courts still frequently apply it to Establishment Clause challenges, and many courts and commentators understand the neutrality principle and the nonendorsement principle as applications or refinements of *Lemon's* first two elements.

[45] Engel v. Vitale, 370 U.S. 421, 422 (1962).   [46] *Id.* at 431.

Writing for the majority, Justice Hugo Black emphasized that the neutrality principle recognizes "that religion is too personal, too sacred, too holy, to permit its 'unhallowed perversion' by a civil magistrate" and that "governmentally established religions and religious persecutions go hand in hand."[47]

Shortly thereafter, the Supreme Court again relied on the neutrality principle to uphold parents' and students' Establishment Clause challenges to their public schools' choice to begin each day with devotional Bible readings and the Lord's Prayer (rather than with the sort of government-drafted prayers at issue in *Engel*).[48] In so holding, the Court distinguished public schools' Bible readings as part of the secular study of civilization, history, ethics, and literature from Bible readings aimed to advance religion: unlike their teaching that seeks to *promote* religion, the majority observed that public schools' teaching *about* religion does not seek to advance religion in violation of the Establishment Clause.[49]

Two decades later, in *Wallace* v. *Jaffree*, the parents of public school students challenged an Alabama law that authorized a minute of silence "for meditation or voluntary prayer" to start the school day; this statute replaced an earlier law that had simply authorized a minute of silence "for meditation."[50] Concluding that the government impermissibly sought to advance religion, the Court struck down the law as a violation of the neutrality principle. As evidence of the government's impermissible purpose, the Court emphasized the sponsor's statement in which he described his proposal as an effort to return prayer to the public schools. The Court also observed that no secular purpose could explain the government's choice, since the earlier law that authorized a moment of silence already permitted, even if it did not expressly mention, voluntary prayer.

---

[47] *Id.* at 432.
[48] Abington Sch. Dist. v. Schempp, 374 U.S. 203, 222 (1963) ("The wholesome 'neutrality' of which this Court's cases speak thus stems from a recognition of the teachings of history that powerful sects or groups might bring about a fusion of governmental and religious functions or a concert or dependency of one upon the other to the end that official support of the State or Federal Government would be placed behind the tenets of one or of all orthodoxies. This the Establishment Clause prohibits.").
[49] *Id.* at 225 ("It certainly may be said that the Bible is worthy of study for its literary and historic qualities. Nothing we have said here indicates that such study of the Bible or of religion, when presented objectively as part of a secular program of education, may not be effected consistently with the First Amendment. But the exercises here do not fall into those categories. They are religious exercises, required by the States in violation of the command of the First Amendment that the Government maintain strict neutrality, neither aiding nor opposing religion.").
[50] Wallace v. Jaffree, 472 U.S. 38, 56 (1985).

The neutrality principle doomed not only public schools' prayer but also their curricular choices that sought to advance religion. Consider biology teacher Susan Epperson's challenge to Arkansas's law forbidding the teaching of evolution in the public schools, a law modeled on the Tennessee statute famously at issue in the 1925 Scopes Monkey Trial.[51] Relying on the neutrality principle to strike down the state's law, the Court found that Arkansas sought to advance a religious theory of human origins through its curricular choices: "the State may not adopt programs or practices in public schools or colleges which aid or oppose any religion. This prohibition is absolute. It forbids alike the preference of a religious doctrine or the prohibition of theory which is deemed antagonistic to a particular dogma."[52]

The Court returned to this issue more than twenty years later in *Edwards v. Aguillard.* A group of parents, teachers, and religious leaders brought an Establishment Clause challenge against Louisiana's Creationism Act, which forbade public elementary and secondary schools from teaching the theory of evolution unless they also taught the theory of "creation science." Louisiana argued that its law neither forbade the teaching of evolution nor required the teaching of creation science, but instead simply sought to protect academic freedom by ensuring that if one were taught, so too must the other be taught. The Court disagreed, concluding that the state instead sought to advance a religious theory of life's origins in violation of the neutrality principle:

> [T]he Act's primary purpose was to change the science curriculum of public schools in order to provide persuasive advantage to a particular religious doctrine that rejects the factual basis of evolution in its entirety.... . [T]he Creationism Act is designed *either* to promote the theory of creation science which embodies a particular religious tenet by requiring that creation science be taught whenever evolution is taught *or* to prohibit the teaching of a scientific theory disfavored by certain religious sects by forbidding the teaching of evolution when creation science is not also taught.[53]

The neutrality principle has generated mixed results when applied to the government's religious displays or other religious references. As one illustration, the Court relied on the neutrality principle in *Stone v. Graham* when it put a stop to a state's choice to post the Ten Commandments on every public

---

[51] Epperson v. Arkansas, 393 U.S. 97, 98 (1968).   [52] *Id.* at 106–107.

[53] Edwards v. Aguillard, 482 U.S. 578, 592–593 (1987); *see also id.* at 594 ("Teaching a variety of scientific theories about the origins of humankind to schoolchildren might be validly done with the clear secular intent of enhancing the effectiveness of science instruction. But because the primary purpose of the Creationism Act is to endorse a particular religious doctrine, the Act furthers religion in violation of the Establishment Clause.").

classroom wall throughout the state. Underscoring the Commandments' substantive role as a sacred text in the Jewish and Christian faiths (including the Commandments' explicit call to worship and observance of the Sabbath) along with the lack of any identified secular purpose for the government's choice, the Court found that the "pre–eminent purpose for posting the Ten Commandments on schoolroom walls is plainly religious in nature."[54] It continued:

> This is not a case in which the Ten Commandments are integrated into the school curriculum, where the Bible may constitutionally be used in an appropriate study of history, civilization, ethics, comparative religion, or the like. Posting of religious texts on the wall serves no such educational function. If the posted copies of the Ten Commandments are to have any effect at all, it will be to induce the schoolchildren to read, meditate upon, perhaps to venerate and obey, the Commandments. However desirable this might be as a matter of private devotion, it is not a permissible state objective under the Establishment Clause.[55]

On the other hand, in *Lynch* v. *Donnelly*, the Court's majority applied the neutrality principle to reject an Establishment Clause challenge to Pawtucket, Rhode Island's forty-year-old annual Christmas display that featured a Christmas tree, a Santa Clause house, a banner with the message "Seasons Greetings," and a Nativity scene.[56] The Court's majority found the city interested not in advancing religion but instead in achieving secular purposes that included celebrating a national holiday, enticing shoppers to the city's downtown area, and fostering good cheer and good will. In contrast, the dissent remained considerably more skeptical of the government's stated purposes, contending that the city could accomplish these goals without displaying a nativity scene, and criticizing the majority as downplaying the religious character of the crèche in a way itself offensive to religion.

Similar disagreements arise when ascertaining the purposes underlying the government's religious references like "In God We Trust" and "under God." Some feel that the government seeks, through certain facially religious references, to achieve secular goals like creating a spirit of unity or solemnizing an occasion,[57] while others infer a governmental objective to advance religion.

---

[54] Stone v. Graham, 449 U.S. 39, 41 (1980).   [55] *Id.* at 42.
[56] Lynch v. Donnelly, 465 U.S. 668 (1984).
[57] *See* Elk Grove Unified Sch. Dist. v. Newdow. 542 U.S. 1, 36 (2004) (O'Connor, J., concurring in the judgment).

As is true of the noncoercion and nonendorsement approaches, the neutrality principle triggers contestation and controversy, division and disagreement. This test demands religious neutrality of the government's speech, but, as we have seen, not everyone shares this vision of the Establishment Clause and its underlying values. The neutrality principle's critics also object that the exercise of ascertaining the government's purpose more generally, especially but not only the purposes underlying the decisions of multimember legislatures or agencies, exceeds courts' institutional competence – in other words, that the effort to determine the government's "purpose" for its choices is hopelessly inexact.

COMPARING AND CONTRASTING THE THREE APPROACHES IN ACTION

These three approaches are by no means mutually exclusive, and sometimes the Justices conclude that the government's religious speech offends two or even three of them. As an illustration, a majority of the Court struck down a public school's student-delivered prayer at the beginning of its football games in an opinion that employed each of the three approaches.[58]

Nevertheless, as a rough generalization, the government's religious speech by itself violates the noncoercion principle in a smaller universe of disputes than the nonendorsement principle, and the government's speech violates the nonendorsement principle in a slimmer slice of cases than the neutrality principle. In other words, the noncoercion principle is generally the least suspicious, and the neutrality principle the most, of the government's religious speech.

For instance, the government's religious displays almost never threaten the noncoercion principle: "Passersby who disagree with the message conveyed by these displays are free to ignore them, or even to turn their backs ... ."[59] Whether these displays offend the nonendorsement principle, as we've seen, turns on their context: would a reasonable observer, aware of the expression's relevant history and context, understand the government's message as endorsing or denigrating religion or nonreligion? And whether the displays offend

---

[58] Santa Fe Indep. Sch. Dist. v. Doe, 530 U.S. 290 (2000). The majority identified evidence of the government's purpose to advance religion in violation of the neutrality principle, concluded that listeners understood the government's message as endorsing religion in violation of the nonendorsement principle, and found that these prayers in public school settings threatened to coerce their young listeners in violation of the noncoercion principle.

[59] *See Cnty. of Allegheny*, 492 U.S. at 651 (Kennedy, J., concurring in the judgment in part and dissenting in part).

the neutrality principle depends on the governmental decisionmakers' descriptions of their own motives, the historical background and specific series of events leading up to the government's expression, and whether we credit the possibility that, under the circumstances, a secular governmental interest actually motivated the government's expressive choice.

The different approaches also lead to different results for Establishment Clause challenges to a government's expressive choice to adorn its seal or its license plates with a cross, or to reference God in its motto. While these governmental choices rarely offend the noncoercion principle (so long as government does not require individuals to display or join the government's message), lower courts have reached mixed results in applying the non-endorsement and neutrality principles to the government's choices. A federal district court in South Carolina, for instance, found that the state's choice to issue a license plate featuring a cross and the words "I Believe" violated both the nonendorsement and neutrality principles in violation of the Establishment Clause.[60] Another federal court found that an Oklahoma city's official seal that featured a Christian cross, along with several historical symbols, impermissibly endorsed Christianity to the exclusion of other faiths.[61] Yet a divided federal court of appeals upheld Ohio's state motto, "With God, All Things Are Possible;"[62] the majority found that reasonable observers were unlikely to understand the motto as endorsing Christianity, and that a secular purpose of unification animated the state's choice. The dissent, in contrast, found the state's choice motivated by a nonsecular purpose to advance religion, and that a reasonable observer would have understood the motto, with its origins in the gospel of Matthew, as communicating a message endorsing Christianity.

Finally, consider the following hypothetical: Suppose a governor issued a proclamation or a city council issued a resolution, without more, that "Islam is not a religion worthy of respect" or "Muslims are dangerous"?

First, a bit of background. In some cases, challengers offer the government's speech as evidence that constitutionally forbidden purposes motivated the government's hard law actions in violation of the Establishment Clause. Think, for instance, of the constitutional challenges to the Trump administration's "travel ban," its order that restricted entry into the United States by the nationals of several majority-Muslim countries. Alleging that the government's action was impermissibly motivated by anti-Muslim animus in

---

[60] Summers v. Adams, 669 F. Supp. 2d 637 (D.S.C. 2009).
[61] Robinson v. City of Edmond, 68 F.3d 1226 (10th Cir. 1995), *cert. denied*, 517 U.S. 1201 (1996).
[62] ACLU v. Capitol Square Review and Advisory Bd., 243 F.3d 289 (6th Cir. 2001).

violation of the Establishment Clause, the challengers offered statements by Trump and his staff both before and after he became president as evidence of that animus. These statements included, but were not limited to, Trump's call during his campaign "for a total and complete shutdown of Muslims entering the United States," a call that remained on his campaign website several months into his presidency.[63] Several lower courts relied on these and other statements to conclude that the travel ban violated the Establishment Clause.[64]

A sharply divided Supreme Court ultimately held that executive branch decisions about this sensitive foreign affairs matter – admitting and excluding foreign nationals – require courts' deference rather than their suspicion. Applying this deferential review to conclude that independent national security justifications other than anti-Muslim animus could have supported the Administration's decision, a 5–4 majority rejected the Establishment Clause claim.[65]

But the majority did not reject the value of the government's speech as evidence of the government's impermissible motives for its hard law action in other settings that do not demand judicial deference to the executive. And in other cases the Court has relied on government officials' speech as evidence that their hard law actions were motivated by religious hostility in violation of the First Amendment's Free Exercise Clause, which forbids the government from "prohibiting the free exercise" of religion.[66] (Although the Court to date has identified only the Establishment Clause as constraining the government's speech, without more, that disapproves religion, we can imagine that the government's speech that denigrates religion, by itself, could also violate the Free Exercise Clause if and when it sufficiently interferes with an individual's religious exercise. Think, for instance, of the government's threats, discussed in more detail in Chapters 4 and 5.)

So let's return to the hypothetical above. Does the Establishment Clause forbid the government's statement, unaccompanied by its lawmaking or other regulatory action, that "Islam is not a religion worthy of respect" or "Muslims are dangerous"? Your intuition about the answer illuminates your theory of the Establishment Clause and its values.

---

[63] *See* Trump v. Hawaii, 138 S. Ct. 2392, 2435 (2018) (Sotomayor, J., dissenting).

[64] E.g., Cnty. of Santa Clara v. Trump, 250 F. Supp. 3d 497, 508 (N.D. Cal. 2017); *reconsideration denied*, 267 F. Supp. 3d 1214 (N.D. Cal. 2017).

[65] *Trump*, 138 S. Ct. at 2421.

[66] *See* Church of the Lukumi Babalu Aye, Inc. v. City of Hialeah, 508 U.S. 520, 540–541 (1993); Masterpiece Cakeshop, Ltd. v. Colorado Civil Rights Comm'n, 138 S. Ct. 1719, 1729–1730 (2018).

Here the government's speech runs afoul of the neutrality principle, as it clearly takes sides on religious matters (although we can imagine other, more ambiguous, statements in which the government's anti-Muslim animus might be less clear). The neutrality principle's advocates understand the Establishment Clause to strip the government of the constitutional power to speak, as well as act, when motivated by an interest in advancing some religions over others, or in promoting religion over nonreligion.

The government's speech as posited here also offends the nonendorsement principle, as it disparages a specific religion, communicating a message that identifies Islam's adherents as outsiders to the community. Again, we can imagine some more ambiguous statements in which the meaning of the government's message would be contested, where reasonable observers might disagree about whether the message is one of disapproval.[67] But not here.

Whether the government's speech as hypothesized here violates the non-coercion principle is a closer question. Those who are reluctant to describe the government's speech as coercive may argue that here the government's speech commands or threatens nothing, that it requires no interaction or behavioral response by its listeners, and instead simply reflects the government's opinion, and no more. On the other hand, some might understand the proclamation as reflecting the government's efforts to convert adherents away from Islam, in other words its speech that puts "the government's weight behind an obvious effort to proselytize." And some might find the government's statement to carry coercive potential by encouraging others to discriminate against Muslims.[68]

A NOTE ON JUSTICIABILITY

In thinking about this hypothetical (and maybe some of the other disputes discussed in this chapter), you may have wondered whether federal courts even have the constitutional power to resolve the dispute; in other words, you

---

[67] To address these difficulties, law professor Jay Wexler has suggested a bright-line rule that distinguishes government's permissible expressive attacks on policy positions taken by religious individuals or entities from the government's unconstitutional expressive attacks on the religious individuals or groups themselves. *See* Jay Wexler, *Government Disapproval of Religion*, 2013 B.Y.U. L. Rev. 119 (2013). The government's message in my hypothetical is unambiguous, and thus satisfies Wexler's test.

[68] Cnty. of Allegheny v. ACLU, 492 U.S. 573, 661 (1989) (Kennedy, J., concurring in the judgment in part and dissenting in part).

may have wondered whether the dispute is justiciable.[69] Before we proceed to additional second-stage government speech problems in the chapters that follow, let's take a short detour to flag the justiciability issues sometimes raised by constitutional challenges to the government's speech.

Through its justiciability doctrine, the Supreme Court interprets the Constitution to limit the federal judiciary's power to resolve certain disputes. By narrowing the circumstances under which the judiciary will second-guess other governmental actors, the doctrine seeks to respect the separation of powers. The doctrine's objectives also include conserving scare judicial resources by limiting the federal courts' review to concrete disputes that are well-suited for judicial, rather than political, resolution.

Most relevant for our purposes here, the Court's justiciability doctrine includes a requirement that the challenger establish her "standing" to bring the claim – that is, that she allege that the defendant's choice has caused her to suffer, or will imminently cause her to suffer,[70] a "concrete and particularized injury."[71] The requirement of standing seeks to ensure that the plaintiff has a sufficiently personal stake in the dispute to litigate the claim effectively. The requirement also "enables the Court to distinguish genuine injuries from what it has termed 'generalized grievances,' disputes over matters better left to the political [rather than judicial] branches."[72] In other words, that we're unhappy with, even incensed by, our government does not necessarily mean that the federal courts are well-positioned to address our concerns.

To be sure, courts' assessments of whether a challenger has alleged a "concrete and particularized" injury sufficient to satisfy the requirement of standing are sometimes unpredictable, and courts and commentators often identify this as "one of the most confused areas of the law."[73] Rather than provide a comprehensive treatment of the Court's justiciability doctrine, including the requirement of standing, for now I simply observe that the question is not whether constitutional challenges to the government's speech are *ever* justiciable, but rather when and how.

---

[69] Note that a federal court's determination that a dispute is nonjusticiable – and thus that the court lacks the constitutional power to adjudicate it – is entirely distinct from the Supreme Court's denial of certiorari, its discretionary choice to decline to consider an appeal.

[70] *See* City of Los Angeles v. Lyons, 461 U.S. 95, 101 (1983).

[71] Lujan v. Defenders of Wildlife, 504 U.S. 555, 560 (1992).

[72] JAMES E. PFANDER, PRINCIPLES OF FEDERAL JURISDICTION 32 (2006).

[73] ERWIN CHEMERINSKY, FEDERAL JURISDICTION 57 (4th ed. 2003). The doctrine's critics sometimes also "argue that the Court has gone too far in limiting justiciability and preventing federal courts from protecting and vindicating important constitutional rights." *Id.* at 47.

To start, a challenger who alleges that the government's speech has altered or interfered with her choices or opportunities can generally establish standing. This would be true, for instance, of a challenger who alleges that the government's speech has coerced her participation in prayer or other religious observance. For an illustration outside of the Establishment Clause setting, consider *Joint Anti-Fascist Refugee Committee* v. *McGrath* (discussed in more detail in Chapter 5), where several organizations alleged that the federal government's speech designating them as Communist front organizations injured their reputation, and thus their ability to recruit members and raise funds.[74] The Court found that they had established standing:

> [T]he standing of the petitioners to bring these suits is clear. The touchstone to justiciability is injury to a legally protected right and the right of a bona fide charitable organization to carry on its work, free from defamatory statements of the kind discussed, is such a right. It is unrealistic to contend that because the respondents gave no orders directly to the petitioners to change their course of conduct, relief cannot be granted against what the respondents actually did. We long have granted relief to parties whose legal rights have been violated by unlawful public action, although such action made no direct demands upon them. The complaints here amply allege past and impending serious damages caused by the actions of which the petitioners complain.[75]

But what about a plaintiff who alleges only that the government's speech has caused expressive, or dignitary, harm? Has he alleged a sufficiently concrete or particularized injury? Think of Establishment Clause challenges to the government's religious displays, mottos, seals, and other religious references – or to the government's anti-Islam proclamation in the hypothetical above.[76] Notably, the Supreme Court has yet to raise concerns about standing in any of the many Establishment Clause challenges to the

---

[74] 341 U.S. 123 (1951).

[75] *Id.* at 139–140 (citations omitted); *see also* Meese v. Keene, 481 U.S. 465, 473–474 (1987) (holding that the plaintiff established standing; the plaintiff had brought a Free Speech Clause challenge to the government's designation of certain foreign films as "political propaganda," and offered uncontroverted "affidavits support[ing] the conclusion that [he] could not exhibit the films without incurring a risk of injury to his reputation and of an impairment of his political career"); *but see* Laird v. Tatum, 408 U.S. 1 (1973) (holding that the challengers' allegations that the government's surveillance chilled their speech in violation of the First Amendment did not did not suffice to establish standing).

[76] Standing issues have proven especially thorny in Establishment Clause challenges to Congress's funding of religious activities, where courts often conclude that taxpayers unhappy with their government's spending choices do not suffer an injury personal to them sufficient to establish standing. *See* Hein v. Freedom from Religion Found., Inc., 551 U.S. 587

government's religious speech it has considered to date.[77] And lower courts have identified two different ways in which a challenger alleging that the government's religious speech caused expressive harm can satisfy the requirement of standing.[78] One requires the challenger to allege that the government's speech caused him to alter his behavior – for example, by altering his daily commute or taking other action to avoid the government's religious display.[79] The other takes a broader approach, requiring the challenger simply to allege his direct and unwelcome contact with the government's message.[80]

As an illustration, consider the division between the judges on a federal appellate court over the nature of the alleged injury required to satisfy standing to bring an Establishment Clause claim absent any allegation of coercion. The majority required the plaintiff to allege that the government's religious speech caused her to change her behavior:

> Eventually we may need to revisit the subject of observers' standing in order to reconcile this circuit's decisions, but today is not the time … What did provide standing, we held, is that the plaintiffs had altered their daily commute, thus incurring costs in both time and money, to avoid the unwelcome religious display.… . Plaintiffs have not altered their conduct one whit or incurred any cost in time or money. All they have is disagreement with the President's action. But unless all limits on standing are to be abandoned, a feeling of alienation cannot suffice as injury in fact.[81]

The concurring judge contended instead that a plaintiff established standing simply by alleging "direct and unwelcome exposure" to the government's religious speech:

(2007). But here we instead consider Establishment Clause challenges to the government's religious speech.

[77] See Newdow v. Roberts, 603 F.3d 1002, 1014 (D.C. Cir. 2010) (Kavanaugh, J., concurring) ("[T]he Supreme Court's consistent adjudication of religious display and speech cases over a span of decades suggests that the Court has thought it obvious that the plaintiffs in those matters had standing.… . To ignore the import of these cases for the standing analysis, one would have to believe the Supreme Court repeatedly overlooked a major standing problem and decided a plethora of highly controversial cases unnecessarily and inappropriately.").

[78] For discussion of lower courts' various approaches for determining injury-in-fact standing for Establishment Clause purposes, see David Spencer, What's the Harm? NonTaxpayer Standing to Challenge Religious Symbols, 34 Harv. J.L. & Pub. Pol'y 1071, 1075 (2011); Note, NonTaxpayer Standing, Religious Favoritism, and the Distribution of Government Benefits: The Outer Bounds of the Endorsement Test, 123 Harv. L. Rev. 1999, 2004–2006 (2010).

[79] E.g., Freedom from Religion Found., Inc. v. Obama, 641 F.3d 803 (7th Cir. 2011).

[80] E.g., Suhre v. Haywood Cty., 131 F.3d 1083 (4th Cir. 1997).

[81] Freedom from Religion Foundation, Inc. v. Obama, 641 F.3d 803, 807 (7th Cir. 2011).

Nor, as the majority suggests, must the plaintiffs alter their behavior in order to have a cognizable injury ... We stated that a plaintiff can also satisfy the standing requirement by establishing that he is subject to direct and unwelcome exposure to religious messages. .... The rule in every other circuit that has considered the question is that while an allegation of a change in behavior is sufficient to confer standing, it is not required.[82]

We'll return to questions about standing in some of the chapters to come.

❋   ❋   ❋

The noncoercion, nonendorsement, and neutrality principles offer a range of approaches for thinking about the second-stage problem of whether and when the government's religious speech violates the Establishment Clause. I don't seek to persuade you that one approach is better than another within the Establishment Clause context, nor that whatever works for the Establishment Clause necessarily works in other constitutional settings. Instead my point is that these approaches illustrate available tools for thinking about second-stage government speech problems more generally. Once we solve the first-stage problem by determining that the government itself is speaking, we can then ask which harms, if any, the government's speech inflicts on its targets and whether the relevant constitutional provision protects us from those harms. We can also (or instead) ask about the government's motivations for speaking, and whether the constitutional provision at issue protects us from a government inspired by those purposes. Our answers to and our preferences among these questions will be informed in part by our theory of the values underlying the constitutional provision in question.

With this as background, we turn next to another second-stage government speech problem: when, if ever, does the government's speech violate the Equal Protection Clause?

---

[82] *Id.* at 810–811 (Williams, J., concurring); *see also* Arizona Civil Liberties Union v. Dunham, 112 F. Supp. 2d 927, 933 (D. Ariz. 2000) (finding injury-in-fact standing for plaintiff challenging town's proclamation of "Bible Week:" "That the Proclamation is announced rather than displayed does not preclude unwelcome direct contact with the Proclamation via news reports. A reported Proclamation can be more invasive than a visual display due to the pervasiveness of media coverage. To avoid the Proclamation, Plaintiffs would be faced not with the option of merely altering a travel route. Rather, they would need to avoid the media entirely, an option close to impossible in this age. Moreover, no such avoidance is required.").

3

The Government's Speech and Equality

Imagine that you're a ninth-grader sitting in class at your public school. This week, your teacher is lecturing on the school's required sex education component, and starts today's discussion by announcing: "Our state's legislature wants you to know that homosexuality is not a lifestyle acceptable to the general public, and that homosexual conduct is a criminal offense under the laws of our state."[1] Maybe you wonder if you're gay. Maybe you've never thought much about it. Maybe you and your family believe, as your church teaches, that homosexuality defies the will of God. Maybe your friends use slurs to describe folks they suspect of being gay. Maybe your parents are gay. Does the government's speech change how you, or your classmates, act? How you feel? Does the government's speech violate the Constitution?

The last chapter explored whether and how the government's speech "establishes" religion in violation of the Establishment Clause. This chapter considers whether and how the government's speech violates the Equal Protection Clause, which forbids the government from "deny[ing] any person within its jurisdiction the equal protection of the laws."[2]

THE DIVERSITY AND COMPLEXITY OF THE GOVERNMENT'S SPEECH ABOUT EQUALITY

This chapter starts with a brief but illustrative sketch of the government's wide-ranging speech about equality. We'll see heroes, villains, and, as is so often the

---

[1] See ALA. CODE § 16-40A-2(c)(8) (2017); TEX. HEALTH & SAFETY CODE ANN. § 85.007(b)(2) (West 2017) & 163.002(8) (West 2017).

[2] Ratified in the aftermath of the Civil War, the Fourteenth Amendment's Equal Protection Clause constrains state and local governments. The Supreme Court later interpreted the Fifth Amendment's Due Process Clause that binds the federal government to include a requirement of equal protection. Bolling v. Sharpe, 347 U.S. 497 (1954).

case with humans and with governments, some that are hard to characterize. These stories show that some of the challenges that confront us today are far from new, even if they sometimes feel different in degree and occasionally in kind. The more we attend to the government's speech, the better (one hopes) our thinking about it: recognizing the diverse array of the government's speech about equality helps illuminate the importance and difficulty of the second-stage government speech problems sometimes generated by that speech.

The Good (If Sometimes Complicated)

Through its speech, the government can assert moral and political leadership in the nation's ongoing struggles against bigotry and hatred. Consider President Lyndon B. Johnson's nationally televised exhortation that "We Shall Overcome" in response to the violent attacks on those marching for African-Americans' voting rights in Selma, Alabama.[3] Think too of President Barack Obama's appeals for justice and grace when eulogizing the African Americans murdered by a white supremacist they had welcomed into their South Carolina church.[4]

The government's choices about whom and what to honor in our public places can also communicate its views about equality and inclusiveness. As one of many examples, think of the boulevards and schools named after civil rights icon Martin Luther King Jr. Among the most expressive of the government's choices is its decision to fly the Confederate flag above or adjacent to its capitol, or to feature Confederate monuments in its public spaces – and the government's choice to take down these displays is equally expressive. As New Orleans Mayor Mitch Landrieu explained his city's decision first to erect, and much later to remove, its statues honoring Confederate leaders:

> The historic record is clear: the [] statues were not erected just to honor these men, but as part of the movement which became known as The Cult of the Lost Cause. This "cult" had one goal – through monuments and through other means – to rewrite history to hide the truth, which is that the

3   *See* RICK PERLSTEIN, NIXONLAND: THE RISE OF A PRESIDENT AND THE FRACTURING OF AMERICA 9 (2008). LBJ continued: "It is wrong—deadly wrong—to deny any of your fellow Americans the right to vote in this country. . . . Their cause must be our cause, too. Because it is not just Negroes, but really it is all of us, who must overcome the crippling legacy of bigotry and injustice." *Id.*
4   *See* President Barack Obama, Eulogy for Charleston Pastor, the Rev. Clementa Pinckney (June 26, 2015) (transcript available at https://www.washingtonpost.com/news/post-nation/wp/2015/06/26/transcript-obama-delivers-eulogy-for-charleston-pastor-the-rev-clementa-pinckney) [https://perma.cc/7MH4-QRLB].

Confederacy was on the wrong side of humanity.... These statues are not just stone and metal. They are not just innocent remembrances of a benign history. These monuments purposefully celebrate a fictional, sanitized Confederacy; ignoring the death, ignoring the enslavement, and the terror that it actually stood for. After the Civil War, these statues were a part of that terrorism as much as a burning cross on someone's lawn; they were erected purposefully to send a strong message to all who walked in their shadows about who was still in charge in this city.... . Surely we are far enough removed from this dark time to acknowledge that the cause of the Confederacy was wrong. And in the second decade of the 21st century, asking African Americans—or anyone else—to drive by property that they own; occupied by reverential statues of men who fought to destroy the country and deny that person's humanity seems perverse and absurd.... . Here is the essential truth: we are better together than we are apart.[5]

Through its apologies the government can unite and heal. Congress offered an official apology for the government's World War II internment of 120,000 Japanese Americans: "For these fundamental violations of the basic civil liberties and constitutional rights of these individuals of Japanese ancestry, the Congress apologizes on behalf of the Nation."[6] Later still, the Solicitor General's office, the office that represents the federal government in the Supreme Court, apologized for its falsehoods when defending the internment from constitutional challenge.[7]

Even better when the government, through its speech, rejects appeals to division and hatred in the midst of crisis (rather apologizing long afterward). President George W. Bush repudiated anti-Muslim bigotry in a speech at a mosque immediately after the 9/11 attacks, in which he emphasized Islam as a religion of peace and highlighted the "incredibly valuable contribution[s]" Muslim Americans make to the United States as "doctors, lawyers, law professors, members of the military, entrepreneurs, shopkeepers, moms and dads." He underscored that Americans' failure to treat their fellow citizens with respect "represent[s] the worst of humankind," asserting that "[t]hose who

[5] *See* Mitch Landrieu, Mayor of New Orleans, On the Removal of Confederate Monuments in New Orleans (May 23, 2017) (transcript available at https://www.nytimes.com/2017/05/23/opinion/mitch-landrieus-speech-transcript.html) [https://perma.cc/8639-LH2B].

[6] *See* DAVID COLE, ENGINES OF LIBERTY: THE POWER OF CITIZEN ACTIVISTS TO MAKE CONSTITUTIONAL LAW 169 (2016) ("In 1988, Congress passed and Reagan signed the Civil Liberties Act, which provided $20,000 for each interned Japanese American, and contained an extraordinary official apology.").

[7] Neal Katyal, *Confession of Error: The Solicitor General's Mistakes during the Japanese-American Internment Cases*, U.S. DEP'T OF JUST. ARCHIVES (May 20, 2011) [https://perma.cc/884T-HP2E].

feel like they can intimidate our fellow citizens ... should be ashamed of that kind of behavior."[8] In a similar vein, in 2010 New York Mayor Michael Bloomberg defended plans to build an Islamic cultural center near the lower Manhattan site of the former World Trade Center:

> Let us not forget that Muslims were among those murdered on 9/11 and that our Muslim neighbors grieved with us as New Yorkers and as Americans. We would betray our values—and play into our enemies' hands—if we were to treat Muslims differently than anyone else. In fact, to cave to popular sentiment would be to hand a victory to the terrorists—and we should not stand for that.[9]

But governments – like most institutions and indeed all of humanity – are riddled with contradictions, inconsistencies, and mixed motives. The government's aims when extolling equality are often inspired by strategic as much as by moral objectives. After years of resisting the women's suffrage movement, for instance, President Woodrow Wilson finally relented, in great part because of his need for women's support for the nation's World War I efforts. He made a special, and unprecedented, appearance in the Senate to plead personally for the Senate's ratification of the Nineteenth Amendment: "This war could not have been fought ... if it had not been for the services of women ... not merely in the fields of effort in which we have been accustomed to see them work, but wherever men have worked and upon the very skirts and edges of the battle itself."[10] "Wilson's unprecedented appearance in the Senate created controversy," law professor William Ross notes, as no president previously had made such a direct appeal on the Senate floor.[11] (The Senate, however, did not pass the Amendment until the following year, and it was finally ratified the year thereafter.)

As another illustration of the government's often complicated motives when speaking about equality, foreign policy goals inspired the federal government's Cold War speech opposing segregation as much as humanitarian aspirations. As legal historian Mary Dudziak explains:

[8] President George W. Bush, Remarks by the President at Islamic Center of Washington, D.C. (Sept. 17, 2001) (transcript available at https://georgewbush-whitehouse.archives.gov/news/releases/2001/09/20010917-11.html) [https://perma.cc/4QQB-X3KM].

[9] Michael R. Bloomberg, Mayor of New York City, Defending Religious Tolerance: Remarks at the Mosque Near Ground Zero (Aug. 3, 2010) (transcript available at http://www.huffingtonpost.com/michael-bloomberg/mayor-bloomberg-on-the-ne_b_669338.html) [https://perma.cc/3RRH-CCJ9].

[10] WILLIAM G. ROSS, WORLD WAR I AND THE AMERICAN CONSTITUTION 180–181 (2017).

[11] *Id.*

U.S. government officials realized that their ability to promote democracy among peoples of color around the world was seriously hampered by continuing racial injustice at home. In this context, efforts to promote civil rights within the United States were consistent with and important to the more central U.S. mission of fighting world communism. The need to address international criticism gave the federal government an incentive to promote social change at home.[12]

Along these lines, President Eisenhower publicly identified the damage of Little Rock, Arkansas's resistance to desegregation not in terms of its harm to African-Americans but instead to American prestige abroad: "[O]ur enemies are gloating over this incident and using it everywhere to misrepresent our whole nation. We are portrayed as a violator of those standards of conduct which the peoples of the world united to proclaim the Charter of the United Nations." He called upon white Arkansans to stop their resistance so that "a blot upon the fair name and high honor of our nation in the world will be removed."[13]

For another example of how the government's laudable speech can be complicated, recall the early years of the AIDS epidemic. The 1986 "Surgeon General's Report on Acquired Immune Deficiency Syndrome" was hailed as "a call to arms against the epidemic, complete with marching orders. For one of the first times, the problem of AIDS was addressed in purely public health terms, stripped of politics."[14] As U.S. Surgeon General C. Everett Koop wrote in the report:

> At the beginning of the AIDS epidemic many Americans had little sympathy for people with AIDS. The feeling was that somehow people from certain groups "deserved" their illness. Let us put those feelings behind us. We are fighting a disease, not people. Those who are already afflicted are sick people and need our care as do all sick patients. The country must face this epidemic as a unified society. We must prevent the spread of AIDS while at the same time preserving our humanity.[15]

But the Surgeon General's office only delivered this important message after five years of silence, a time when tens of thousands of Americans were

---

[12] Mary Dudziak, Cold War Civil Rights: Race and the Image of American Democracy 12 (2002).

[13] *Id.* at 133.

[14] Randy Shilts, And the Band Played On: Politics, People, and the AIDS Epidemic 587 (1987).

[15] Office of the Surgeon General, Report on Acquired Immune Deficiency Syndrome (1986).

dead or dying, with hundreds of thousands more to come. As journalist and author Randy Shilts observed, "Koop's interest was historic for its impact, not its timeliness."[16] Even though the government's public education frequently provides a powerful antidote to public health crises, the many potential federal, state, and local government actors equipped to speak to the AIDS epidemic struggled for years to overcome their political fears, and thus their silence, as the disease's death toll climbed.

The Bad and the Ugly

The government's speech sometimes explicitly demonizes, disparages, and divides. Consider President Andrew Johnson's 1867 annual message to Congress, in which he characterized African Americans as possessing less "capacity for government than any other race of people. No independent government of any form has ever been successful in their hands. On the contrary, wherever they have been left to their own devices they have shown a constant tendency to relapse into barbarism."[17] Around the same time and along the same lines, a report by a Reconstruction-era Florida state commission "praised slavery as a 'benign' institution deficient only in its inadequate regulation of black sexual behavior."[18] In 1907, Mississippi Governor James Vardaman declared, "[I]f it is necessary every Negro in the state will be lynched; it will be done to maintain white supremacy."[19]

Flash forward to the mid-twentieth century when, in the aftermath of the Supreme Court's decision in *Brown* v. *Board of Education*, many Southern governments and their officials engaged in an expressive campaign of "massive resistance" to attack the Court's legitimacy and thus undermine enforcement of its desegregation orders. "The whole point of the Southern [campaign] was to confuse legal and moral issues and to undermine any sense of inevitability a

[16] Randy Shilts, and the Band Played on: Politics, People, and the AIDS Epidemic 588 (1987).
[17] Eric Foner, Reconstruction 180 (1988); *see also* Dorothy Overstreet Pratt, Sowing the Wind: The Mississippi Constitutional Convention of 1890 74–75 (2018) (describing how a Mississippi state constitutional convention committee urged repeal of the Fifteenth Amendment because "the white people only are capable of conducting and maintaining the government" and "the negro race, even if its people were educated, [are] wholly unequal to such great responsibility if they should come into control of such government").
[18] Eric Foner, Reconstruction 200 (1988).
[19] Chris Danielson, The Color of Politics: Racism in the American Political Arena Today 43 (2013).

Supreme Court decision normally commands," historian Numan Bartley explains. "The propaganda barrage undermined the validity of the right of dissent and became a part of a general effort to stamp out the expression of unorthodox thought throughout the South."[20]

To these ends, Southern state legislatures expressed themselves through a variety of resolutions declaring the Court's decision "null, void, and of no effect"[21] and announcing their "condemnation of and protest against the illegal encroachment of the central government"[22] As Bartley notes, these "resolutions per se were statements of policy – or in some cases protest – without direct force and certainly without constitutional sanction, as Virginia's own attorney general pointed out. Yet the sound and fury surrounding inter-position signified a deadly serious intent."[23] At the same time, a number of state and local governments made the expressive choice to fly the Confederate flag or incorporate it into their state symbols: Georgia redesigned its flag in 1956 to include the Confederate logo, and in 1962, South Carolina placed the Confederate flag atop its capitol.[24] The governmental preachers of discrimin-ation included George Wallace, who climbed the Alabama state capitol's steps at his 1963 inauguration as governor, to declare:

> Today I have stood, where once Jefferson Davis stood, and took an oath to my people. It is very appropriate then that from this Cradle of the Confederacy, this very Heart of the Great Anglo-Saxon Southland, that today we sound the drum for freedom as have our generations of forebears before us done, time and time again, through history. Let us rise to the call of freedom-loving blood that is in us and send our answer to the tyranny that clanks its chains upon the South. In the name of the greatest people that have ever trod this earth, I draw the line in the dust and toss the gauntlet before the feet of tyranny ... and I say ... segregation today ... segregation tomorrow ... segregation forever.[25]

---

[20] NUMAN V. BARTLEY, THE RISE OF MASSIVE RESISTANCE 117, 189 (1969).
[21] H.R.J. Res. 42, 1956 Leg., Spec. Sess. (Ala. 1956); H. Res. 185, 1956 Gen. Assemb., Reg. Sess. (Ga. 1956).
[22] S.J. Res. S.514, 1956 Gen. Assemb., Reg. Sess. (S.C. 1956).
[23] NUMAN V. BARTLEY, THE RISE OF MASSIVE RESISTANCE 133 (1969).
[24] *See* James Forman, Jr., *Driving Dixie Down, Removing the Confederate Flag from Southern State Capitols*, 101 YALE L.J. 505, 505 (1991).
[25] George Wallace, Governor of Alabama, Inaugural Address (Jan. 14, 1963) (Jan. 14, 1963) (transcript available at https://web.utk.edu/~mfitzge1/docs/374/wallace_seg63.pdf) [https://perma.cc/57DF-E4RB].

(As an example of governmental counterspeech – that is, its speech in rebuttal to others' speech – contrast Jimmy Carter's inaugural address as Georgia governor eight years later: "The time of racial segregation is over."[26])

The campaign for massive resistance exemplified well-organized and well-financed government speech – in this case, the government's speech committed to defend segregation and repress opposing views. For instance, in 1956 the state of Mississippi created its State Sovereignty Commission; officially charged with protecting the state from federal encroachment and usurpation, "the Commission in actuality was the state's secret intelligence arm, committed and devoted to the perpetuation of racial segregation in Mississippi."[27] The Commission "sent ghost-written editorials to newspapers around the country and bought ads in 500 daily and weekly papers. By April 1964, the group had distributed over a million pamphlets and mailings, Sovereignty Commission records indicate."[28] Years later a federal court described the commission's work, accomplished largely through its speech:

> The Commission used several patterns in attempting to thwart desegregationists. The first was simply to warn local officials prior to boycotts, meetings, and voter registration drives, leaving the response to the local authority. The Commission also harassed individuals who assisted organizations promoting desegregation or voter registration. In some instances, the Commission would suggest job actions to employers, who would fire the targeted moderate or activist. The Commission caused applications for commissions as notaries public to be denied. The Commission maintained and distributed lists of people reported to be supporters of civil rights organizations or who supported public measures toward moderation or desegregation. These lists were made available to other law enforcement agencies. . . . The avowed intent of the Commission and its co-conspirators was to chill or preclude the Plaintiffs from speech, assembly, association, and the petition of government.[29]

The government's expressive choices have undercut equality in many other ways as well. Around the same time as the campaign of massive resistance, a

[26] Jimmy Carter, Governor of Georgia, Inaugural Address (Jan. 12, 1971) (transcript available at https://www.jimmycarterlibrary.gov/assets/documents/inaugural_address_gov.pdf) [https://perma.cc/XLX2-XZ3F].

[27] ACLU v. Mississippi, 911 F.2d 1066 (5th Cir. 1990).

[28] Douglas A. Blackmon, *Silent Partner: How the South's Fight to Uphold Segregation Was Funded Up North*, WALL ST. J., (June 11, 1999) http://www.slaverybyanothername.com/other-writings/silent-partner-how-the-souths-fight-to-uphold-segregation-was-funded-up-north/ [https://perma.cc/M3XM-63G7].

[29] ACLU v. Mabus, 719 F. Supp. 1345 (S.D. Miss. 1989), *vacated and remanded on other grounds*.

Senate subcommittee charged with investigating "The Employment of Homosexuals and Other Sex Perverts in Government" concluded that "[o]ne homosexual can pollute a Government office." It went on:

> In the opinion of this subcommittee homosexuals and other sex perverts are not proper persons to be employed in Government for two reasons; first, they are generally unsuitable, and second, they constitute security risks. . . . . [O]ur investigation has shown that the presence of a sex pervert in a government agency tends to have a corrosive influence upon his fellow employees. These perverts will frequently attempt to entice normal individuals to engage in perverted practices.[30]

Some states continue to insist that their public schools engage in homophobic expression. As of 2018, for example, Alabama and Texas still require public schools' sex education curricula to include "[a]n emphasis, in a factual manner and from a public health perspective, that homosexuality is not a lifestyle acceptable to the general public" and to assert that "homosexual conduct is a criminal offense under the laws of this state."[31] (Even though the Supreme Court ruled in 2003 that laws prohibiting same-sex sexual behavior are unconstitutional,[32] several state legislatures have yet to repeal those laws, which thus remain on the books even though unenforceable. The legislatures' failure to repeal them is itself an expressive choice.).

At times the government's speech includes its deliberate wartime effort to instill or exacerbate the public's fear and hatred of certain individuals or communities. In so doing, government speakers have often targeted immigrants, the government's critics, and others perceived as outsiders. As legal scholar Geof Stone observes, "Fear has proved a potent political weapon."[33]

The government generally defends its wartime fearmongering speech as a necessary response to emergent threats to national security. But vulnerable

---

[30] S. Doc. No. 81–241, at 4 (1950); *see also id.* ("[I]t is generally believed that those who engage in overt acts of perversion lack the emotional stability of normal persons. In addition there is an abundance of evidence to sustain the conclusion that indulgence in acts of sex perversion weakens the moral fiber of an individual to a degree that he is not suitable for a position of responsibility.").

[31] ALA. CODE 16-40A-2(c)(8) (2017); TEX. HEALTH & SAFETY CODE ANN. 85.007(b)(2) (West 2017) & 163.002(8) (West 2017). For additional examples of state laws requiring the delivery of the government's anti-gay expression in the public schools, see Clifford Rosky, *Anti-Gay Curriculum Laws*, 117 COLUM. L. REV. 1463 (2017).

[32] Lawrence v. Texas, 539 U.S. 558 (2003).

[33] Geoffrey R. Stone, *Free Speech in the Age of McCarthy: A Cautionary Tale*, 93 CALIF. L. REV. 1387, 1388–1389 (2005).

individuals and groups pay a steep price when the government chooses its targets based on stereotypes and falsehoods rather than on evidence. Government speakers during World War I invited hatred of German immigrants in the United States, as President Wilson, for example, claimed that "the agents and dupes of the Imperial German Government" were actively engaged in a "sinister intrigue" within the United States, and that "many of our own people were corrupted."[34] The government's fearmongering speech in World War II included that which ultimately deprived its targets of their physical liberty. Dissenting from the Supreme Court's decision in *Korematsu v. United States*,[35] Justice Frank Murphy described how the government's reports justifying its internment – that is, its imprisonment – of Japanese Americans were riddled with racist stereotypes and falsehoods:

> That this forced exclusion was the result in good measure of this erroneous assumption of racial guilt rather than bona fide military necessity is evidenced by the Commanding General's Final Report on the evacuation from the Pacific Coast area. In it he refers to all individuals of Japanese descent as "subversive," as belonging to "an enemy race" whose "racial strains are undiluted," and as constituting "over 112,000 potential enemies ... at large today" along the Pacific Coast. In support of this blanket condemnation of all persons of Japanese descent, however, no reliable evidence is cited to show that such individuals were generally disloyal, or had generally so conducted themselves in this area as to constitute a special menace to defense installations or war industries, or had otherwise by their behavior furnished reasonable ground for their exclusion as a group.
>
> . . . .
>
> A military judgment based upon such racial and sociological considerations is not entitled to the great weight ordinarily given the judgments based upon strictly military considerations. Especially is this so when every charge relative to race, religion, culture, geographical location, and legal and economic status has been substantially discredited by independent studies made by experts in these matters.[36]

The Court's majority infamously disagreed, holding that the government's action, concededly based on race and national origin, did not deny its targets the equal protection of the laws. Not until 2018 did the Supreme Court finally make clear that *Korematsu* "was gravely wrong the day it was decided."[37]

---

[34] President Woodrow Wilson, Address on Flag Day (June 14, 1917) (transcript available at https://www.presidency.ucsb.edu/node/206616) [https://perma.cc/U6C4-MPE5].

[35] 323 U.S. 214 (1944).   [36] *Id.* at 235–240 (Murphy, J., dissenting).

[37] Trump v. Hawaii, 138 S. Ct. 2392, 2423 (2018).

State and local governments also engage in fearmongering speech that stereotypes individuals and communities. Maine Governor Paul LePage announced at a 2016 press conference: "You try to identify the enemy and the enemy right now, the overwhelming majority of people coming in, are people of color or people of Hispanic origin."[38] For a time the New York Police Department's (NYPD) training materials included videos that portrayed Muslims in stereotypically negative and inaccurate ways; one of the films declared that "the true agenda of much of Islam in America" is "to infiltrate and dominate America."[39] Then-Attorney General Eric Holder ultimately repudiated the FBI's use of similar training materials, observing that such materials "really have a negative impact on our ability to communicate effectively."[40]

In short, the government's speech on matters of equality is both consequential and complicated. The government often speaks in an effort to engage ongoing national conversations about race, gender, national origin, sexual orientation, and more – and this speech can be valuable even when controversial, even when painful. On the other hand, the government's speech that communicates hatred or hostility toward certain individuals or groups can encourage private parties' discriminatory behavior, deter its targets from exercising their rights, and deliver messages of exclusion and second-class status. Like all hateful words, the government's hateful speech hurts. But the government's hateful speech sometimes hurts differently, and more dangerously, precisely because of its governmental source.

WHEN, IF EVER, DOES THE GOVERNMENT'S SPEECH DENY ITS TARGETS "THE EQUAL PROTECTION OF THE LAWS"?

Thinking about whether and when the Equal Protection Clause limits the government's speech requires us to wrestle anew with what it means for the government to "deny to any person within its jurisdiction the equal protection

[38] Amber Phillips, *LePage Doubles Down: "The Enemy Right Now" Is "People of Color or People of Hispanic Origin,"* WASH. POST (Aug. 27, 2016) https://www.washingtonpost.com/news/the-fix/wp/2016/08/26/this-is-gov-paul-richard-lepage-i-would-like-to-talk-to-you-about-your-comments-about-my-being-a-racist-you-expletive [https://perma.cc/88XN-XEER].

[39] *See* Michael Powell, *In Police Training, a Dark Film on U.S. Muslims,* N.Y. TIMES (Jan. 23, 2012), http://www.nytimes.com/2012/01/24/nyregion/in-police-training-a-dark-film-on-us-muslims.html?pagewanted=all.

[40] Spencer Ackerman, *Attorney General: FBI Hurt Terror Fight with "Violent Muslim" Training,* WIRED (Nov. 8, 2011, 2:45 PM), https://www.wired.com/2011/11/holder-fbi-islamophobia.

of the laws." In other words, determining when the government's speech violates the Equal Protection Clause forces us to identify our theory of that Clause and its values, our answers to the questions "Why does the Constitution include the Equal Protection Clause? What goals does the Clause seek to achieve, and what harms does it strive to prevent?"

As Chapter 1 explained, the government's speech generally advances free speech values so long as the message's governmental source is transparent. This is because the government's expression exposes its priorities to the electorate, informing the public's political conversations and choices. Even the government's hateful speech reveals a great deal about that government that can valuably shape the public's decisions and facilitate democratic self-governance. That the government's speech may be consistent with free speech values, however, does not mean that it is necessarily consistent with equal protection values, as very different purposes underlie the two constitutional protections.

The values animating the Equal Protection Clause are themselves deeply contested, as courts, policymakers, and scholars have long debated whether we should understand the Constitution's commitment to equality as driven by anticlassification or instead antisubordination commitments.

Anticlassification and Antisubordination Theories of the Equal Protection Clause

Anticlassification theory understands the Equal Protection Clause's core value as forbidding the government from classifying, or distinguishing among, individuals based on race or other class status regardless of the government's motive for its distinction.[41] In the context of race, for example, the anticlassification perspective views the Constitution as barring the government from "reduc[ing] an individual to an assigned racial identity for differential treatment."[42] Anticlassification theory is driven by the moral commands of colorblindness: "[o]ne of the principal reasons race is treated as a forbidden classification is that it demeans the dignity and worth of a person to be judged by ancestry instead of by his or her own merit and essential qualities."[43] But

---

[41] This chapter uses the term "class status," rather than "protected class status," to refer not only to those classifications that the Supreme Court has already identified as triggering heightened scrutiny (race, national origin, gender, and a few other characteristics), but also those that the Court has yet to characterize (for example, LGBTQ status).

[42] Parents Involved in Cmty. Schs. v. Seattle Sch. Dist. No. 1, 551 U.S. 701, 795 (2007) (Kennedy, J., concurring in part and dissenting in part).

[43] Rice v. Cayetano, 528 U.S. 495, 517 (2000).

instrumental concerns about inflaming racial divisions also inform the anti-classification view: in Justice Clarence Thomas's words, governmental classifications are "precisely the sort of government action that pits the races against one another, exacerbates racial tension, and 'provoke[s] resentment among those who believe that they have been wronged by the government's use of race.'"[44] Anticlassification advocates generally conclude that the government's race-based classifications with immediate and obvious effects – its laws or other actions in which "the government distributes burdens or benefits on the basis of individual racial classification" – violate the Equal Protection Clause.[45] Whether the government's speech, unaccompanied by its lawmaking or other regulatory action, offends an anticlassification understanding of the Equal Protection Clause depends on whether we think that the government's speech, by itself, "classifies" on bases that trigger suspicion and in ways that deny the equal protection of the law.

Antisubordination theory, in contrast, understands the Equal Protection Clause to bar the government's actions that have the intent or the effect of perpetuating long-standing racial and other hierarchies, thus disadvantaging those who have historically suffered discrimination or political vulnerability. The antisubordination perspective also understands the Clause to permit the government's actions that have the intent or effect of undercutting those hierarchies. Like anticlassification theory, antisubordination theory draws from both moral and instrumental rationales; it considers the government's maintenance of subordinating hierarches both morally repugnant and instrumentally disastrous, and finds "no moral or constitutional equivalence between a policy that is designed to perpetuate a caste system and one that seeks to eradicate racial subordination."[46] Whether the government's speech, unaccompanied by its hard law, offends an antisubordination approach to the Equal Protection Clause turns on whether it perpetuates traditional patterns of subordination.

To illustrate the points of agreement and disagreement between the two theories, consider the decision in *Brown* v. *Board of Education*, where the Supreme Court held that public schools' race-based segregation of their students violated the Equal Protection Clause.[47] Here anticlassification and antisubordination perspectives converge to support the Court's decision: the government classified students based on race, and the government

---

[44] *Parents Involved*, 551 U.S. at 759–760 (Thomas, J., concurring).
[45] *Id.* at 719 (plurality opinion).
[46] Adarand Constructors, Inc. v. Pena, 515 U.S. 200, 243 (1995) (Stevens, J., dissenting).
[47] 347 U.S. 483 (1954).

perpetuated racial subordination by subjecting African-American students to inferior educational opportunities. But some disputes force us to choose between the two theories. For example, affirmative action programs that consider race as a plus-factor to expand employment and educational opportunities for those historically denied them generally offend anticlassification theorists (because the government is considering race in its decision-making) while appealing to antisubordination theorists (because the government is seeking to dismantle racial hierarchies).

The anticlassification and antisubordination perspectives reflect different answers to the questions: "What values does the Equal Protection Clause protect? A commitment to end the government's classifications on certain bases? Or instead a commitment to end long-standing racial and other hierarchies?" Just as our theory of the Establishment Clause often drives our choice among noncoercion, nonendorsement, or neutrality approaches to that Clause's protections, so too is the case with the Equal Protection Clause. Our intuitions about the sorts of governmental effects and governmental motives that violate the Clause turn on whether, when push comes to shove, we prefer an anticlassification or antisubordination understanding of the Clause.

With this as background, next we ask and answer a familiar series of questions about the consequences of, and the motivations underlying, the government's speech. First, does the government's speech change its targets' choices or opportunities to their disadvantage, and does the Equal Protection Clause bar the government from causing those changes? Next, does the government's speech inflict expressive, or dignitary, harm upon its targets by communicating hostility to or disrespect for its targets based on their race or other class status, and does the Equal Protection Clause bar the government from inflicting that harm? Finally, is the government's speech motivated by animus or other discriminatory intent and, if so, does the Equal Protection Clause bar the government from speaking for those reasons?

FOCUSING ON GOVERNMENT EXPRESSION'S EFFECTS: SPEECH THAT CHANGES ITS TARGETS' CHOICES AND OPPORTUNITIES IN DISCRIMINATORY WAYS

One approach to second-stage government speech problems focuses on the effects, the harmful consequences, of the government's speech, identifying discriminatory change in its targets' choices or opportunities as the constitutionally forbidden harm. As we'll see, the government can achieve these changes by directing its speech to either of two different audiences: the government's speech may cause third parties to deny opportunities to, or otherwise discriminate against, class members; and the government's speech directly to its targets may change their opportunities and choices to their disadvantage.

We can expect disagreement about whether and when the government's voice, by itself, achieves these constitutionally forbidden effects – just as we saw disagreements among advocates of the noncoercion principle about whether and when government's religious speech coerces its listeners' choices in violation of the Establishment Clause. The quicker we are to find a causal connection between the government's speech and discriminatory changes in its targets' opportunities and choices, the more we encourage the government to think twice about its expressive choices, and the more we protect its targets from the harms of that speech. But the more we constrain the government's speech, the more we may also cramp its communication in counterproductive ways. This recurring tension forces us to grapple with important and difficult questions about the requisite causal connection between the government's speech and discriminatory consequences.[48]

The Government's Speech That Commands or Coerces Discrimination

The Supreme Court interprets the Equal Protection Clause to forbid the government from intentionally distinguishing based on race, gender, or certain other characteristics (except in rare circumstances where the government can justify its choice under heightened, or suspicious, scrutiny).[49] The Court has also interpreted the Clause to forbid the government's speech that commands, threatens, or otherwise coerces others to discriminate on these bases. Consider the following illustration: in the 1960s, New Orleans city officials issued a statement announcing their intent to enforce trespass law to prevent the desegregation of restaurants and other public accommodations. In *Lombard* v. *Louisiana*, the Supreme Court found that the city's statement by itself

---

[48] In Washington v. Davis, the Supreme Court held that government actions that impose a discriminatory effect based on protected class status do not violate the Equal Protection Clause unless accompanied by a facial classification or some other evidence of the government's intent to distinguish based on protected class status. 426 U.S. 229, 239 (1976). Here we address situations in which government's speech references class status on its face, and explore the circumstances under which we should understand the government's speech to be imposing a discriminatory effect as well.

[49] E.g., Brown v. Board of Education, 347 U.S. 483 (1954); United States v. Virginia, 518 U.S. 515 (1996).

commanded others to continue to segregate, and that that command violated the Equal Protection Clause:

> As we interpret the New Orleans city officials' statements, they here deter-
> mined that the city would not permit Negroes to seek desegregated service in
> restaurants. Consequently, the city must be treated exactly as if it had an
> ordinance prohibiting such conduct. We have just held ... that where an
> ordinance makes it unlawful for owners or managers of restaurants to seat
> whites and Negroes together, a conviction under the State's criminal pro-
> cesses employed in a way which enforces the discrimination mandated by
> that ordinance cannot stand. Equally the State cannot achieve the same
> result by an official command which has at least as much coercive effect as
> an ordinance.[50]

In other words, if the Equal Protection Clause forbids New Orleans from enacting an ordinance requiring restaurants to segregate, then it also forbids the city from commanding continued segregation, or threatening punishment for those who resist, since that speech is functionally indistinguishable from the government's own discrimination. This presents an easy case, in part because it does not require us to choose between anticlassification and antisubordination theory: here the government's speech classified based on race, and it perpetuated racial subordination in the form of segregation.

The Government's Speech That Encourages Others to Discriminate

What if the government's speech does not command, threaten, or otherwise coerce its listeners, but instead encourages them to discriminate against others based on targets' race or other class status?[51] In *Anderson v. Martin*, the Court held that the government's racially identifying speech on a ballot violated the Equal Protection Clause because it enabled and encouraged voters to discriminate based on race. In so holding, the Court explained how the government's speech facilitated voters' discriminatory decision-making:

> [This case] has nothing whatever to do with the right of a citizen to cast his
> vote for whomever he chooses and for whatever reason he pleases or to

---

[50] 373 U.S. 267, 273 (1963).

[51] Recall from Chapter 2 that, in the Establishment Clause context, advocates of the noncoercion principle ask only whether the government's religious speech *coerces* its listeners' behavior. As we'll see, there are other ways to describe the potential causal connections between the government's speech and changes in its targets' choices, and we can understand the government's speech in some of those circumstances to violate specific constitutional provisions.

receive all information concerning a candidate which is necessary to a proper
exercise of his franchise. It has to do only with the right of a State to require or
encourage its voters to discriminate upon the grounds of race. In the abstract,
Louisiana imposes no restriction upon anyone's candidacy nor upon an
elector's choice in the casting of his ballot. But by placing a racial label on
a candidate at the most crucial stage in the electoral process – the instant
before the vote is cast – the State furnishes a vehicle by which racial
prejudice may be so aroused as to operate against one group because of race
and for another.[52]

The Court enjoined the statute's enforcement, concluding "that the com-
pulsory designation by Louisiana of the race of the candidate on the ballots
operates as a discrimination against appellants."[53] Did the government command voters to discriminate based on race, or threaten them if they did not?
No. But as the Court pointed out, "[T]hat which cannot be done by express
statutory prohibition cannot be done by indirection."[54]

"The vice," the Court made clear, lies "in the placing of the power of the
State behind a racial classification that induces racial prejudice at the polls."[55]
This is an empirical prediction – and, in my view, an accurate one – that the
government's speech in this setting will cause some voters to discriminate
based on race. Through its speech, the government designated, and thus
classified, candidates based on race. And it did so in a subordinating way, by
talking about candidates' race at a critical point in voters' decision-making at a
time and in a place when African-Americans' voting rights were under siege.

In other circumstances where courts must determine whether the government has unconstitutionally caused a nongovernmental party to take action
that the Constitution forbids the government itself to undertake, the Supreme
Court tells us that the government "normally can be held responsible for a
private decision only when it has exercised coercive power or has provided
such significant encouragement, either overt or covert, that the choice must in
law be deemed to be that of the State."[56] In both *Lombard* and *Anderson*, we
can see the requisite causal connection between the government's speech and
discriminatory consequences. In *Lombard*, the government threatened the
exercise of its coercive power against those who resisted its command to
segregate. In *Anderson*, the government encouraged voters' discriminatory
decisions based on race. Although we can imagine other situations in which
the parties contest the causal connection between the government's speech

---

[52] 375 U.S. 399, 402–403 (1964).   [53] *Id.* at 401–402.   [54] *Id.* at 404.   [55] *Id.* at 402.
[56] Blum v. Yaretsky, 457 U.S. 991, 1004 (1982).

and discriminatory change in its targets' choices and opportunities, those causal questions – however difficult – are neither new nor uncommon.

The Government's Speech That Alters or Interferes with Its Targets' Opportunities in Discriminatory Ways

Next we turn to the effects of the government's speech not on third parties but instead on its targets themselves, more specifically on their choices and opportunities. Under what circumstances does the government's speech to those listeners, by itself, limit or otherwise disadvantage their opportunities in violation of the Equal Protection Clause?

Long-standing antiharassment law recognizes that speech can inflict discriminatory, and thus unlawful, effects on targets' educational or job opportunities when it forces its targets to endure miserable environments because of their race, gender, or other class status. More specifically, a wide range of federal, state, and local statutes prohibit discrimination by public and private actors in education, employment, housing, and other settings, with the illegal discrimination interpreted to include verbal harassment that is sufficiently severe or pervasive to create a hostile environment.[57] When the harassing speaker is a government entity, that speech can also violate the Equal Protection Clause, as federal courts have made clear that "harassment by state actors violates the Fourteenth Amendment . . . ."[58] Verbal harassment in the government's workplace, by itself, is sometimes sufficiently severe or pervasive to violate the Equal Protection Clause.[59]

---

[57] *E.g., Meritor Savings Bank v. Vinson*, 477 U.S. 57, 67 (1986) (interpreting federal statute prohibiting job discrimination to forbid unwelcome workplace speech on the basis of protected status that is sufficiently severe or pervasive to create a hostile work environment and alter the terms and conditions of employment); *Harris v. Forklift Systems, Inc.*, 510 U.S. 17, 21 (1993) (same); *Davis v. Monroe Cnty. Bd. of Educ.*, 526 U.S. 629, 633 (1999) (interpreting federal statute prohibiting sex discrimination in federally funded educational activities to forbid "harassment that is so severe, pervasive, and objectively offensive that it effectively bars the victim's access to an educational opportunity or benefit").

[58] Tuggle v. Mangan, 348 F.3d 714, 720 (8th Cir 2003); *see also* Williams v. Herron, 687 F.3d 971, 978 (8th Cir. 2012), *cert. denied*, 568 U.S. 1160 (2013) ("[S]ection 1983 sexual harassment claims are treated the same as sexual-harassment claims under Title VII.").

[59] *E.g.,* Wright v. Rolett Cnty., 417 F.3d 879, 882 (8th Cir. 2005)), *cert. denied*, 546 U.S. 1173 (2005) (concluding that verbal harassment, by itself, can constitute unconstitutional sexual harassment under 42 U.S.C. section 1983 and describing daily "use of vulgar, sexist language in the sheriff's office"); Kopman v. City of Centerville, 871 F. Supp. 2d 875, 888 (S.D.S.D. 2012) (denying defendants' motion for summary judgment on a section 1983 claim for compensatory and punitive damages where the government official's harassing workplace speech "permeated and poisoned [the plaintiff's] work environment").

Think of a government official's racist, misogynist, or other harassing speech to workers in the public workplace that is sufficiently severe or pervasive to create a hostile work environment and alter the terms and conditions of employment. The coercive potential of the government's workplace speech can be severe, as workers confronted with a governmental employer's harassing speech on the job have limited ability to leave or rebut because of their economic dependence on their continued employment. Here the government's expression can change its targets' job opportunities in a discriminatory way. Just as compelling public employees to endure miserable conditions for discriminatory reasons (for example, relegating targets to an unheated office in the dead of winter based on race or gender) violates equal protection, so too does forcing them to endure a gauntlet of verbal abuse. The government's harassing speech that alters the terms and conditions of employment based on race or sex classifies based on race and sex, and perpetuates long-standing subordination.

To be sure, constitutional claims of this sort are not easy to win. Challengers must often show a long-standing pattern of epithets, slurs, and more to establish that the government's speech is sufficiently severe or pervasive to alter the terms and conditions of employment.[60] And governmental immunities (discussed in more detail in Chapter 7) often limit the government's liability for monetary damages. My point for now is that sometimes the government's harassing speech, by itself, alters its targets' job opportunities in violation of the Equal Protection Clause.

Relatedly, the government's speech based on protected class status sometimes deters its targets from pursuing certain opportunities as effectively as an outright command. Consider a government employer that says or writes "Only whites need apply." Here too the government's speech offends both anticlassification and antisubordination understandings of the Equal Protection Clause: it classifies its targets' job opportunities based on race, and it perpetuates long-standing hierarchies by reserving those opportunities for whites. We can imagine other governmental expression that discourages its targets from seeking certain opportunities. Consider the effect, on a gay or lesbian worker planning to apply for a government position, of the Senate subcommittee report stating that "[i]n the opinion of this subcommittee homosexuals and other sex perverts are not proper persons to be employed in Government."[61]

---

[60] *See id.*

[61] *See* S. REP. No. 81–241, at 4 (1950). Note that a congressional report itself is immune from liability under the Speech and Debate Clause, discussed in more detail in Chapter 7. But no

In short, both anticlassification and antisubordination theorists can understand the Equal Protection Clause to forbid the government's speech that commands, threatens, and coerces third parties to discriminate; the government's speech that encourages third parties to discriminate; and the government's speech that creates a hostile environment or otherwise disadvantages its targets' opportunities. We can understand the Equal Protection Clause to prohibit the government's speech that achieves those effects, even as we can disagree about *when* the government's speech, without more, does so.

FOCUSING ON GOVERNMENT EXPRESSION'S EFFECTS: SPEECH THAT INFLICTS EXPRESSIVE HARM BY DENIGRATING ITS TARGETS BASED ON CLASS STATUS

Another approach to this second-stage government speech problem maintains a focus on the consequences of the government's speech, and asks when, if ever, the Equal Protection Clause forbids the government's speech that inflicts harmful effects *other* than disadvantaging its targets' choices and opportunities in discriminatory ways. More specifically, does the Equal Protection Clause deny the government the power simply to *say* that its targets are inferior or second-class citizens because of their race or other class status? If so, how do we determine whether the government has communicated this message of inferiority? (As we'll see, the perceived difficulty of the second question leaves some reluctant to answer "yes" to the first).

Recall the nonendorsement approach to second-stage Establishment Clause problems, which interprets the Clause to prohibit the government's speech about religion that inflicts expressive, or dignitary, harm without more. Remember, more specifically, that adherents of the nonendorsement principle identify equality and inclusiveness as among the key values informing the Clause, and thus conclude that the government commits a constitutional wrong when its speech sends a message of inferiority based on religion or nonreligion entirely apart from whether it coerces its listeners. As Richards Pildes and Niemi explain:

> On this view, the *meaning* of a governmental action is just as important as what that action *does*. Public policies can violate the Constitution not only because they bring about concrete costs, but because the very meaning they convey demonstrates inappropriate respect for relevant public values. On this

---

such immunity would attach if some other governmental entity, like the Office of Personnel Management, issued the same report, or uttered the same statement.

unusual conception of constitutional harm, when a governmental action expresses disrespect for such values, it can violate the Constitution.[62]

An emphasis on expressive, or dignitary, harm thus identifies the constitutional wrong as the government's communication of this disrespect, regardless of whether it causes material disadvantage to its targets (or even regardless of whether it distresses its targets, as their emotional resilience does not erase the dignitary harm).

Those who identify equality and inclusiveness as among the key values underlying the Establishment Clause may well share a similar view of the Equal Protection Clause, the constitutional provision that is all about equality. If we understand the Equal Protection Clause to require that government treat individual members of the polity with equal respect and equal concern regardless of class status, then the government's speech alone may violate this constitutional commitment when it denigrates its targets, when it communicates exclusion or inferiority based on that class status. (And the more the government denigrates a group, the easier it becomes to treat them differently, and not just talk about them differently.)

If we understand the Equal Protection Clause to prohibit the government from inflicting discriminatory expressive harm, the next question is whether and when the government's message in fact inflicts that harm. Remember that the nonendorsement principle's adherents in the Establishment Clause setting ask whether a reasonable observer would understand the government's message as endorsing or denigrating religion (or nonreligion). So too would an expressive harm approach to the Equal Protection Clause turn on whether a reasonable listener understands the government's message to disparage its targets based on their race or other class status. Assessments of a message's meaning can be hotly contested, but law has long wrestled with related questions. Most relevant, statutory antidiscrimination law looks to the perceptions of a reasonable target when determining whether harassing speech in the workplace is sufficiently severe or pervasive to create a hostile environment and alter the terms and conditions of the target's employment.[63]

One's comfort or discomfort with an expressive harm approach to the Equal Protection Clause likely turns in part on one's theory of the Clause and the values it protects. Those who adopt an antisubordination perspective may feel

---

[62] Richard Pildes & Richard Niemi, *Expressive Harms, "Bizarre Districts," and Voting Rights: Evaluating Election-District Appearances after* Shaw v. Reno, 92 MICH. L. REV. 483, 507 (1993).

[63] *See* Harris v. Forklift Systems, Inc., 510 U.S. 17, 21–23 (1993).

that the government's speech violates the Clause when it delivers a message that reinforces traditional hierarchies, as would be the case of the government's speech that denigrates the competence, or advocates the exclusion, of women or people of color. Under this view, the government's expression of concern for some groups does not necessarily involve disparagement of others: teaching African-American history is not the same as teaching white supremacy, and recognizing that race has mattered in American life is not the same as disparaging white people.

In contrast, those who adopt an anticlassification perspective may be reluctant to characterize the government's speech that disparages its targets for their class status as a "classification" – a distribution of benefits and burdens – for equal protection purposes. Under this view, the difference between "hard" and "soft" power, between the government's regulatory action and its speech, may be especially relevant to a constitutional provision that demands "the equal protection of *the laws*."

But some anticlassification adherents might emphasize the theory's roots in both moral and instrumental rationales to conclude that the government's hateful speech is not only morally offensive in demeaning its targets but also instrumentally dangerous by contributing to social divisions and instability. Recall that "[o]ne of the principal reasons race is treated as a forbidden classification is that it demeans the dignity and worth of a person to be judged by ancestry instead of by his or her own merit and essential qualities."[64] As some of the illustrations offered at the beginning of this chapter make clear, the government's speech can certainly express the government's demeaning judgment of a person based on ancestry rather than on merit.[65] Interpreting the Equal Protection Clause to forbid the government's infliction of expressive harm based on race or other class status would doom these expressive choices.[66]

In short, the government's speech that denigrates its targets based on certain class statuses communicates a message that is subordinating and thus

---

[64] Rice v. Cayetano, 528 U.S. 495, 517 (2000).

[65] E.g., ERIC FONER, RECONSTRUCTION 180 (1988) (quoting President Andrew Johnson's state of the union address in which he claimed that "wherever [African-Americans] have been left to their own devices they have shown a constant tendency to relapse into barbarism").

[66] As another example, the Court's majority identified expressive harm as among the injuries inflicted by federal law that excluded same-sex couples from the federal definition of marriage. See United States v. Windsor, 570 U.S. 744, 772 (2013) ("And it humiliates tens of thousands of children now being raised by same-sex couples. The law in question makes it even more difficult for the children to understand the integrity and closeness of their own family and its concord with other families in their community and in their daily lives.").

repugnant to many antisubordination theorists. And the government's speech that denigrates its targets on these bases may or may not classify its targets in ways that disturb anticlassification theorists.[67]

Criticisms of an expressive harm approach to the Equal Protection Clause are reminiscent of those levelled against the nonendorsement approach to the Establishment Clause. Those who are skeptical worry that efforts to assess the government's expressive meaning inevitably lead to inconsistent, unpredictable, and unprincipled results. Relatedly, some may fear that the indeterminacy and thus uncertainty of this inquiry threaten to deter the government's laudable expressive efforts to promote equal protection values. They may also wonder about further unintended, and damaging, consequences, as constitutional constraints on the government's transparent expression of bigotry might drive that bigotry underground in ways that impede political mobilization in opposition.[68]

FOCUSING ON THE GOVERNMENT'S PURPOSES WHEN SPEAKING: THE GOVERNMENT'S SPEECH MOTIVATED BY ANIMUS

Next we turn from the possible consequences of the government's speech from an Equal Protection perspective to consider instead the government's motivations for speaking. (As noted in the Introduction, in this book I generally use the terms "intentions," "purposes," and "motivations" interchangeably.[69] We can, and in certain contexts should, recognize shades of distinction among these terms, but for now I put those subtleties aside.)

Now we consider whether the Equal Protection Clause forbids the government's speech motivated by animus regardless of its effect – in other words,

---

[67] *See* Bush v. Vera, 517 U.S. 952, 980 (1996) ("Significant deviations from traditional districting principles, such as the bizarre shape and noncompactness demonstrated by the districts here, cause constitutional harm insofar as they convey the message that political identity is, or should be, predominantly racial.").

[68] But it's also true that the cognitive effort required by government speakers who must then express bigotry in more veiled ways may be valuable in and of itself; in other words, there may be value in giving the government reason to take care with its expressive choices. *See* Int'l Refugee Assistance Project v. Trump, 857 F.3d 554, 600 (4th Cir. 2017) ("To the extent that our review chills campaign promises to condemn and exclude entire religious groups, we think that a welcome restraint."), *vacated and remanded* by Trump v. Int'l Refugee Assistance Project, 138 S. Ct. 353 (2017).

[69] *See* Richard H. Fallon, Jr., *Constitutionally Forbidden Legislative Intent*, 130 HARV. L. REV. 523, 534–535 (2016) (observing that courts often use these terms synonymously).

apart from whether it harms its targets' opportunities or inflicts expressive harm.[70] Does the Equal Protection Clause constrain the government's speech motivated by animus?

The government's intentions are relevant to courts' assessment of whether its lawmaking or other regulatory actions violate the Equal Protection Clause. The Court's Equal Protection Clause doctrine – that is, its body of law interpreting and applying the Clause – treats the government's actions with great suspicion when those actions intentionally distinguish among individuals on certain bases.[71] When courts find that the government intends to draw such distinctions, they treat the government's choices with suspicion; in other words, the government bears the burden of showing an unusually tight connection between its choice and an extremely strong government interest, a burden that the government usually fails to meet.[72]

On several occasions the Court has also held that the government's lawmaking and other regulatory actions automatically violate the Equal Protection Clause when motivated by the government's "bare desire to harm" – its animus - because such a motivation "cannot constitute a legitimate

---

[70] Of course, we can anticipate that when the government intends to send a hurtful message, it will also often succeed in doing so. Perhaps for this reason, the Court has sometimes characterized the constitutional injury involving animus as involving both purpose and effect. *See* United States v. Windsor, 570 U.S. 744, 775 (2013) ("The federal statute is invalid, for no legitimate purpose overcomes the purpose and effect to disparage and to injure those whom the State, by its marriage laws, sought to protect in personhood and dignity.").

[71] Under the Supreme Court's equal protection doctrine, the government's intent is generally necessary to a finding that the government's action violated the Clause; in other words, the Court does not apply heightened scrutiny to government actions that have a discriminatory effect based on protected class status unless accompanied by the government's intent to draw distinctions based on protected class status. Washington v. Davis, 426 U.S. 229, 239 (1976). Although this section focuses on the government's speech motivated by animus, we can imagine situations in which the government's speech has some other discriminatory motive, like paternalism or self-interest. In those cases, if we understand the Equal Protection Clause to constrain the government's speech when motivated by discriminatory intent, without more, we'd apply heightened scrutiny to the government's speech inspired by that intent

[72] For example, the Court applies strict scrutiny to the government's intentional distinctions based on race, which requires the government to show that its distinction is necessary to achieving a compelling government interest. And the Court applies a form of intermediate (but still very suspicious) scrutiny to the government's intentional distinctions based on gender, which requires the government to show that its distinction is substantially related to achieving an important government interest. For the rare exception of a governmental program that survives strict scrutiny, see Grutter v. Bollinger, 539 U.S. 306 (2003) (upholding the University of Michigan School of Law's consideration of race as a plus-factor in its admissions decisions as narrowly tailored to achieving the school's compelling educational interest in a diverse student body).

governmental interest" under any level of scrutiny.[73] More specifically, in *U.S. Dep't of Agriculture v. Moreno*, the Supreme Court struck down a federal limitation on those eligible for food stamps that it found to be motivated by "a bare congressional desire to harm a politically unpopular group" ("hippies," in Congress's terms, who formed households of unrelated folks).[74] In *City of Cleburne v. Cleburne Living Center*, the Court nullified a city's decision to deny a zoning permit to a group home for individuals with mental disabilities because the Court found the decision based "on an irrational prejudice against" those individuals.[75] In *Romer v. Evans*, the Court invalidated Colorado's state constitutional amendment that barred local jurisdictions from protecting their citizens from sexual orientation discrimination, concluding that Colorado's action was "inexplicable by anything but animus toward the class it affects."[76] And in *United States v. Windsor*, the Court struck down a federal law that excluded same-sex couples from its definition of marriage once it found that the law had "the purpose and effect to disparage and to injure" those couples.[77] Finally, in *Trump v. Hawaii*, the majority suggested that a governmental choice "'inexplicable by anything but animus'" would violate the Constitution (even as it concluded that motivations other than animus could support the Administration's travel ban restricting the nationals of several majority-Muslim countries from entering the United States).[78] In determining whether a government's lawmaking or other regulatory action was motivated by animus or other discriminatory intent, the Court has looked to decision-makers' own statements, the historical background of the government's choice, the specific sequence of events leading up to its choice, any departures from normal processes in making the choice, and any lack of a relationship between the government's choice and its stated ends (which would create doubt about the credibility of the government's self-described purposes).[79]

So if the Equal Protection Clause limits the government's power to *act* when motivated by animus – its hostility toward or strong dislike for certain individuals or groups – does it also limit the government's power to *speak*,

---

[73] *See* U.S. Dep't of Agriculture v. Moreno, 413 U.S. 528, 534 (1973) ("For if the constitutional conception of 'equal protection of the laws' means anything, it must at the very least mean that a bare congressional desire to harm a politically unpopular group cannot constitute a legitimate governmental interest.").

[74] *Id.*   [75] 473 U.S. 432, 450 (1985).   [76] 517 U.S. 620, 632 (1996).

[77] 570 U.S. 744, 775 (2013).   [78] 138 S. Ct. 2392, 2420–2421 (2018).

[79] *See* Village of Arlington Heights v. Metropolitan Housing Corp., 429 U.S. 252, 266–268 (1977); *see also* WILLIAM D. ARAIZA, ANIMUS: A SHORT INTRODUCTION TO BIAS IN THE LAW 89–104 (2017).

without more, when motivated by animus? Those who answer "yes" may do so for instrumental reasons: if the government speaks with a "bare desire to harm," it is probably more likely actually to cause harm. Those who answer "yes" may do so based on moral intuitions: it's just wrong for the government to try to hurt people through words as well as deeds. And they may answer "yes" based on a theory of the government's constitutional power: the Constitution does not empower the government to try to harm us or to otherwise try to achieve objectives that are not public-regarding. As the Court declared in *Romer*, "We must conclude that Amendment 2 classifies homosexuals not to further a proper legislative end but to make them unequal to everyone else. This Colorado cannot do. A State cannot so deem a class of persons a stranger to its laws."[80]

For an illustration of how an animus inquiry might apply to the government's speech, consider public schools' curricular decisions, decisions that communicate the ideas and values that the government chooses to impart.[81] Imagine, for example, a public school that announces that it will offer electives in white supremacy – the theory that the white race is superior to all others – that no one is required to attend or teach. (This example is not so far-fetched: during the Southern campaign for massive resistance in the 1950s and 1960s, "[s]egregationists sometimes sought positively to promote the teaching of white supremacy in the public schools."[82]). As another example, in 2010, the state of Arizona put a stop to Tucson's Mexican American Studies program.[83] Teachers, students, and parents challenged Arizona's decision on equal protection grounds, alleging that it was motivated by animus against Latinos. A federal district court found that the law's enactment and enforcement were motivated by the government's animus.[84] Although the state's action in this case constituted hard law because it docked noncompliant districts 10% of their state education funding, we can imagine softer counterparts, where a public school simply announces that it will stop teaching Latino history, and the same evidence reveals that animus inspired its choice.

To be sure, the Court's animus doctrine triggers substantial controversy even when used to strike down governmental *actions* as violating the Equal Protection Clause, much less its speech. The doctrine's detractors charge that it is not only unworkable, but also threatens instrumental harm of its own. To

---

[80] *Romer*, 517 U.S. at 635.
[81] *See* Bd. of Regents of Univ. of Wisconsin Sys. v. Southworth, 529 U.S. 217, 235 (2000).
[82] Numan V. Bartley, The Rise of Massive Resistance 225 (1969).
[83] *See* González v. Douglas, 269 F. Supp. 3d 948 (D. Ariz. 2017).
[84] *González*, 269 F. Supp. 3d at 965–973.

elaborate, critics of the animus doctrine object that the judicial effort to ascertain the government's motives is too indeterminate and subjective an inquiry, especially when multiple decision-makers with mixed, and sometimes mysterious, motives are involved. They also fear that branding governmental decision-makers as motivated by animus denigrates those decision-makers themselves, exacerbating social conflict and polarization. Along these lines, legal scholar Steven Smith is among those to argue that the Court's animus doctrine fuels more division and exclusion rather than less: "[i]t is hard to imagine a jurisprudence better calculated to undermine inclusiveness, destroy mutual respect, and promote cultural division."[85]

To illuminate the three approaches' various strengths and limitations, let's apply them to a few problems, both real and hypothetical.

COMPARING AND CONTRASTING THE THREE APPROACHES IN ACTION

Consider an Equal Protection Challenge brought by African Americans to their state's choice to display the Confederate flag on its property or as part of its state flag.

If we focus on harm to protected class members' choices and opportunities, we ask whether the flag's display commanded, coerced, or encouraged third parties to discriminate against African Americans; whether it reasonably deterred African Americans from seeking certain opportunities; or (if displayed in public workplaces or schools) whether it created a racially hostile environment. If we focus on expressive harm, we ask whether reasonable onlookers would understand the flag to communicate a message of racial inferiority or second-class status. And if we focus on the government's purpose for its choice, we ask whether the government's choice was motivated by the government's discriminatory intent, such as animus toward African Americans.

We can see these various approaches at work – or not – in the handful of lower court decisions to date that have considered Equal Protection Clause challenges to governments' display of the Confederate flag. All of these courts rejected the claims, with several ruling against the challengers on the merits and one, more recently, rejecting the challenge for lack of standing. In so holding, all of the courts appeared to conclude that the government's choice to display the Confederate logo would violate the Equal Protection Clause *only* if its choice caused a discriminatory change in its targets' choices or

---

[85] *See* Steven D. Smith, *The Jurisprudence of Denigration*, 48 U.C. Davis L. Rev. 675, 700 (2014).

opportunities through "specific factual evidence to demonstrate that the [] flag presently imposes on African-Americans as a group a measurable burden or denies them an identifiable benefit."[86] None found evidence of such a burden. All of the courts rejected, implicitly or explicitly, the possibility that the Equal Protection Clause forbids the government's infliction of expressive harm, without more. Several of the courts acknowledged that the government's initial choice to display the flag was motivated by a discriminatory purpose, but none considered the possibility that the Equal Protection Clause prohibits the government's speech motivated by animus or other discriminatory purpose apart from any discriminatory effect on its targets' choices or opportunities.

More specifically, in *NAACP* v. *Hunt,* the Eleventh Circuit found that Alabama's expressive choice to fly the Confederate flag above the state capitol dome inflicted no discriminatory harm on African Americans. The panel concluded simply that whites as well as African Americans were offended by the flag's display, and that such offense did not establish the requisite discriminatory harm for equal protection purposes: "[T]here is no unequal application of the state policy; all citizens are exposed to the flag. Citizens of all races are offended by its position."[87]

Several years later, in *Coleman* v. *Miller,* the Eleventh Circuit rejected an equal protection challenge to Georgia's incorporation of the Confederate flag logo into its own state flag design.[88] There the plaintiff alleged that "the flag's Confederate symbol, which is often used by and associated with hate groups such as the Ku Klux Klan, inspires in him fear of violence, causes him to devalue himself, and sends an exclusionary message to Georgia's African-American citizens."[89] In other words, the plaintiff alleged, among other things, that the flag inflicted expressive harm by sending a message of African-Americans' inferiority and exclusion. The panel, however, declined to credit expressive harm as an injury forbidden by the Equal Protection Clause:

---

[86] Coleman v. Miller, 117 F.3d 527, 529–530 (11th Cir. 1997), *cert. denied,* 523 U.S. 1011 (1998) (requiring that the challenger "first demonstrate that the flying of the [] flag produces disproportionate effects along racial lines, and then prove that racial motivation was a substantial or motivating factor behind the enactment of the flag legislation").

[87] 891 F.2d 1555, 1562 (11th Cir. 1990); *see also* Daniels v. Harrison Cnty. Bd., 722 So. 2d 136, 139 (Miss. 1998) (rejecting a constitutional challenge to a county's display of confederate flag on beaches and other county property: "As in *Hunt,* the record in the present case contains no indication that the flying of the single Confederate Flag at Eight Flags serves to deprive any citizens of this State of any constitutionally protected right.").

[88] *Coleman,* 117 F.3d at 527.   [89] *Id.* at 529.

After carefully reviewing the record, and drawing all inferences in the light most favorable to appellant, we find no evidence of a similar discriminatory impact imposed by the Georgia flag. ...He testified that the Confederate symbol in the Georgia flag places him in imminent fear of lawlessness and violence and that an African-American friend of his, upon seeing the Georgia flag in a courtroom, decided to plead guilty rather than litigate a traffic ticket. This anecdotal evidence of intangible harm to two individuals, without any evidence regarding the impact upon other African-American citizens or the comparative effect of the flag on white citizens, is insufficient to establish "disproportionate effects along racial lines." Coleman also offered the affidavit of another witness who testified that, in his opinion, the flying of the flag promotes violence against blacks and continues to represent a symbol of Georgia's efforts against integration. This mere allegation, without any accompanying support, also is not sufficient to demonstrate a disproportionate racial effect.[90]

But the court left open the possibility that evidence that the government's display encouraged third parties to discriminate against African Americans could establish a violation: "We recognize that a government action may in some instances violate the Constitution because it encourages private discrimination. There is no evidence in the record of this case, however, that connects the Georgia flag to private discrimination or racial violence."[91]

More recently, in *Moore v. Bryant*, a federal district court dismissed, for lack of standing, an equal protection challenge to Mississippi's incorporation of the Confederate flag logo into its state flag; the state also required its flag to be displayed "in close proximity" to all public schools, where students must be taught the "proper respect" for the flag.[92] Recall (as discussed in more detail in Chapter 2) that to establish standing, a plaintiff must allege that he suffered a concrete and particularized injury as a result of the defendant's choice. Here, the challenger alleged that his regular exposure to the flag caused him to fear for his safety, to feel like a second-class citizen, and to experience emotional distress. The court found this insufficient to establish standing, requiring that the plaintiff instead allege a discriminatory change in his opportunities: "Without sufficient facts that Moore is *treated* differently because of the state flag, this argument that he *feels* like a second-class citizen does not give rise to

---

[90] *Id.* at 530 (citations omitted); *see also id.* ("In order to demonstrate disproportionate impact along racial lines, appellant must present specific factual evidence to demonstrate that the Georgia flag presently imposes on African-Americans as a group a measurable burden or denies them an identifiable benefit.").
[91] *Id.* at 530 n.6.   [92] Miss. Code. Ann. Sec. 37-13-5.

a legal injury."[93] The judge thus implicitly rejected the notion that the Equal Protection Clause prohibits the government's speech that inflicts expressive harm absent any discriminatory change in its targets' choices and opportunities.

On appeal, the Fifth Circuit agreed that the challenger had not established standing. It too required the challenger to allege that Mississippi's expressive display of the Confederate logo resulted in a discriminatory injury to his choices and opportunities. In so holding, the court acknowledged but distinguished Establishment Clause precedent in which courts apply the nonendorsement principle to find standing when plaintiffs simply allege direct and unwelcome exposure to the government's religious display:

> The reason that Equal Protection and Establishment Clause cases call for different injury-in-fact analyses is that the injuries protected under the Clauses are different. The Establishment Clause prohibits the Government from endorsing a religion, and thus directly regulates Government speech if that speech endorses religion. Accordingly, Establishment Clause injury can occur when a person encounters the Government's endorsement of religion. The same is not true under the Equal Protection Clause: the gravamen of an equal protection claim is differential governmental treatment, not differential governmental messaging.[94]

Even if the flag communicates a governmental message of inequality, the Fifth Circuit tells us, the Equal Protection Clause does not forbid the government from inflicting such expressive harm. The Establishment Clause is different, according to the Fifth Circuit. But if we adopt the nonendorsement principle in the Establishment Clause context (and we may or may not), that's because we believe that equality and inclusiveness are key values underlying that Clause. Why wouldn't a similar emphasis on expressive harm be appropriate in the Equal Protection Clause context, a Clause assuredly steeped in equality values? The Fifth Circuit offers little explanation, but its emphasis on "differential governmental treatment" suggests that it adopts an anti-classification understanding of the Equal Protection Clause, and finds no classification here.

The Fifth Circuit also rejected the plaintiff's claim that the flag's display in and near courtrooms, where his work as a prosecutor required him to encounter it, created a hostile work environment. In its words, "analogizing Plaintiff's equal protection claim to a hostile work environment claim fails for the same

---

[93] Moore v. Bryant, 205 F. Supp. 3d 834, 853 (S.D. Miss. 2016).
[94] Moore v. Bryant, 853 F.3d 245, 250 (5th Cir. 2017), *cert. denied*, 138 S. Ct. 468 (2017).

reason that the Establishment Clause analogy fails: under Title VII, exposure to a hostile work environment alone is the injury; under the Equal Protection Clause it is not." But courts have repeatedly held that a government employer that creates a hostile environment based on protected class status can violate the Equal Protection Clause.[95] Allegations of a hostile work environment, if proven, demonstrate that the government has altered the terms and conditions of employment, and has thus both classified and subordinated, based on race. To be sure, hostile environment claims based on the government's speech alone are tough to win. But whether the display of the flag creates a hostile environment in any given workplace in violation of the Equal Protection Clause should be a context-specific inquiry on the merits.[96]

Finally, several of these courts concluded that state governments *intended* to communicate a message of white supremacy with their initial choice to display the Confederate flag. In the words of the 11th Circuit:

> The current flag design was adopted during a regrettable period in Georgia's history when its public leaders were implementing a campaign of massive resistance to the Supreme Court's school desegregation rulings. . . . As many of Georgia's politicians and citizens openly resisted the Supreme Court's desegregation rulings, increasing numbers of white Southerners began expressing renewed interest in their Confederate heritage. It was in this environment of open hostility to the Supreme Court's civil rights rulings and of developing interest in Confederate history that the Georgia General Assembly acted to re-design its state flag. It chose as an official state symbol an emblem that historically had been associated with white supremacy and resistance to federal authority.[97]

Another panel explained that Alabama raised the Confederate flag above its capitol dome in 1963 when Attorney General Robert F. Kennedy traveled to the state capitol to discuss then-Governor George Wallace's announced plan to block the admission of black students to the University of Alabama.[98]

---

[95] E.g., Tuggle v. Mangan, 348 F.3d 714, 720 (8th Cir 2003); Williams v. Herron, 687 F.3d 971, 978 (8th Cir. 2012).

[96] See JAMES E. PFANDER, PRINCIPLES OF FEDERAL JURISDICTION 30–31 (2006) ("Standing focuses on the interests of the parties to the dispute, but standing decisions invariably reflect judicial views about the fitness of the legal question for judicial resolution. Questions about fitness, in turn, often implicate the merits of the dispute, and open the Court to criticism that its standing doctrine lacks principle.").

[97] Coleman, 117 F.2d at 528–530.

[98] Hunt, 891 F.2d at 1558; see also Daniels, 722 So. 2d at 139–140 (Banks, J., concurring) ("Quite recently, many state governments adopted the battle flag as a symbol of continued support of white supremacy, segregation and discrimination against persons of black African descent.").

And before dismissing the challenge in *Moore* v. *Bryant* for lack of standing, federal district court Judge Carlton Reeves offered a lengthy discussion of governments' discriminatory purpose in displaying the Confederate logo, detailing the Confederacy's goal of racial supremacy,[99] and governments' efforts to keep that objective alive during the campaign of massive resistance by erecting Confederate monuments and displaying the Confederate flag. Judge Reeves's dictum itself reflects government speech about government speech:

> It should go without saying that the emblem has been used time and time again in the Deep South, especially in Mississippi, to express opposition to racial equality. Persons who have engaged in racial oppression have draped themselves in that banner while carrying out their mission to intimidate or do harm.[100]

In short, Judge Reeves, like several of the other courts, found evidence that governments' display of the flag had a subordinating purpose. But like the other courts considering related claims, he did not consider the possibility that the Equal Protection Clause might forbid the government's expressive choice if motivated by the government's animus or other discriminatory purpose alone, absent any discriminatory change in its targets' choices or opportunities.

Finally, return to the example that opened this chapter: Alabama and Texas state law that requires public schools' sex education curriculum include "[a]n emphasis, in a factual manner and from a public health perspective, that homosexuality is not a lifestyle acceptable to the general public" and that "homosexual conduct is a criminal offense under the laws of our state."

If we focus on harm to class members' choices or opportunities, we ask whether a challenger can show that the government's speech commanded, coerced, or encouraged third parties to discriminate against gay or lesbian students; whether it deterred those students from seeking certain opportunities; or whether it created a hostile educational environment. It's not hard to

---

[99] For an explanation of the original Confederacy's roots in white supremacy from one of the Confederacy's founders, see Alexander Stephens, Vice-President of the Confederate States of America, Cornerstone Speech (Mar. 21, 1861) ("Our new government['s] . . . foundations are laid, . . . its cornerstone rests, upon the great truth that the negro is not equal to the white man; that slavery, subordination to the superior race, is his natural and normal condition. This, our new government, is the first, in the history of the world, based upon this great physical, philosophical, and moral truth."), available at http://teachingamericanhistory.org/library/document/cornerstone-speech/.

[100] *Moore*, 205 F.Supp.3d at 844.

imagine that the government's speech could encourage other students to bully or harass LGBTQ students, especially given the government's misleading assertion that same-sex sexual behaviour is a criminal offense (yes, laws criminalizing such behaviour remain on Alabama's and Texas's books but those laws are no longer enforceable because the Supreme Court has held them to be unconstitutional.) And the government's speech means that lesbian and gay students face an obstacle to educational success that others don't face when the government tells them and their classmates that theirs is not a life acceptable to the general public. At the same time, we can expect disputes about the causal connection between the government's speech and those discriminatory consequences, including disputes about whether the government's speech rises to the level of a hostile environment.

If we focus on expressive harm, we ask whether reasonable onlookers would understand the government to be communicating a message of inferiority or second-class status. As is so often the case, this turns on who constitutes a reasonable observer – a lesbian or gay teenager or the child of lesbian or gay parents? Someone whose religion teaches that same-sex sexual behavior is morally wrong? Someone who hasn't thought about it much? Your preference for an antisubordination or anticlassification understanding of the Equal Protection Clause likely informs your choice.

And if we focus on the motivations for the government's speech, we ask whether the government's speech was motivated by its animus, or other discriminatory intent, based on sexual orientation. The state would likely argue that its choice was motivated not by hostility or dislike but instead by its moral and pedagogical views about healthy sexual behavior. But the Court at times has signaled that moral disapproval in this context is a type of animus. For example, in *Windsor*, as evidence of the government's animus in enacting the Defense of Marriage Act (DOMA), the Court's majority opinion pointed to a House committee report explaining that DOMA expresses "both moral disapproval of homosexuality, and a moral conviction that heterosexuality better comports with traditional (especially Judeo-Christian) morality."[101] And years earlier, Justice O'Connor wrote, "Moral disapproval of this group, like a bare desire to harm the group, is an interest that is insufficient to satisfy rational basis review under the Equal Protection Clause."[102] To be sure, the

---

[101] United States v. Windsor, 570 U.S. 744, 770–771 (2013).
[102] Lawrence v. Texas, 539 U.S. 558, 582 (2003) (O'Connor, J., concurring).

Court's dissenters contest the premise that animus and moral disapproval are indistinguishable.[103]

These problems force us to think hard about the meaning of equality, about when the government's speech threatens our conception of equality, and about our hierarchy of values when we weigh the costs and benefits of constraining the government's speech related to equality. We can see the cleavages, the points of contention. The government's speech violates the Equal Protection Clause when it results in certain discriminatory effects, but some will be quicker than others to find those effects. And whether the Equal Protection Clause forbids the government's denigrating messages that inflict expressive harm or the government's messages inspired by animus turns in part on whether we prefer an anticlassification or antisubordination approach as well as on our assessment of courts' institutional competence to ascertain expressive meaning or governmental purpose. These difficulties may mean that even the nastiest of the government's expressive choices may only rarely violate the Constitution. But the answer to the question "When does the government's speech violate the Equal Protection Clause" is not "never," but instead "sometimes."

We confront similarly hard and important problems in the next chapter when we consider when, if ever, the Due Process Clause restrains the government's speech, including its lies and other falsehoods, its disclosure of intimate information, and its cruel and humiliating speech.

---

[103] *Windsor*, 570 U.S. at 795 (Scalia, J., dissenting) ("As I have observed before, the Constitution does not forbid the government to enforce traditional moral and sexual norms.").

4

The Government's Speech and Due Process

Imagine that you walk out your front door one morning, only to find the police waiting for you. They arrest you, charging that you recently bought drugs in violation of state law. An officer advises you that you have the right to remain silent and that you have the right to a lawyer – and then tells you that unless you waive those rights and talk to the police immediately, the local judge will pronounce you an unfit parent and order your five-year-old daughter taken from you. That's not true – but you don't know that, as this is your first encounter with the criminal justice system. Does the government's lie violate the Constitution –more specifically, the Due Process Clause?

The Due Process Clause prohibits the government from depriving any person "of life, liberty or property without due process of law."[1] The government violates procedural due process protections when it takes away an individual's life, liberty, or property without providing her a meaningful opportunity to be heard. The government violates substantive due process protections (regardless of the presence of procedural safeguards) when it denies life, liberty, or property without adequate justification.

This chapter addresses whether and when the government's speech – including the government's lies and other falsehoods, the government's disclosure of private information through its speech, and its speech that humiliates its targets – deprives its targets of life, liberty, or property in violation of the Due Process Clause.[2]

But first, to remind us how the government's expressive choices are so often complicated, at times salutary and at times malign, I start with a brief tour of

---

[1] The Fifth Amendment's Due Process Clause constrains the federal government, while the Fourteenth Amendment's Due Process Clause applies to state and local governments.

[2] The next chapter considers whether and when the government's speech that takes these forms violates the First Amendment's Free Speech or Free Press Clauses.

the government's lies and other falsehoods.[3] I focus on the government's lies because the wide array of their audiences, topics, motives, and effects trigger unusually challenging constitutional questions. As we'll see, these challenges are such that the government's most catastrophic speech – like its lies about its justifications for war – may be among those most resistant to constitutional redress.

THE VARIETY AND COMPLEXITY OF THE GOVERNMENT'S LIES

Lies, whatever their source, so often sting because they leave us feeling disrespected and betrayed. So too of the government's lies. But the government's lies are also different from, and at times more dangerous than, the lies of nongovernmental speakers: the government's lies sometimes wreak harm that only the government can inflict.

The government's lies are often contemptible and, at the same time, ever so human and thus all too familiar. Because lies seem endemic to the human condition, we shouldn't be surprised to find that our government engages in them as well, as of course it is filled with human beings as flawed (and as virtuous) as the rest of us. We hope to elect a government that we can trust even as we remain distrustful of it.

The government's lies, like our own, are often complicated. The government's motives for lying and the consequences of its lies, again like our own, are many and motley. We lie frequently, for a variety of reasons, with a wide array of consequences. At times our falsehoods are selfish or cruel, at other times compassionate or constructive. When discussing the lies of nongovernmental parties more generally, Justice Breyer reminds us that some have instrumental and even moral value:

> False factual statements can serve useful human objectives, for example: in social contexts, where they may prevent embarrassment, protect privacy, shield a person from prejudice, provide the sick with comfort, or preserve a child's innocence; in public contexts, where they may stop a panic or otherwise preserve calm in the face of danger; and even in technical, philosophical, and scientific contexts, where (as Socrates' methods suggest)

---

[3] I'll use the term "lie" to mean a speaker's deliberately or recklessly false assertion of fact made with the intention that the listener believe it to be true. The government also can mislead the public in many other ways, both intentionally and unintentionally – for example, by keeping material information secret from the public or by accidentally misleading the public through mistakes and inaccuracies.

examination of a false statement (even if made deliberately to mislead) can promote a form of thought that ultimately helps realize the truth.[4]

For these reasons we may feel that some lies by nongovernmental speakers are harmless or even helpful – like those told to protect privacy, to flatter, to calm, and to comfort.

So too may some lies by the government strike us as innocuous or even valuable if they help accomplish important public objectives: think of undercover police officers' lies about their identities, told to discover and stop wrongdoing. (But some argue that even the government's public-regarding lies still injure. Along these lines, some legal scholars assert that law enforcement officers' lies to secure confessions undercut citizens' willingness to trust and cooperate with the police, ultimately frustrating law enforcement's effectiveness to the public's detriment.[5]) Other illustrations include governmental lies to achieve certain domestic and foreign policy goals like the Kennedy administration's lies during the Cuban missile crisis about the extent of its knowledge of the location of Soviet missiles, and the negotiated terms of their withdrawal from Cuba. Arthur Sylvester, Kennedy's Assistant Secretary of Defense, even proposed a governmental *duty to lie* in related circumstances:

> Government officials as individuals do not have the right to lie politically or to protect themselves, but they do always have the duty to protect their countrymen.... Sometimes, and those times are rare indeed, Government officials may be required to fulfill their duty by issuing a false statement to deceive a potential enemy, as in the Cuban missile crisis.[6]

Sometimes the government lies about the existence or scope of a government program. When Francis Gary Powers and his U-2 aircraft were shot down in Soviet airspace, President Eisenhower's first public statement was a lie: he claimed that the plane was merely an off-track weather aircraft when in

[4] United States v. Alvarez, 567 U.S. 709, 733 (2012) (Breyer, J., concurring).
[5] *E.g.*, I. Bennett Capers, *Crime, Legitimacy, and Testilying*, 83 IND. L.J. 835, 835–842 (2008) (contending that public perceptions that law enforcement officers engage in deceit and other illegitimate behavior discourage public compliance with the law); Deborah Young, *Unnecessary Evil: Police Lying in Interrogations*, 28 CONN. L. REV. 425, 458–459 (1996) ("As knowledge of police lying spreads, trust of police will decrease and citizens will be less likely to come forward and talk honestly with police. Critical evidence may remain undiscovered or undisclosed.").
[6] *See* Arthur Sylvester, *The Government Has the Right to Lie*, SATURDAY EVENING POST, Nov. 18, 1967.

fact it was a Central Intelligence Agency spy plane on a reconnaissance mission.[7] More recently, Obama administration officials misrepresented the sweep of the federal government's domestic surveillance and data collection. As legal scholar Mary-Rose Papandrea recounts:

> [I]n March 2013 Senator Ron Wyden directly asked James Clapper, the Director of National Intelligence: "[D]oes the NSA collect any type of data at all on millions, or hundreds of millions, of Americans?" Clapper stated that the government did not collect such data, at least "not wittingly." After the Snowden leaks made clear that this response was false, Clapper explained that his response was the "least untruthful" answer he could give when asked about a classified program in an open session.[8]

The government's deliberate falsehoods include those for its political gain and sometimes its political survival. To these ends, the government sometimes lies about its own actions to avoid legal and political accountability. Think, for instance, of the government's deliberately false claims that a government official or agency acted in compliance with law, like Nixon administration officials' lies to conceal criminal activity in the aftermath of Watergate and Reagan administration officials' lies denying their illegal activities in Nicaragua.[9]

The government's falsehoods to justify its military intervention threaten death and other shattering harms. President Polk misrepresented the incidents leading the United States to engage in war with Mexico in the nineteenth century,[10] Lyndon Johnson's administration did the same of the incidents that triggered broader U.S. involvement in Vietnam in the twentieth century,[11] and George W. Bush's administration followed suit in the twenty-first century when, to support its invasion of Iraq, it misrepresented the evidence of Iraq's

---

[7]   *See* JIM NEWTON, EISENHOWER: THE WHITE HOUSE YEARS 313–315 (2011).

[8]   Mary-Rose Papandrea, *Leaker Traitor Whistleblower Spy: National Security Leaks and the First Amendment*, 94 B.U. L. REV. 449, 467 (2014) (quoting Current and Projected National Security Threats to the United States: Hearing Before the S. Select Comm. on Intelligence, 113th Cong. 66 (2013) (statements of Sen. Ron Wyden, Member, S. Select Comm. on Intelligence and James R. Clapper, Director of National Intelligence) and Interview by Andrea Mitchell with James Clapper, Dir. of Nat'l Intelligence (June 8, 2013) (transcript archived at http://perma.cc/SJF4-FJ7K).

[9]   *See* ERIC ALTERMAN, WHEN PRESIDENTS LIE 240–241, 279–288 (2004).

[10] *See* Peter W. Morgan, *The Undefined Crime of Lying to Congress: Ethics Reform and the Rule of Law*, 86 Nw. U. L. REV. 177, 216–221 (1992).

[11] *See* GEOFFREY R. STONE, PERILOUS TIMES: FREE SPEECH IN WARTIME 517 (2004) ("[The Pentagon Papers] revealed that the American government had systematically lied to the American people about the nature, purpose, conduct, and consequences of an ongoing war.").

purported weapons of mass destruction.[12] Writing about the Vietnam War, journalist David Wise describes the devastating results of these sorts of misrepresentations:

> Often, in the foreign policy and national security area, what the government says *is* the news. The Tonkin Gulf episode was a classic illustration of this. The public was told that on August 4 two American warships on "routine patrol" had, in Defense Secretary Robert McNamara's words, been under "continuous torpedo attack" by North Vietnamese PT boats; in response, Lyndon Johnson ordered the first bombing attack on North Vietnam and pushed the Tonkin Gulf resolution through Congress, thereby acquiring a blank check to escalate the war. Later it became clear that there had been much confusion and considerable doubt within the government as to whether any PT-boat attack had taken place at all. The public, however, had to rely entirely on Lyndon Johnson and Robert McNamara for their news of the incident. If the details seem unimportant in the larger tapestry of the war, we need only recall that at the time 163 Americans had died in Vietnam.[13]

At times the government lies about what it is actually doing in wartime. The Nixon administration lied not only about its decision to bomb Cambodia but also about its intervention in Laos: just days after its Pentagon assured anti-war Senators that there were no American ground troops in Laos, "the White House admitted that at least twenty-seven Americans had died fighting" there.[14] Relatedly, the government sometimes lies about its wartime setbacks. The government misrepresented the extent of its losses at Pearl Harbor, and elsewhere, during World War II.[15] And Defense Secretary Robert McNamara reported great military progress in Vietnam to an audience of journalists just

---

[12] *See* Susan A. Brewer, Why America Fights: Patriotic and War Propaganda from the Philippines to Iraq 245 (2009) ("At the United Nations, Powell detailed Iraq's nuclear ambitions, biological and chemical weapons, and ties to Al Qaeda. Later, it would be revealed that the facts he cited were known to be fake or unreliable, under dispute at the CIA, the Defense Intelligence Agency, the Energy Department, and the International Atomic Energy Agency.").

[13] David Wise, The Politics of Lying: Government Deception, Secrecy, and Power 27–28 (1973).

[14] *See* Rick Perlstein, Nixonland: The Rise of a President and the Fracturing of America 463 (2008).

[15] *See* Allan M. Winkler, The Politics of Propaganda: The Office of War Information 1942–1945 49 (1978) ("Ever since the Japanese attack on Pearl Harbor the American public suspected that the United States Navy was trying to hide its losses.... [P]ublic indignation grew even more intense when the Navy finally admitted months after the May 1942 battle of the Coral Sea the extent of the losses there.").

minutes after telling government analyst Daniel Ellsberg, in private, that 100,000 additional American troops had resulted in no improvement (Ellsberg was so disillusioned by these lies that he later leaked the Pentagon Papers to the press to ensure their public exposure.[16])

Both military and civilian leaders at times lie not only to the American public and to foreign audiences, but also to themselves:

> After the escalation, General William Westmoreland, the commander of U.S. forces, banned the CIA from pegging the number of enemy fighters at more than 399,000. There were actually over 600,000. That number included guerrillas, and to count them would acknowledge the insurgency had popular support. They lied, as well, to one another. When McNamara came to visit, commanders doctored maps and records to make the enemy looks small and the ARVN, the South Vietnamese army, look bigger.[17]

Relatedly, after reviewing the Pentagon Papers and their documentation of the government's lies about its involvement in Vietnam, political theorist and philosopher Hannah Arendt concluded that the government's lies were "destined chiefly, if not exclusively, for domestic consumption, for propaganda at home, and especially for the purpose of deceiving Congress. The Tonkin incident, where the enemy knew all the facts and the Senate Foreign Relations Committee none, is a case in point."[18] As historian Susan Brewer reminds us more generally in recounting governmental propaganda during World Wars I and II, "wars begin because diplomats tell lies to journalists and then believe what they read."[19]

The government's lies inflict damaging unintended consequences when they contribute to public doubts about the government's credibility. More than one commentator has suggested that the public's perception that the government had lied to it in World War I left Americans, two decades later, reluctant to believe the government's reports of Nazi barbarities. As historian Barbara Tuchman observed:

> Take the question of German atrocities in 1914. Nothing requires more careful handling because, owing to post-war disillusions, "atrocity" came to be a word one did not believe in. It was supposed because the Germans had

---

[16] *See* GEOFFREY R. STONE, PERILOUS TIMES: FREE SPEECH IN WARTIME 501 (2004).

[17] *See* RICK PERLSTEIN, NIXONLAND: THE RISE OF A PRESIDENT AND THE FRACTURING OF AMERICA 170 (2008).

[18] HANNAH ARENDT, CRISES OF THE REPUBLIC 14 (1972).

[19] SUSAN A. BREWER, TO WIN THE PEACE: BRITISH PROPAGANDA IN THE UNITED STATES DURING WORLD WAR II 7 (1997) (quoting Viennese satirist Karl Kraus).

not, after all, cut off the hands of Belgian babies, neither had they shot hostages nor burned Louvain. The results of this disbelief were dangerous because when the Germans became Nazis people were disinclined to believe they were as bad as they seemed and appeasement became the order of the day.[20]

As this small sampling illustrates, the government's lies are complicated. At times they threaten distinct and especially serious damage precisely because of their governmental source. That the government's lies and other falsehoods hurt us, however, does not always mean that the Constitution forbids them.

As discussed in Chapter 2, the Supreme Court's justiciability doctrine requires, among other things, that a plaintiff allege a "concrete and particularized," rather than generalized, injury to establish his standing – and unless the plaintiff can establish standing, the federal courts do not have the constitutional power to hear his claim. This and other justiciability requirements (like the political question doctrine) seek to respect the separation of powers, divert more collective injuries to the political process for redress, and protect federal courts' workload from disputes they are not well-positioned to resolve. For this reason, the government's speech that inflicts more concrete and individualized harms is more amenable to constraint through constitutional litigation than its speech that inflicts more diffuse harms, like the damage caused by the government's lies to avoid political and legal accountability, or to justify its military actions. That lies' harms are less tangible or more diffuse does not mean that they're painless or unimportant: indeed, they can be deeply dangerous, threatening to corrode our democracy. But the nature of their harms might mean that law, especially constitutional law, holds limited capacity to address them.

Consider the vexing problems presented by the government's lies about its deployment of military force, lies that threaten dire harms together with substantial enforcement difficulties. Imagine a president's lies to Congress and to the public in her State of the Union address about the reasons for U.S. military intervention. These falsehoods threaten a range of ruinous injuries, both individual and collective, as they can lead to the loss of lives by both civilians and soldiers, the disastrous diversion of national resources, and a substantial loss in public trust. Yet establishing the link between the president's lie and the actual decision to go to war (and the resulting deprivation of life, liberty, and property) will no doubt be difficult, as many factors influence that causal chain. Furthermore, we may worry that partisan rather than

---

[20] Barbara Tuchman, Practicing History 43 (1981).

principled interests might motivate constitutional litigation challenging the president's assertions as lies, and that the judiciary might be reluctant to second-guess the choices of the president when exercising her powers as commander-in-chief. Relatedly, we may fear that lies' constitutional constraint will inadvertently chill the government's valuable speech. These concerns may lead many to prefer nonconstitutional responses as the best among imperfect options. Discussed at more length in Chapter 7, these responses include aggressive congressional oversight of the executive's claims, enhanced statutory protections for whistle-blowers who expose government falsehoods, protest and pushback from the press and the people themselves, even impeachment.

These complexities suggest, perhaps to our frustration, that the government's most catastrophic lies may be those most resistant to constitutional redress. Our expectations of the government's truthfulness may be unenforceable, through constitutional litigation, in many settings.

But not in all. Next we consider how the government's lies and other expressive choices sometimes endanger life, liberty, or property in violation of the Due Process Clause.

WHEN, IF EVER, DOES THE GOVERNMENT'S SPEECH DEPRIVE ITS TARGETS OF "LIFE, LIBERTY, OR PROPERTY"?

In thinking through the second-stage government speech problem of whether and when the government's speech violates the Due Process Clause, we ask a series of familiar questions about the consequences of, and the motivations underlying, the government's speech. When we interrogate its consequences, we consider whether the government's speech deprives its listeners of specific liberties in ways akin to the government's lawmaking or other regulatory actions. Examples include law enforcement officers' lies to those in custody that coerce their targets' involuntary waiver of constitutional rights, the government's falsehoods or disclosures that unduly burden women's exercise of their reproductive rights, and the government's falsehoods that deny their targets' meaningful exercise of voting rights. When we turn to the expressive, or dignitary, consequences of the government's speech, we consider whether its speech humiliates or shames its targets because they have exercised protected liberties. Finally, when we turn from the consequences of the government's speech to the government's purposes when speaking, we ponder whether the Due Process Clause denies the government the power to speak for certain reasons, for example, when the government speaks to interfere with its targets' protected liberties or to inflict pain. Our theory of the Due Process

Clause and the nature of the liberty and property interests that it protects (and relatedly, our theory of when the government infringes those interests) often drives our doctrinal preferences, our reactions to the various approaches for considering these second-stage government speech problems.

FOCUSING ON THE EFFECTS OF THE GOVERNMENT'S EXPRESSION: SPEECH THAT COERCES OR UNDULY BURDENS ITS TARGETS' LIBERTIES

The government's lies, threats, and other expressive choices can deprive their targets of liberty in violation of the Due Process Clause in a variety of ways. Sometimes the government's speech leads directly to its targets' imprisonment, and thus their loss of physical liberty. And sometimes the government's speech coerces or otherwise interferes with its targets' exercise of their constitutional rights.

The Government's Speech That Deprives Its Targets of Physical Liberty

A prosecutor's lies to a judge or jury offend the Due Process Clause when they lead to a defendant's imprisonment, thus depriving him of physical liberty.[21] As an illustration on a large scale, the government's World War II lies resulted in Japanese-American citizens' detention, and thus their loss of physical liberty. As lawyer and political science professor Peter Irons summarizes:

> The evidence of the government's misconduct in these cases is clear and compelling, and rests on the government's own records. It reveals that high government officials, including the Solicitor General, knowingly presented the Supreme Court with false and fabricated records, both in briefs and oral arguments, that misled the Court and resulted in decisions that deprived the petitioners in these cases of their rights to fair hearings of their challenges to military orders that were based, not on legitimate fears that they—and all Japanese Americans—posed a danger of espionage and

---

[21] *See Davis v. Zant,* 36 F.3d 1538 (11th Cir. 1994) (concluding that a prosecutor's knowingly false statements to the jury that a key government witness had not confessed to murder were fundamentally unfair and thus a violation of due process); *United States v. Kalfayan,* 8 F.3d 1315 (9th Cir. 1993) (concluding that a prosecutor's knowingly false statement to the jury that an absent witness could have refused to testify was willful prosecutorial misconduct of a sufficiently prejudicial nature to violate due process).

sabotage on the West Coast, but rather reflected the racism of the general who promulgated the orders.[22]

Yet, in *Korematsu v. United States*, a majority of the Supreme Court infamously found that the federal government's action, concededly based on race and national origin, did not violate its equal protection obligations;[23] the Court's majority failed even to mention the due process and habeas corpus implications of the government's actions. Only recently did the contemporary Court finally make clear that *Korematsu* "was gravely wrong the day it was decided" as a matter of equal protection law (still no mention of due process or habeas corpus).[24]

Offered to justify the government's imprisonment of its targets, these governmental lies directly led to the deprivation of physical liberty. Other government statements that falsely or inaccurately assert an individual's misconduct or dangerousness can also deprive their targets of liberty in very direct ways. Think, for example, of a government's false statement that an individual is sufficiently dangerous to be included on a "no-fly" list and thus barred from international air travel.[25]

The Government's Speech That Coerces the Waiver of Constitutional Rights in the Criminal Justice Setting

Government expression's potential to coerce its listeners varies with its setting, and the criminal justice setting is among the most coercive of environments. For this reason, the Supreme Court told us in *Miranda v. Arizona*, the Constitution compels law enforcement officers who exert physical and legal control over their listeners to disclose available constitutional protections to protect those listeners from coercion and deception:

> We have concluded that without proper safeguards the process of in-custody interrogation of persons suspected or accused of crime contains inherently compelling pressures which work to undermine the individual's will to resist

---

[22] PETER IRONS, UNFINISHED BUSINESS: THE CASE FOR SUPREME COURT REPUDIATION OF THE JAPANESE AMERICAN INTERNMENT CASES 4 (2013).

[23] United States v. Korematsu, 323 U.S. 214 (1944). But not everyone on the Court agreed. As discussed in Chapter 3, for example, Justice Murphy's scathing dissent called out the government's racist falsehoods. *Id.* at 235–240 (Murphy, J., dissenting).

[24] Trump v. Hawaii, 138 S. Ct. 2392, 2423 (2018).

[25] *See* Latif v. Holder, 28 F. Supp. 3d 1134 (D. Or. 2014) (noting that the Department of Homeland Security's inadequate process for addressing inaccurate listings on its No-Fly list threatened constitutionally protected liberty interests).

and to compel him to speak where he would not otherwise do so freely. In order to combat these pressures and to permit a full opportunity to exercise the privilege against self-incrimination, the accused must be adequately and effectively apprised of his rights and the exercise of those rights must be fully honored.... For those unaware of the privilege, the warning is needed simply to make them aware of it – the threshold requirement for an intelligent decision as to its exercise. More important, such a warning is an absolute prerequisite in overcoming the inherent pressures of the interrogation atmosphere. It is not just the subnormal or woefully ignorant who succumb to an interrogator's imprecations, whether implied or expressly stated, that the interrogation will continue until a confession is obtained or that silence in the face of accusation is itself damning and will bode ill when presented to a jury.[26]

Not only have courts interpreted the Due Process Clause to require the government to make certain truthful disclosures in the criminal justice setting, but sometimes they have also interpreted the Clause to forbid the government's lies in that setting. More specifically, law enforcement officers' lies violate the Due Process Clause when they coerce their listeners into relinquishing their constitutional rights, like the right to be free from compelled self-incrimination, the right to a lawyer, or the right to refuse a warrantless search.

Coercion is the key here, according to most courts: law enforcement officials' lies do not violate the Due Process Clause when they reflect "mere strategic deception" rather than coercion. Under this view, coercion unacceptably frustrates individuals' liberty to decide freely whether to waive a constitutional right, while "mere strategic deception" helps achieve public benefits that outweigh its more limited costs to individual liberty.[27]

To be sure, we can expect disagreement and dispute about the meaning of "coercion." Legal scholar Christopher Slobogin has synthesized the case law to identify two types of police interrogators' lies as "clearly illegitimately

---

[26] Miranda v. Arizona, 384 U.S. 436, 467–468 (1966).
[27] *See* Illinois v. Perkins, 496 U.S. 292, 296–297 (1990) (finding no constitutional violation when an undercover law enforcement officer posed as a fellow inmate to whom a jailed suspect made damaging admissions: "*Miranda* forbids coercion, not mere strategic deception by taking advantage of a suspect's misplaced trust in one he supposes to be a fellow prisoner"); United States v. Byram, 145 F.3d 405, 408 (1st Cir. 1998) ("But trickery is not automatically coercion. Indeed, the police commonly engage in such ruses as suggesting to a suspect that a confederate has just confessed or that police have or will secure physical evidence against the suspect. While the line between ruse and coercion is sometimes blurred, confessions procured by deceits have been held voluntary in a number of situations.").

coercive," rather than "mere strategic deception."[28] First, courts routinely find that police lies about the target's constitutional rights coerce the waiver of such rights and thus violate constitutional protections. In other words, the government's lies about the existence or exercise of constitutional rights can be the practical equivalent of its refusal to honor those rights altogether. These include the government's misrepresentations about the legal consequences of waiving a constitutional right, as was the case, for instance, where local law enforcement officials assured a suspect that they would not prosecute if he spoke freely to them with federal officers in the room – without making clear that he could, and would, still be prosecuted by federal prosecutors under federal rather than state law.[29] As another illustration, the Supreme Court found a suspect's consent to a search to be coerced when given in response to law enforcement officers' lies that they had a warrant.[30]

Second, courts often characterize police interrogators' lies as coercive if the assertions would be coercive if true – that is, if a reasonable person would not resist them by remaining silent, requesting counsel, or otherwise exercising her constitutional rights.[31] Recall the not-so-hypothetical example that opened the chapter: law enforcement officers' lies to a parent that her child will be taken from her unless she waives her constitutional rights. Most of us would not feel free to rebuff the government by continuing to claim our rights – and indeed, the Court found these sorts of lies to be unconstitutionally coercive.[32] In a similar vein, a court found law enforcement officers' lies to be coercive in violation of the Due Process Clause when they falsely told a suspect that doctors were trying to save his child's life and needed him to explain the circumstances under which he injured the child.[33]

---

[28] Christopher Slobogin, *Lying and Confessing*, 39 TEX. TECH. L. REV. 1275, 1276 (2007).

[29] *See* United States v. Rogers, 906 F.2d 189 (5th Cir. 1990).

[30] Bumper v. North Carolina, 391 U.S. 543, 550 (1968) ("When a law enforcement officer claims authority to search a home under a warrant, he announces in effect that the occupant has no right to resist the search. The situation is instinct with coercion—albeit colorably lawful coercion. Where there is coercion there cannot be consent.").

[31] *See* Christopher Slobogin, *Lying and Confessing*, 39 TEX. TECH. L. REV. 1275, 1276 (2007).

[32] *See* Lynumn v. Illinois, 372 U.S. 528, 534 (1963) ("[T]he petitioner's oral confession was made only after the police had told her that state financial aid for her infant children would be cut off, and her children taken from her, if she did not 'cooperate.' These threats were made while she was encircled in her apartment by three police officers and a twice convicted felon who had purportedly 'set her up.' There was no friend or adviser to whom she might turn. She had had no previous experience with the criminal law, and had no reason not to believe that the police had ample power to carry out their threats. We think it clear that a confession made under such circumstances must be deemed not voluntary, but coerced.").

[33] *See* People v. Thomas, 8 N.E.3d 308, 314–315 (N.Y. 2014).

Government expression's coercive potential can vary with the audience as well as with the subject matter. For instance, teenagers' youth and inexperience may leave them especially vulnerable to police interrogation tactics that include lies. Recognizing this, the Supreme Court has held that whether a young person questioned by police at school reasonably believes he is not free to leave – which would trigger *Miranda's* requirement that the police read him his rights – may turn on his age.[34] Even better, legal scholar Justin Driver suggests, to hold that the school setting's coercive potential is such that the police should always inform young people of their rights when questioning them at school.[35]

Courts generally find that law enforcement officers' lies are *not* coercive for Due Process Clause purposes when they conclude that a reasonable person could and would simply respond to the government's speech by exercising his constitutional rights to remain silent or wait for a lawyer. Courts generally consider this to be true of police officers' lies about whether a codefendant has confessed or whether there's a witness, lies about the existence of physical evidence, and lies about the results of a polygraph test.[36] So too of most undercover officers' lies about their identity, when the target is free simply to walk away from the conversation. Courts in these settings often expect that targets would and could reasonably respond in any of a variety of ways other than relinquishing their constitutional rights.[37] For example, the Court held that an undercover officer's false claim about his identity did not coerce the suspect's invitation of that undercover agent into his home for a drug sale.[38]

But philosophers, courts, and commentators have long disagreed over the meaning of coercion, and some of us will be quicker than others to feel that the government's speech coerces a target's relinquishment of her constitutional rights. Recall debates among adherents of the noncoercion principle in

[34] J.D.B. v. North Carolina, 564 U.S. 261 (2011).
[35] JUSTIN DRIVER, THE SCHOOLHOUSE GATE: PUBLIC EDUCATION, THE SUPREME COURT, AND THE BATTLE FOR THE AMERICAN MIND 237 (2018).
[36] *See* Deborah Young, *Unnecessary Evil: Police Lying in Interrogations*, 28 CONN. L. REV. 425, 429–432 (1996).
[37] *See* Christopher Slobogin, *Lying and Confessing*, 39 TEX. TECH. L. REV. 1275, 1276 (2007). You may be wondering whether undercover law enforcement officers' lies about their identity are a type of governmental lie about the source of speech that violates the transparency principle described in Chapter 1. Keep in mind that that earlier discussion focused on first-stage government speech problems, namely, whether the government could claim the government speech defense to Free Speech Clause claims that it was regulating others' speech rather than speaking itself. In this chapter we explore instead situations where there's no question that the government is speaking, and we are instead considering the second-stage problem of whether and when the government's speech violates the Due Process Clause.
[38] Lewis v. United States, 385 U.S. 206, 211 (1966).

the Establishment Clause setting about whether and when the government's religious speech coerces its targets. There Justice Anthony Kennedy urged a functional, context-sensitive approach to this inquiry in the public schools: "Law reaches past formalism. And to say a teenage student has a real choice not to attend her high school graduation is formalistic in the extreme."[39] Similarly, in the criminal justice setting, Justices John Paul Stevens and Thurgood Marshall were among those to urge the Court to adopt a functional, rather than formalist, understanding of the government's speech and its coercive power. For instance, Justice Stevens dissented from the majority's failure to treat as coercive law enforcement officers' deliberately false assurances to an attorney that they were not questioning his client. Stevens argued that such lies are the functional equivalent of refusing to allow a suspect to consult with his attorney in violation of the right to counsel: "In my view, as a matter of law, the police deception of [the suspect's lawyer] was tantamount to deception of [the suspect] himself. It constituted a violation of [his] right to have an attorney present during the questioning that began shortly thereafter."[40] As another example, Justice Marshall dissented from the Court's tolerance of an undercover officer's lies about his identity (posing as a fellow inmate) to a suspect in custody, asserting that any questioning of a suspect while in custody is inherently coercive. "The psychological pressures inherent in confinement increase the suspect's anxiety, making him likely to seek relief by talking with others .... and the constant threat of physical danger peculiar to the prison environment may make him demonstrate his toughness to other inmates by recounting or inventing past violent acts," Marshall observed. "Thus, the pressures unique to custody allow the police to use deceptive interrogation tactics to compel a suspect to make an incriminating statement."[41]

My point for now is simply that the government's lies, threats, and other expressive choices sometimes coerce or deny its targets' constitutional rights in violation of the Due Process Clause, even as we can and will disagree about when that's the case. And while the body of relevant judicial precedent outside the criminal justice setting is slim, we can nevertheless build upon this analysis to identify other circumstances in which the government's speech interferes with its targets' constitutionally protected liberties in violation of the

[39] Lee v. Weisman, 505 U.S. 577, 595 (1992).
[40] Moran v. Burbine, 475 U.S. 412, 463 (1986) (Stevens, J., dissenting) ("In my opinion there can be no constitutional distinction—as the Court appears to draw [—] between a deceptive misstatement and the concealment by the police of the critical fact that an attorney retained by the accused or his family has offered assistance, either by telephone or in person.").
[41] Illinois v. Perkins, 496 U.S. 292, 307–308 (1990) (Marshall, J., dissenting).

Due Process Clause. As we tread on less familiar ground, our reactions to these various possibilities will likely turn, at least in part, on our theory of the Due Process Clause, on our views about how broadly to define the "liberty" and "property" protected by the Clause.

The Government's Speech That Unduly Burdens Women's Reproductive Rights

The Supreme Court has held that the liberties protected by the Due Process Clause include a woman's right to choose an abortion, as that choice implicates her rights to control her body and to decide whether and when to become a parent.[42] And the government often speaks to pregnant women about their reproductive choices, including abortion – sometimes through the government's own brochures, pamphlets, or online materials, and sometimes by requiring health care providers to deliver the government's script to the women they serve. This speech sometimes takes place in health care environments that can be coercive: as the Court has noted, women seeking abortions at health care facilities can be considered captive "by medical circumstances" – i.e., with limited possibilities for exit or rebuttal.[43] We can envision how the government's speech – say, threats of retaliation against women who choose an abortion, or falsehoods about the legal consequences of abortion – could coerce a woman's reproductive decisions.

But the government's choices, including its expressive choices, need not rise to the level of coercion to violate the Supreme Court's abortion-specific approach to substantive Due Process Clause protections.[44] In *Planned Parenthood of Southeastern Pennsylvania v. Casey*, the Court applied a new "undue burden" test to the government's regulation of abortion.[45] Under this test, the government may not pose an "undue burden" to a woman seeking an abortion; the Court explained that a "finding of an undue burden is a

---

[42] Planned Parenthood of Southeastern Pennsylvania v. Casey, 505 U.S. 833 (1992).

[43] *See* Madsen v. Women's Health Ctr., Inc., 512 U.S. 753, 768 (1994).

[44] Normally, the Court applies strict scrutiny to a governmental choice that infringes a fundamental right; this requires the government to show that its choice is narrowly tailored to serve a compelling government interest, a burden that the government rarely meets. E.g., Zablocki v. Redhail, 434 U.S. 378 (1978) (applying suspicious scrutiny to strike down a state law that infringed the fundamental right to marry by denying marriage licenses to those not in compliance with their child support obligations). Even as *Casey* claimed to reaffirm *Roe v. Wade*'s holding that a woman's right to choose an abortion is a fundamental right protected by the Due Process Clause test, it applied a new undue burden test to the government's restrictions on abortion, a test that is more forgiving of the government than strict scrutiny.

[45] *Casey*, 505 U.S. at 877–878.

shorthand for the conclusion that a state regulation has the purpose or effect of placing a substantial obstacle in the path of a woman seeking an abortion of a nonviable fetus."[46] This understanding of the Due Process Clause permits the government to try to persuade a woman not to have an abortion, but the means it chooses to further this interest "must be calculated to inform the woman's free choices, not hinder it."[47]

The Court fleshed out its "undue burden" analysis more recently in *Whole Woman's Health v. Hellerstedt*.[48] There it considered a Due Process Clause challenge to a Texas law that, among other things, required clinics providing abortions to meet the standards for surgical medical centers even if they did not perform surgeries; this and the law's other requirements threatened to shut down most of Texas's licensed abortion providers.[49] Balancing evidence of the regulation's (considerable) burden to women seeking an abortion against its (minimal, if any) benefits to women's health and safety, a divided Court concluded that the Texas law unduly, and thus unconstitutionally, burdened women's right to choose an abortion. In other words, if the government places a significant burden on a woman seeking an abortion without offering a meaningful benefit, *Whole Woman's Health* suggests that that burden is undue in violation of the Due Process Clause.

With that as background, let's turn to whether and when the government's *speech* about abortion poses an impermissible undue burden. The Court offered some guidance in *Casey* when it considered whether a state law that required doctors to deliver the government's speech intended to discourage women from obtaining an abortion violated the Due Process Clause. The Court held that Pennsylvania's requirement that doctors give "truthful, non-misleading information about the nature of the abortion procedure, the attendant health risks and those of childbirth and the probable gestational age of the fetus," information about medical assistance for childbirth, information about child support from the father, and a list of agencies that provide adoption and other services as alternatives to adoption, did not unduly burden women's reproductive choices:

> In short, requiring that the woman be informed of the availability of information relating to fetal development and the assistance available should she decide to carry the pregnancy to full term is a reasonable measure to ensure an informed choice, one which might cause the woman to choose childbirth over abortion. This requirement cannot be considered a substantial obstacle to obtaining an abortion, and, it follows, there is no undue burden.... [T]he

---

[46] *Id.* at 877.   [47] *Id.* at 877–878.   [48] 136 S. Ct. 2292 (2016).   [49] *Id.* at 2301–2302.

right protected by *Roe* is a right to decide to terminate a pregnancy free of undue interference by the State. Because the informed consent requirement facilitates the wise exercise of that right, it cannot be classified as an interference with the right *Roe* protects.[50]

In other words, the Court found that the government's accurate speech about abortion informed, rather than interfered with, women's reproductive choices.

But the Court's formulation signals that the undue burden test constrains the government's speech that places "a substantial obstacle" in the path of a woman seeking an abortion. And as legal scholar Jessie Hill points out, the government's false or misleading assertions about abortion's health consequences do not inform a woman's choice but instead manipulate, and thus unduly burden, it.[51] Think, for instance, of Arizona's 2015 law requiring abortion providers to deliver the government's claim that a nonsurgical abortion is reversible after it has begun.[52] (Arizona repealed the law the following year after the ACLU challenged it in court.[53]).

To be sure, courts to date have devoted little attention to whether and when the government's speech about abortion poses a constitutionally impermissible undue burden – and the Supreme Court's constitutional approach to abortion rights more generally is increasingly unstable in light of recent changes in the Court's composition. But under the Court's current Due Process Clause framework, we can envision how the government's speech

[50] *Casey*, 505 U.S. at 883, 887.
[51] *See* Jessie Hill, *Sex, Lies, and Ultrasound*, 89 U. COLO. L. REV. 421, 448 (2018) ("[M]isleading or deceptive information cannot meaningfully serve the purpose of informing a woman's choice. And indeed, the available empirical evidence confirms that a woman's knowledge about the actual risks of abortion is decreased rather than increased by the sorts of misleading information provided by the most recent spate of informed consent laws.").
[52] *See* Rick Rojas, *Arizona Orders Doctors to Say Abortions with Drugs May Be Reversible*, N.Y. TIMES (Mar. 31, 2015), https://www.nytimes.com/2015/04/01/us/politics/arizona-doctors-must-say-that-abortions-with-drugs-may-be-reversed.html [https://perma.cc/3EFW-R2HK]. As another example, South Dakota requires doctors to inform women seeking abortions that abortions are associated with increased risk of suicide and suicide ideation, even though these claims are medically contested. *See* S.D. Codified Laws § 34-23A-10.1(1)(e)(ii) (2018). The Eighth Circuit upheld South Dakota's requirement in a review deferential to, rather than skeptical of, the government's medical assertions. *See* Planned Parenthood Minn. v. Rounds, 686 F.3d 889, 894 (8th Cir. 2012).
[53] *See* ACLU of Arizona, https://www.acluaz.org/en/cases/planned-parenthood-arizona-v-brnovich (last visited Dec. 27, 2018) [https://perma.cc/Q787-ASMV] ("On May 17, 2016, less than one year after we filed suit, the Governor signed a new law that effectively repeals the statute being challenged in this case.").

sometimes poses an undue burden to women's constitutionally protected reproductive rights.[54]

The Government's Speech That Denies Voting Rights

As the Court has explained, "[t]he right to vote freely for the candidate of one's choice is of the essence of a democratic society, and any restrictions on that right strike at the heart of representative government."[55] The government's speech can interfere with, and thus injure, individuals' voting rights in at least two ways. First, some governmental falsehoods and other speech can interfere with individuals' ability to cast a ballot. Second, some governmental falsehoods and other speech can manipulate individuals' choices when casting their ballots. As we'll see, the first is more amenable to constitutional constraint than the second.

First, some falsehoods interfere with individuals' ability to cast a vote at all. Examples include lies about the mechanics of voting (like lies about the dates of an election, the location of polls, and the times at which the polls close) and lies about the legal consequences of voting (like false claims that individuals in certain communities could be arrested if they try to vote).[56] Private parties' lies of this sort can be regulated by statute without running afoul of the First Amendment,[57] and we can also understand the Constitution to prohibit these lies when told by the government. Consider a secretary of state's office – the office charged with administering elections within that state – that lies to certain audiences about where polls are located or when the polls will close in hopes of depressing their vote and increasing its political allies' reelection prospects. By preventing or deterring some who

---

[54] This chapter explores how the government may violate the Due Process Clause when its speech coerces, unduly burdens, or otherwise impermissibly interferes with *listeners'* ability to exercise constitutional rights. But the government sometimes violates *speakers'* Free Speech Clause rights when it forces unwilling nongovernmental speakers to display or deliver the government's message. *See* Comprehensive Health of Planned Parenthood of Kan. & Mid-Mo., Inc. v. Templeton, 954 F. Supp. 2d 1205, 1219 n.16 (D. Kan. 2013).

[55] The Supreme Court has characterized the right to vote as a fundamental right protected under the Fourteenth Amendment's Equal Protection Clause (with respect to state and local governments) and under the Fifth Amendment's Due Process Clause (with respect to the federal government). Reynolds v. Sims, 377 U.S. 533, 555 (1964).

[56] *See* Gilda R. Daniels, *Voter Deception*, 43 IND. L. REV. 343, 343–353 (2010) (detailing lies of this type, primarily by private parties).

[57] *See* James Weinstein, *Free Speech and Domain Allocation: A Suggested Framework for Analyzing the Constitutionality of Prohibition of Lies*, 71 OKLA. L. REV. 168 (2018).

intend to vote from doing so, these lies are functionally indistinguishable from the government's choice to lock the doors to the polls. In other words, these governmental lies – like the government's lies about the existence or exercise of constitutional rights more broadly – directly deprive their targets of a constitutionally protected right.

Other falsehoods can block some voters' access to the ballot through a more attenuated causal chain. Consider false assertions by the same secretary of state's office about the incidence of voter fraud, proffered to support restrictions on access to the ballot for partisan gain. Deliberate or reckless falsehoods alleging widespread voter fraud date back to America's founding and the bitter disputes between the Republican and Federalist parties.[58] More recently, President Trump claimed – without evidence – that "[i]n addition to winning the Electoral College in a landslide, I won the popular vote if you deduct the millions of people who voted illegally" and "[s]erious voter fraud in Virginia, New Hampshire and California – so why isn't the media reporting on this? Serious bias – big problem!"[59] By themselves, these falsehoods don't directly block individuals' access to the polls. But they can lead to laws that restrict individuals' right to cast a ballot – and for this reason, courts should apply the most rigorous review to ensure that those laws do not rest on falsehoods.[60]

---

[58] *See* ERIC BURNS, INFAMOUS SCRIBBLERS: THE FOUNDING FATHERS AND THE ROWDY BEGINNINGS OF AMERICAN JOURNALISM 377 (2006) (recounting that Thomas Jefferson encouraged pamphleteer and journalist James Callender's claim that John Adams had engaged in voter fraud).

[59] Donald J. Trump (@realDonaldTrump), TWITTER (Nov. 27, 2016, 12:30 PM), https://twitter.com/realdonaldtrump/status/802972944532209664 [https://perma.cc/UB5E-8PJU]; Donald J. Trump (@realDonaldTrump), TWITTER (Nov. 27, 2016, 4:31 PM), https://twitter.com/realdonaldtrump/status/803033642545115140 [https://perma.cc/45TC-BR9U]. Studies refute Trump's charge. *E.g.*, CHRISTOPHER FAMIGHETTI ET AL., BRENNAN CTR. FOR JUSTICE, NONCITIZEN VOTING: THE MISSING MILLIONS 1 (2017) (finding that election officials flagged only about thirty incidents of suspected noncitizen voting for further investigation or prosecution out of 23.5 million votes cast in the 2016 election, and that forty out of forty-two jurisdictions studied reported no known incidents of noncitizen voting).

[60] *See* Harper v. Virginia State Bd. of Elections, 383 U.S. 663, 667 (1966) (explaining that strict scrutiny applies to the government's infringement of the fundamental right to vote); North Carolina State Conference of NAACP v. McCrory, 831 F.3d 204 (4th Cir. 2016), *cert. denied*, 137 S. Ct. 1399 (2017) (enjoining state's restriction on registration and voting that disproportionately harmed African Americans after finding the restriction to be motivated by discriminatory racial intent); Fish v. Kobach, 840 F.3d 710 (10th Cir. 2016) (upholding preliminary injunction of state law that required additional documentation in order to register to vote).

Second, some governmental falsehoods don't deny individuals' access to the ballot, but can affect voters' decisions when casting their ballots. Sometimes the ballot language itself includes the government's false or misleading speech that alters voter's choices.[61] In 2008, for example, Illinois' state ballot inaccurately stated that "THE FAILURE TO VOTE THIS BALLOT IS THE EQUIVALENT OF A NEGATIVE VOTE."[62] Think too of the government's lies or deliberate misrepresentations about the identity of a candidate, her party affiliation, even whether she's the incumbent.[63] Falsehoods of this nature are particularly likely to affect voters' choices because listeners so commonly rely on these factors as heuristics, or mental shortcuts, for decision-making.

Much more commonly, government speakers lie about their own behavior or performance to enhance their reelection prospects. Consider, for instance, a department of labor's lie that deliberately misstates unemployment rates to improve the incumbent's prospects in an upcoming election – in other words, a governmental lie about a substantive matter that may or may not influence some voters' decisions given the multitude of reasons that inform voters' choices. These lies are less amenable to constitutional constraint in part because of the greater difficulties in establishing a causal connection between the lie and its targets' voting decisions. And constitutional or other legal efforts to prohibit campaign-related lies threaten substantial dangers of their own, as they may chill valuable political speech and encourage selective, and partisan, enforcement.

[61] *See* Caruso v. Yamhill County, 422 F.3d 848, 863–864 (9th Cir. 2005), *cert. denied,* 547 U.S. 1071 (2006) (raising the possibility that the government's ballot language could violate the Due Process Clause if it were "so misleading as to deceive voters about the subject of the measure at issue").

[62] Chi. Bar Ass'n v. White, 898 N.E.2d 1101, 1104 (Ill. App. Ct. 2008) (ordering the Secretary of State to issue a corrective notice). Some state statutes and state constitutions also constrain false or misleading ballot language. Remedies can include preelection corrective notices and occasionally even post-election voidance of the result. *See* Bradley v. Hall, 251 S.W.2d 470, 472 (Ark. 1952) (finding ballot language to be misleading in violation of state law when it enabled the legislature to legalize new service charges but was instead described as empowering the legislature to enact laws "to authorize, define, and limit" such charges); Ex parte Tipton, 93 S.E.2d 640, 644 (S.C. 1956) (invalidating election results where the ballot language described a proposed state constitutional amendment as providing a debt limitation when in fact it removed a debt limitation).

[63] *See* Smith v. Cherry, 489 F.2d 1098, 1102–1103 (7th Cir. 1973), *cert. denied,* 417 U.S. 910 (1974) (finding possible due process violation when state election officials issued a ballot that knowingly misidentified a sham candidate as the nominee, when the sham candidate quickly resigned upon his election, and was replaced by the officials' preferred candidate).

The Government's Disclosure of Private Information

So far we've focused primarily on the government's false and misleading speech that can endanger rights protected by the Due Process Clause. But the government's speech that reveals accurate, but constitutionally protected, information may also violate substantive due process rights. The government holds the capacity, as government, to collect all sorts of information: sometimes the government deliberately collects information, and sometimes the government stumbles across it. Either way, the government then possesses the power to disclose that information through its speech. Think, for instance, of the government's disclosure of a woman's reproductive history to deter women from seeking abortions. Or the government's disclosure of other often-private matters like sexual orientation or disability without adequate justification.

Again, our reaction to this possibility largely turns on our views about how broadly to define the "liberty" and "property" interests protected by the Due Process Clause. The Supreme Court has occasionally suggested, without yet holding, that the Due Process Clause protects certain private information from the government's disclosure.[64] In the meantime, some lower courts and commentators have specifically urged that the Due Process Clause protects us from the government' disclosures, and threats to disclose, certain intimate information like "sexual, medical, and mental health information."[65] Consider, for example, *Sterling* v. *Borough of Minersville*,[66] a heartbreaking case in which a small town police officer happened across two young men in a car, only to find them engaged in consensual sexual conduct. The officer warned one, 18-year-old Marcus Wayman, that he would inform the young man's grandfather that Marcus was gay unless Marcus confessed to his grandfather himself. Marcus told his friend that he would kill himself instead – and promptly did just that upon his release from the police's custody. In denying the government's claim of qualified immunity (discussed in more detail in Chapter 7), the appellate court interpreted the Due Process Clause to mean "that matters of personal intimacy are protected from threats of disclosure" by the government.

---

[64] *See* Whalen v. Roe, 429 U.S. 589, 599 (1977) (suggesting individuals' constitutionally protected interest in avoiding disclosure of personal matters).

[65] *See* Scott Skinner-Thompson, *Outing Privacy*, 110 Nw. U. L. Rev. 159, 205 (2015).

[66] 232 F.3d 190, 192 (3rd Cir. 2000).

The Government's Speech That Inflicts Reputational Harm

Consider next the question whether the Due Process Clause constrains the government's defamatory falsehoods that directly injure their targets' reputation. Although reputational harm is a harm protected from private encroachment by common law and sometimes by statutory law, whether it is a harm that the Constitution forbids the government from inflicting is a separate question. In other words, whether reputation itself is a liberty or property interest protected from the government's deprivation by the Due Process Clause remains contested.

The Supreme Court considered an aspect of this question in 1976 in *Paul v. Davis*, where it rejected a procedural due process challenge to a local police department's creation and distribution of a flyer that identified the challenger as one of several "Active Shoplifters,"[67] even though the pending shoplifting charges against him had not been proven and were later dismissed. The challenger sought a name-clearing hearing: the chance to appear before a neutral tribunal to explain why the government's damaging description of him was untrue. A divided Court held that the government's defamation does not trigger procedural due process unless it causes some additional harm, like job loss or other economic harm, on top of stigmatic injury. Dissenting Justice William Brennan objected to the majority's narrow understanding of the harm to liberty interests necessary to trigger procedural due process review; he feared that the "logical and disturbing corollary of this holding is that no due process infirmities would inhere in a statute constituting a commission to conduct *ex parte* trials of individuals, so long as the only official judgment pronounced was limited to the public condemnation and branding of a person."

The Court's decision in *Paul* continues to generate criticism. Law professor Barbara Armacost, for example, characterizes the Court's holding as ignoring the unique reputational harms of government defamation in the criminal context: "[B]ecause governmental officials have a virtual monopoly on criminal enforcement, the power to cause this kind of reputational harm is uniquely governmental.... The words and actions of police officers and prosecutors are viewed as official declarations of the law enforcement arms of government."[68] She describes the government's defamatory assertion that an individual has engaged in criminal conduct as akin to an adjudication that should thus trigger procedural due process protections.

---

[67] 424 U.S. 693, 697 (1976).
[68] Barbara E. Armacost, *Race and Reputation: The Real Legacy of* Paul v. Davis, 85 Va. L. Rev. 569, 622 (1999).

Still others argue that the government deprives its targets of liberty or property interests in violation of substantive (and not just procedural) due process protections when its defamatory falsehoods inflict reputational harm.[69] Under this approach, regardless of the availability of a name-clearing hearing or other procedural protection, the government's defamatory lies violate substantive due process protections when they lack an adequate justification. The Supreme Court in *Paul* expressly declined to foreclose this possibility,[70] and has more recently suggested that substantive due process guarantees might apply to the government's defamatory lies.[71]

FOCUSING ON GOVERNMENT EXPRESSION'S HARMFUL EFFECTS: EXPRESSIVE HARM

So far this chapter has considered whether and how the government's speech may coerce, unduly burden, or otherwise impermissibly interfere with targets' constitutionally protected liberties. But the government's speech may inflict expressive, or dignitary, harm even when it does not alter or deter its targets' choices. As we've seen, expressive harm describes the dignitary injury inflicted by the government's speech that treats its targets as outsiders to the community, that fails to treat them with some baseline level of respect and concern.

There's little judicial precedent to date on whether the Due Process Clause forbids the government's speech that causes expressive harm. But legal scholar Toni Massaro has written with grace and power about the harms of the government's shaming speech more generally – that is, the government's speech that humiliates its targets:

> The shamers belong to the proper community, and the shamed ones do not. Consequently, modern shaming is not reintegrative—an attempt to reestablish the bond between the norm-breaker and the relevant community through shaming followed by reacceptance—as it has been deployed relatively effectively and humanely, in some face-to-face, socially cohesive

---

[69] *See* Ronald J. Krotoszynski, Jr., *Fundamental Property Rights*, 85 GEO. L.J. 555, 590–607 (1997) (proposing that government defamation should be understood as infringing a fundamental property interest in reputation and thus triggering strict scrutiny as a matter of substantive due process).

[70] *Paul*, 424 U.S. at 711 n.5 ("Our discussion in Part III is limited to consideration of the procedural guarantees of the Due Process Clause and is not intended to describe those substantive limitations upon state action which may be encompassed within the concept of 'liberty' expressed in the Fourteenth Amendment.").

[71] *See* Conn. Dep't of Pub. Safety v. Doe, 538 U.S. 1, 9 (2003) (Souter, J., concurring).

cultures. Rather, it is a call for *humiliation* of offenders, first by the state and then—less predictably but likely nonetheless—by the offenders' community.[72]

In other words, through its shaming or humiliating speech, the government can declare certain individuals to be outsiders to the community. Although Massaro's work does not claim that the government's infliction of expressive harm violates the Constitution, it invites the question whether freedom from the government's humiliation is a liberty interest protected by the Due Process Clause.

Turn again to the reproductive rights setting. Earlier we examined the possibility that the government's speech about abortion sometimes impermissibly interferes with women's reproductive rights when it places a substantial obstacle in the path of a woman seeking an abortion. Law professor Jessie Hill additionally proposes that the government's false or misleading speech about abortion can inflict expressive harm in violation of the Due Process Clause apart from any effect on women's choices:

> The likely outcome of providing the sorts of misinformation about abortion described in this article is not that the woman will carry to term. Rather, the more likely outcome is that she will terminate the pregnancy anyway, while experiencing fear, guilt, and shame as a result of the false and stigmatizing information that she is given. . . . [T]he harm of government-mandated lies of all sorts in the abortion context is that they stigmatize women seeking abortions by casting abortion in an extremely negative light, causing emotional injury and distress.[73]

In other words, even if the government's false or misleading speech about abortion does not deter women from obtaining an abortion, it may still inflict expressive harm.

Yet, as we've seen in the Establishment and Equal Protection Clause settings, whether the Constitution forbids the government from inflicting expressive harm remains contested. A focus on expressive harm invites substantial indeterminacy concerns, concerns that efforts to identify the point at

---

[72] Toni M. Massaro, *The Meaning of Shame: Implications for Legal Reform*, 3 Psych., Pub. Pol'y, & L. 645, 647 (1997).

[73] Jessie Hill, supra note 51; *see also* Nelson Tebbe, *Government Nonendorsement*, 98 Minn. L. Rev. 648, 688 (2013) ("Imagine, for instance, that the government positioned an employee outside the entrance to a local abortion clinic, with instructions to shout at every woman entering the clinic, saying that abortion is immoral and that she should immediately cancel any plans to end her pregnancy through artificial means. Many people will have an intuition that an extreme form of such action would offend due process.").

which the government's speech inflicts impermissible expressive harm are hopelessly subjective and unpredictable. This, in turn, exacerbates worries that interpreting the Due Process Clause to forbid the government from inflicting these dignitary harms strains courts' institutional competence and discourages valuable government speech.

FOCUSING ON THE GOVERNMENT'S PURPOSES WHEN SPEAKING: THE GOVERNMENT'S INTENT TO INTERFERE OR TO INJURE

So far this chapter has focused on whether and when the Due Process Clause forbids the government's speech that causes certain consequences. When we focus on the effects of the government's speech on its listeners, that a governmental falsehood is intentional is often irrelevant: the interference with the listener's rights is often simply inflicted by the falsity and not by the speaker's intent to mislead. Think about the government's misrepresentations about the consequences of waiving one's rights in the criminal justice setting, or about the health risks of abortion: the listener's choices may be influenced by the false information regardless of whether the statement was knowingly or instead accidentally false. The government's *intent* to mislead or hurt its listener, on the other hand, is key to an inquiry that focuses on the government's purposes when speaking. Here we turn to the possibility that the Due Process Clause denies the government the power to speak for certain reasons.

The government's speech to accomplish purposes that we find wrongful can offend both our moral intuitions and our understanding of the government's constitutionally legitimate power: many of us feel that it's just wrong for the government to try to hurt us, and that the Constitution denies the government the power to seek to achieve objectives that are not public-regarding. Understanding the Due Process Clause to limit the government's speech inspired by certain wrongful purposes addresses both of these concerns. This, in turn, requires us to identify which purposes should be considered wrongful under the Due Process Clause, and when the government speaks for those purposes.

The Government's Speech That Seeks to Interfere with Women's Reproductive Choices

This chapter earlier discussed the Supreme Court's abortion-specific Due Process Clause doctrine, which prohibits the government's choices that have "the purpose or effect of placing a substantial obstacle in the path of a woman seeking an abortion of a nonviable fetus."[74] Courts considering Due Process Clause challenges to the government's restrictions on abortion to date have focused almost exclusively on the "effects" prong of the Court's test such that the "purpose" prong has received little, if any, attention. But under the purpose prong, the Due Process Clause also forbids the government's speech intended to interfere with, rather than inform, a woman's reproductive choices.

A "law enacted for the purpose of undermining abortion rights expresses governmental contempt for constitutional rights, and for women's liberty," law professor Thomas Colby writes. "Such a law is inherently wrongful. The government's seeking to undermine this constitutional liberty is detrimental to society at large, regardless of whether it is successful in its pursuit."[75] In other words, even if the government is unsuccessful in impeding women's access to abortion, its effort to do so may be a constitutional wrong. Colby summarizes: "The state may urge the woman to 'choose life,' but it has to respect the fact that the choice is the woman's to make, not the state's. . . . Efforts to convince the woman to make a different choice are permissible, but efforts to hinder, impede, or take away the woman's choice are not."[76] Under this view, the government may seek to convince, to persuade – but not to coerce or impede. As we've seen, this is a difficult but not unfamiliar distinction, and we'll return to it again in the next chapter.

The Government's Speech Intended to Injure

In rare circumstances, the government's intent to inflict pain or cruelty through its speech may run afoul of the Due Process Clause. As the Supreme Court has explained, "Since the time of our early explanations of due process, we have understood the core of the concept to be protection against arbitrary action . . . . [that is,] the exercise of power without any reasonable justification in the service of a legitimate government objective."[77] When determining whether executive branch action violates such substantive due process protections, the Court has considered whether "the behavior of the governmental officer is so egregious, so outrageous, that it may fairly be said to shock the

---

[74] *Casey,* 505 U.S. at 877.

[75] Thomas B. Colby, *The Other Half of the Abortion Right,* 20 U. Pa. J. Con. L. 1043, 1053 (2018).

[76] *Id.* at 1077; *see also id.* at 1078 ("And—though there is very little case law on the point—it is a commonly held intuition that the state generally may not act with the purpose of hindering, rather than just discouraging, the exercise of constitutional rights.").

[77] Cnty. of Sacramento v. Lewis, 523 U.S. 833, 845–846 (1998).

contemporary conscience."[78] The government's motive, its intent to hurt or harm its targets, is key to this inquiry: "[C]onduct intended to injure in some way unjustifiable by any government interest is the sort of official action most likely to rise to the conscience-shocking level."[79]

The Due Process Clause thus may forbid the government's lies and other expressive choices inspired by its intent to injure.[80] The Court itself has noted the possibility that the government's lies could cross this line, even while declining to find that police officers did so when they deliberately misled a suspect's attorney about their plans to question his client: "We do not question that on facts more egregious than those presented here police deception might rise to a level of a due process violation."[81] More recently, a federal court found that law enforcement officers' misrepresentations shocked the conscience when they falsely claimed that they had a warrant to extract drugs involuntarily from a suspect's vagina such that she then extracted them herself.[82] In another case, three Ninth Circuit judges urged in dissent that law enforcement officers' lies shocked the conscience in violation of the Due Process Clause when they recruited random targets to commit a fictional crime (robbing a drug house that did not exist) for which the targets were ultimately prosecuted and convicted. "Massively involved in the manufacture of the crime, the [officers'] actions constitute conduct disgraceful to the federal government," one judge wrote. "It is not a function of our government

---

[78] *Id.* at 847 n.8; *see also* Rochin v. California, 342 U.S. 165, 172 (1952) (holding that sheriff's instruction to hospital doctor to pump suspect's stomach, against suspect's will, to retrieve evidence was sufficiently outrageous to violate substantive due process protections). More recently, advocates asserted that a Trump Administration policy shocked the conscience in violation of the Due Process Clause by separating parents from their children while the parents contested their removal from the United States and without a determination that they are unfit or present a danger to their children. Editorial Board, Opinion, *A Judge Says Trump's Family Separation Policy "Shocks the Conscience." We Agree.*, WASH. POST: THE POST'S VIEW (June 27, 2018) https://www.washingtonpost.com/opinions/a-judge-says-trumps-family-separation-policy-shocks-the-conscience-we-agree/2018/06/27/438860c4-7a28-11e8-aeee-4d04c8ac6158_story.html [https://perma.cc/XJ6P-MBH3].

[79] *Lewis*, 523 U.S. at 849. In *Lewis*, the Court found that a police officer's allegedly reckless highspeed pursuit of two teens that resulted in one's death did not shock the conscience because it was spontaneous rather than deliberate and did not involve an intent to cause harm. *Id.* at 854–855. While this approach constrains the government's outrageous choices regardless of their effects, actual harm to its targets contributes to a finding of outrageousness.

[80] *See* Daniels v. Williams, 474 U.S. 327, 331 (1986) (explaining that substantive due process protects against the arbitrary exercise of government power and thus "bar[s] certain government actions regardless of the fairness of the procedures used to implement them").

[81] Moran v. Burbine, 475 U.S. 412, 432 (1986).

[82] United States v. Anderson, No. 5:13-cr-24, 2013 WL 5769976, at *12 (D. Vt. Oct. 24, 2013), *rev'd on other grounds*, 772 F.3d 969 (2d Cir. 2014).

to entice into criminal activity unsuspecting people engaged in lawful conduct; not a function to invent a fiction in order to bait a trap for the innocent; not a function to collect conspirators to carry out a script written by the government."[83]

To date, however, courts have very rarely applied the shocks-the-conscience test to constrain government action of any sort, much less its speech, perhaps for fear that the test is unacceptably subjective and thus indeterminate. But after an extensive review of the test and its history, law professors Jane Bambauer and Toni Massaro concluded that "the problems anticipated by critics are more theoretical than actual," that the test is no more subjective than tort law, and that judges have been appropriately restrained in applying it.[84] Indeed, courts not uncommonly assess the outrageousness of speech in other contexts – for example, in determining whether a defendant's lies or other expressive choices satisfy the outrageousness element of an intentional infliction of emotional distress claim. There courts rely on a number of factors, considering not only the liar's malicious intent to injure, but also (and relatedly) whether she abused a position of authority, whether her conduct was repeated rather than isolated, and whether she knew her target to be especially vulnerable.[85]

So the available precedent is slim. But an intuition that our government should not behave outrageously in speaking to, and otherwise dealing with, us supports the notion that the Constitution places some curbs on the government's cruelty. Focusing on the government's purposes when speaking as key to a Due Process Clause violation also offers a limiting principle that some may find attractive. We might well feel empathy for the challenges faced by the government decisionmakers who have to make expressive choices,

---

[83] United States v. Black, 733 F.3d 294, 318 (9th Cir. 2013) (Noonan, J., dissenting); *see also* United States v. Black, 750 F.3d 1053, 1054 (9th Cir. 2014) (en banc) (Reinhardt, J., dissenting) ("While trolling in a bar, the paid CI [confidential informant] successfully tempted a randomly-selected person to participate in the (fictional) crime by offering him the opportunity to obtain a huge financial benefit. After the CI put the participant in touch with the government agent, the agent urged the participant to bring others into the plot, played the principal role in devising and executing the imaginary crime, and then walked the defendants through a script that ensured lengthy prison sentences for committing a crime that did not exist.").

[84] Jane R. Bambauer & Toni M. Massaro, *Outrageous and Irrational*, 100 MINN. L. REV. 281, 285 (2015); *see also Rochin*, 342 U.S. at 169 ("In dealing not with the machinery of government but with human rights, the absence of formal exactitude, or want of fixity of meaning, is not an unusual or even regrettable attribute of constitutional provisions.").

[85] *See* RESTATEMENT (SECOND) OF TORTS § 46 cmt. d, cmt. e (1965) (identifying, as examples of outrageous conduct, lies told to inflict pain or to manipulate the target's choices to the liar's advantage).

sometimes in settings of great urgency and uncertainty. It's human to make mistakes, to be careless, especially in our speech. Government speakers, like the rest of us, need some breathing room, some space to err. But we need not leave government speakers room to be cruel, to be purposefully hurtful, or to seek other wrongful objectives. Government speakers, like the rest of us, can more easily control their venality than their carelessness.

5

The Government's Speech, Free Speech, and a Free Press

Suppose that you're an outspoken critic of your state's governor and her policies on immigration. Suppose too that, in retaliation for your speech, the head of the state patrol spreads lies about you to your employer – falsely claiming that his office has received evidence that you're a thief and a drug abuser – and your employer fires you as a result. Does the government's speech violate the Constitution?

When the government itself is speaking, as discussed in Chapter 1, then the Free Speech Clause rules that constrain the government *as regulator* do not apply. This chapter considers possible Free Speech and Press Clause constraints on the government as *speaker*. It investigates whether and how the government's speech can endanger the protections provided by the First Amendment's Free Speech and Free Press Clauses, which deny the government the power to "abridg[e] the freedom of speech, or of the press."

Traditional First Amendment theory and doctrine counsel that counterspeech – speech that rebuts or resists speech – is the preferred response, rather than regulation, to the speech we find objectionable. And the government itself can be a valuable source of counterspeech. At its best, the government speaks truth to power both public and private, amplifying the voices of the powerless and protecting the public interest. Think again of the Surgeon General's 1964 report on the dangers of cigarettes, a report that informed the public while challenging the tobacco industry's preferred narrative. The government's speech also delivers great value even when – and sometimes perhaps precisely because – it discomfits, even enrages, us. The Pentagon Papers illustrate both sides of the government speech coin: commissioned by Defense Secretary Robert McNamara for the government's use and written by government employees and contractors, the Papers themselves exemplify the government's speech that documented and ultimately exposed the government's lies and other destructive expressive choices.

But our history and continuing experience reveal a variety of ways in which the government's expression frustrates free speech values by distorting the truth and suppressing others' speech. At times the government deploys its speech as a weapon to quash less powerful speakers, to smother expression with which it disagrees. This, in turn, can undermine the core values that inform the First Amendment's Free Speech Clause.[1]

More specifically, the government's lies can frustrate democratic self-governance, the value most commonly identified at the heart of the Free Speech Clause.[2] Just as a government's criminal sanction or economic reprisal to punish or silence those who seek to expose its wrongdoing endanger democratic self-governance, so too do the government's lies to prevent or deter such exposure. And, like lies more generally, the government's lies can frustrate the search for truth and the dissemination of knowledge, especially with respect to scientific or national security matters where the government has unusual expertise or selective access to the information in question. Just as the government's efforts to prohibit the dissemination of certain facts contrary to its own preferred narrative undermine the enlightenment values that underlie the Free Speech Clause, so too can the government's lies that successfully distort public discussion.

The government's expressive attacks on individuals and institutions to discredit and silence their speech also undermine free speech values. These efforts are particularly effective when the government's targets are limited in their ability to fight back; this can be the case when they cannot attract the same media and public attention, or when they are politically or otherwise vulnerable. Senator Joseph McCarthy, among others, demonstrated how to capture media attention and partisan gain through outrageous attacks and unfounded charges against his targets.[3] The Senate's Permanent Subcommittee on Investigations, led by McCarthy, as well as the House Un-American Activities Committee (HUAC), engaged in expression that

---

[1] *See* Thomas L. Emerson, *First Amendment Doctrine and the Burger Court*, 68 CAL. L. REV. 422, 423 (1980) (describing the key values underlying the First Amendment's protection of speech to include furthering democratic self-governance, enabling the exercise of individual autonomy, and facilitating the discovery of truth and the dissemination of knowledge).

[2] *See* ALEXANDER MEIKLEJOHN, FREE SPEECH AND ITS RELATION TO SELF-GOVERNMENT (1948).

[3] *See* JAMES B. RESTON, DEADLINE: A MEMOIR 220 (1991) ("Even with a superb [newspaper] staff, we were, I'm sorry to say, intimidated much of the time by the popularity of McCarthy's lies and his charges that his opponents were 'soft on communism.'"); *see also id.* at 216 ("His charges may not have made sense, but they made headlines and they sold a lot of papers. McCarthy knew how to take advantage of this 'cult of objectivity.' He made the front pages by announcing his discovery one day and embellishing it a few days later, and each time he still hit the front pages.").

encouraged private parties' acts of retaliation against its targets. As one HUAC Chair explained, "the committee's goal was to expose Communists and fellow travelers 'before their neighbors and fellow workers,' with the 'confidence' that loyal Americans 'will do the rest of the job.'"[4]

The government's expressive targets have included organizations as well as individual speakers; the consequences of the government's expressive attacks include job loss, property destruction, physical violence, even loss of life. Many of these stories are well-known, others less so. For example, the day after the Attorney General announced in 1966 that he would seek to require the W.E.B. Dubois Club, a civil rights group, to register as a communist front organization, the club's San Francisco office was bombed and its Brooklyn office attacked by a mob.[5] And shortly after senators associated with McCarthy's efforts threatened to disclose that Wyoming Senator Lester Hunt's son had been arrested for soliciting a male police officer, Senator Hunt shot himself in his Capitol Hill office.[6]

These are just a few illustrations of the ways in which the government's expressive choices can undermine free speech values. All deserve our notice and often our concern: we should pay attention to the government's speech about speech and about the press. But as we've seen, that the government's speech is troubling does not always mean that it is unconstitutional, or at least does not always mean that constitutional limitations are readily enforceable. With this in mind, let's consider some possibilities for constitutional constraint of the government's expressive choices that frustrate Free Speech and Free Press Clause values, as well as the difficulties and dangers that inhere in attempting to enforce those constraints.

WHEN, IF EVER, DOES THE GOVERNMENT'S SPEECH "ABRIDGE THE FREEDOM OF SPEECH"?

As we think about the second-stage problem of whether and when the government's speech "abridge[s] the freedom of speech" in violation of the First Amendment, we turn again to our series of questions about the consequences of, as well as the motives underlying, the government's expressive

---

[4] GEOFFREY R. STONE, PERILOUS TIMES: FREE SPEECH IN WARTIME 372 (2004).

[5] *See* Ted Finman & Stewart Macauley, *Freedom to Dissent: The Vietnam Protests and the Words of Public Officials,* 1966 WIS. L. REV. 632, 633 (1966).

[6] *See* Drew Pearson, *Washington Merry-Go-Round,* PRESCOTT EVENING COURIER (June 23, 1954) (describing the incident as "one of the lowest types of political pressure this writer has seen in many years" and an example of "the new technique used by McCarthyites to pressure other senators").

choices. Note that, from a free speech perspective, whatever constitutional rules we identify must apply with equal force to the government's speech about the speech that we love as well as the speech that we hate: the Free Speech Clause constraints, if any, that apply to the government's speech attacking civil rights leaders' speech must be the same as those that apply to the government's speech attacking white supremacists' speech.

FOCUSING ON GOVERNMENT EXPRESSION'S EFFECTS: THE GOVERNMENT'S SPEECH THAT SILENCES OR PUNISHES ITS TARGETS' SPEECH

Recall that the government's religious speech that coerces its targets' participation in religious observances inflicts harmful consequences akin to those sometimes inflicted by the government's lawmaking or other regulatory action. As we've also seen, so too does the government's speech that coerces its targets' decisions about whether to exercise constitutionally protected liberties, like a criminal defendant's right to request a lawyer. The same is true of the government's speech that silences or otherwise coerces its targets' expressive choices: as legal scholar Toni Massaro explains, we should understand the government's speech to violate the Free Speech Clause when it exerts "so much expressive power that its actions are tantamount to direct speech regulation."[7]

Keep in mind that the government's speech can silence or punish its targets' speech by changing the behavior of either of two sets of audiences: the government's speech may cause third parties to retaliate against the government's targets, and the government's speech may directly silence the targeted speakers. The quicker we are to find a causal connection between the government's speech and speech-silencing effects, the more we protect its targets from harm and the more we encourage the government to think twice about its expressive choices. On the other hand, the more we may cramp and discourage the government's speech in counterproductive ways.

The Government's Threats That Silence Speech

The Free Speech Clause permits the government to resist and rebut others' speech through the force of its ideas, but not through its legal, physical, or

---

[7] Toni M. Massaro, *Tread on Me*, 17 U. PA. J. CON. L. 365, 402 (2014); *see also* Am. Commc'n Ass'n v. Douds, 339 U.S. 382, 402 (1950) ("Under some circumstances, indirect 'discouragements' undoubtedly have the same coercive effect upon the exercise of First Amendment rights as imprisonment, fines, injunctions or taxes.").

economic force. When the government uses its lawmaking or other regulatory power to punish dissent – as is the case, for example, when it jails, taxes, or fines its critics – it violates the Free Speech Clause. And under some circumstances, the government can achieve the same results through its expressive choices, as is the case of its speech that threatens, or encourages retaliation against, certain speakers.[8]

Because the government's credible threat to deploy its coercive power is functionally indistinguishable from its actual deployment of that power, the government's speech violates the Free Speech Clause when it threatens speakers with whom it disagrees. The Supreme Court recognized the constitutional injuries inflicted by the government's threats more than a half-century ago in *Bantam Books, Inc. v. Sullivan.*[9] There it considered a First Amendment challenge to a state commission's letters to the distributors of sexually explicit but nonobscene books and magazines, letters stating that the commission found some of their materials "objectionable for sale" to young people and that it planned to share its views with local police departments.[10] The letters also mentioned the Commission's "duty to recommend to the Attorney General prosecution of purveyors of obscenity."[11] The Court ordered a stop to the government's speech, concluding that it threatened protected expression in violation of the Free Speech Clause:

> The appellees are not law enforcement officers; they do not pretend that they are qualified to give or that they attempt to give distributors only fair legal advice. Their conduct as disclosed by this record shows plainly that they went far beyond advising the distributors of their legal rights and liabilities. Their operation was in fact a scheme of state censorship effectuated by extralegal sanctions; they acted as an agency not to advise but to suppress.[12]

Lower courts have similarly enjoined the government's threats that coerce its targets' speech in violation of the First (or, with respect to state and local

---

[8] The First Amendment permits the government to regulate the harm-causing speech of nongovernmental speakers under certain circumstances, like their threats. *See* Watts v. United States, 394 U.S. 705, 705–708 (1969) (defining an unprotected true threat as that which a reasonable person would consider an expression of the speaker's intent to inflict bodily harm). When the government's own speech threatens the same sorts of harm, it is more amenable to constitutional and other legal constraint, especially (but not only) because the government itself is not a First Amendment rightsholder.

[9] Bantam Books, Inc. v. Sullivan, 372 U.S. 58 (1963).   [10] *Id.* at 59–63.   [11] *Id.*

[12] *Id.* at 72; *see also id.* at 67 n. 8 (citing a number of cases in which "threats of prosecution or of license revocation, or listings or notifications of supposedly obscene or objectionable publications or motion pictures, on the part of chiefs of police or prosecutors, have been enjoined").

governments, Fourteenth) Amendment.[13] More recently, for example, a federal appellate court enjoined a sheriff's speech that sought to shut down sexually explicit advertisements through false threats of legal action:

> [E]ven in his official capacity the sheriff can express his distaste for Backpage and its look-alikes; that is, he can exercise what is called "[freedom of] government speech." A government entity, including therefore the Cook County Sheriff's Office, is entitled to say what it wants to say—but only within limits. It is not permitted to employ threats to squelch the free speech of private citizens.[14]

And as another federal appellate court emphasized:

> What matters is the distinction between attempts to convince and attempts to coerce. A public-official defendant who threatens to employ coercive state power to stifle protected speech violates a plaintiff's First Amendment rights, regardless of whether the threatened punishment comes in the form of the use (or, misuse) of the defendant's direct regulatory or decisionmaking authority over the plaintiff, or in some less-direct form.[15]

Again, we can expect disagreements over whether and when the government's speech permissibly "convinces" or instead unconstitutionally "coerces." This is inevitably a fact-sensitive inquiry, one that requires that we remain attentive to context when assessing the coercive potential of the government's speech.

When will a reasonable listener perceive the government's criticism of her speech as a threat? The more powerful the government speaker, the harder to ignore the possibility that it will unleash its coercive force. In many circumstances, a reasonable listener will more readily experience speech from a police officer as threatening than speech by the head of the public library or county hospital. Reasonable listeners are also more likely to experience the government's speech as threatening when the speaker explicitly invokes its governmental power (for example, by writing a letter on government letterhead or reminding the target of the government's authority).[16] Also relevant is

---

[13] The First Amendment applies to constrain the federal government; the Supreme Court also interprets the Fourteenth Amendment's Due Process Clause to prohibit state and local governments from infringing fundamental rights, rights that include those protected by the First Amendment. E.g., Gitlow v. New York, 268 U.S. 652 (1925).

[14] Backpage.com v. Dart, 807 F.3d 229, 234–235 (7th Cir. 2015) (citations omitted), *cert. denied*, 137 S. Ct. 46 (2016).

[15] Okwedy v. Molinari, 333 F.3d 339, 344 (2nd Cir. 2003).   [16] *See id.*

whether the speech occurs against a backdrop of governmental regulatory action: a bully's threats are more credible when he has a history of fulfilling them.

The Government's Falsehoods That Silence Speech

The last chapter explored how the government's lies (and other speech) sometimes interfere with rights protected by the Due Process Clause. Here we consider how the government's lies (and other speech) sometimes interfere with rights protected by the Free Speech Clause.

When the government's lies and misrepresentations silence its targets' speech as effectively as the government's lawmaking and other regulatory action, they too violate the Free Speech Clause. Through lies and misrepresentations about its targets, for instance, the government can provoke a nongovernmental third party to fire or otherwise punish a targeted speaker. To illustrate, a federal appellate court refused to dismiss a plaintiff's constitutional claim alleging that the government had retaliated against her speech with false and threatening speech of its own that led to her firing.[17] In that case, a county official called the plaintiff's employer after the plaintiff had expressed opposition to the county's proposed highway project at a public meeting; the county official falsely stated that the plaintiff had identified her employer in opposing the project, and asked whether the employer was truly committed to local development. The employer fired the plaintiff shortly thereafter. Focusing on the reasonably foreseeable effects of the government's speech on third parties' choices, the court concluded that the government's expression would violate the Free Speech Clause if intended, and reasonably likely, to encourage its target's employer to fire her in retaliation for her speech.[18] In a similar vein, other lower courts have found that the government's verbal "campaigns of harassment and humiliation" of its target can violate the Free Speech Clause if "reasonably likely to deter" protected speech.[19]

Relatedly, the government's lies about critics or dissenters that inflict reputational or economic injury can silence those speakers in violation of the Free Speech Clause. During the 1950s and 1960s, for example, Mississippi's State Sovereignty Commission circulated damaging falsehoods

---

[17] Paige v. Coyner, 614 F.3d 273 (6th Cir. 2010).　　[18] *Id.* at 276–283.

[19] *See* Coszalter v. City of Salem, 320 F.3d 968, 975–977 (9th Cir. 2003); Addison v. City of Baker City, 2018 WL 6016879 (9th Cir. 2018) ("[T]he district court properly found that [the police chief] had engaged in a campaign of harassment over a period of years"—a verbal campaign directed to the plaintiff's employer that ultimately led to the plaintiff's job loss).

to the employers, friends, and neighbors of citizens who spoke out against segregation. Only decades later, when the Commission's actions became public, did federal courts recognize their injuries to free speech. The Fifth Circuit found that "[c]ommission reports include numerous instances of (often unsubstantiated) allegations of homosexuality, child molestation, illegitimate births, and sexual promiscuity, as well as reports of financial improprieties, drug abuse, and extreme political and religious views."[20] Another federal court concluded:

> The Court also finds that the evidence clearly and convincingly demonstrates that a direct result of the acts of the Commission was to memorialize rumors and statements concerning the Plaintiffs, that there is a substantial likelihood that some of these rumors and statements were untrue, and that there is a substantial likelihood that harms to the reputation of such Plaintiffs would accrue if this information were published without an opportunity for rebuttal.[21]

During the same time period, the FBI spread false information about antiwar protestors and other political dissenters to their spouses, employers, and others. As legal scholar Geof Stone describes in more detail:

> In its effort to destabilize and incapacitate the left, FBI agents wrote letters to employers to cause the firing of antiwar activists; distributed fraudulent college newspapers defaming peace activists; sent anonymous letters to campaign contributors and other supporters of antiwar candidates to sabotage their campaigns; mailed anonymous letters to the spouses of antiwar activists, suggesting that their partners were having extramarital affairs; and spread false rumors that individuals were embezzling funds or secretly cooperating with the FBI.[22]

Here too the government's defamatory speech was not exposed until years later, but we can again understand the Free Speech Clause to prohibit the government's falsehoods like these when they cause a target's firing, or similar injury, in retaliation for, or to silence, her speech. The government's speech that achieves those effects violates the Free Speech Clause, even as we will sometimes disagree about *when* the government's speech, without more, achieves those effects.

---

[20] ACLU v. Mississippi, 911 F.2d 1066, 1070 (5th Cir. 1990).
[21] ACLU v. Mabus, 719 F. Supp. 1345, 1354 (S.D. Miss. 1989).
[22] GEOFFREY R. STONE, PERILOUS TIMES: FREE SPEECH IN WARTIME 490 (2004).

The Government's Disclosures and Designations That Silence Speech

The last chapter briefly considered the possibility that the government's speech that discloses certain private information can violate the Due Process Clause. But sometimes the government discloses information to the public about a speaker with which it disagrees with the effect (and, as we'll discuss later, sometimes the intent) of silencing that speaker: consider, for instance, disclosures about a targeted speaker's sexual orientation, reproductive choices, unpopular political views, and more. And sometimes the government silences or punishes speakers with which it disagrees through derogatory labels or designations of the target's expressive choices.

This was the case, for example, in the 1960s when the Attorney General designated certain nonprofit organizations as "subversive" – in other words, as Communist front organizations. After several of the groups so designated sought declaratory and injunctive relief from the government's statement, the Supreme Court reversed the lower court's dismissal of their claims in *Joint Anti-Fascist Refugee Committee v. McGrath.*"[23] There the Court recognized that the effect of "inclusion in the Attorney General's list of a designation [as 'subversive'] that is patently arbitrary or contrary to fact ... is to cripple the functioning and damage the reputation of those organizations in their respective communities and in the nation."[24] Concurring Justice Hugo Black made the point even more sharply: "In the present climate of public opinion it appears certain that the Attorney General's much publicized findings, regardless of their truth or falsity, are the practical equivalents of confiscation and death sentences for any blacklisted organization not possessing extraordinary financial, political, or religious prestige and influence."[25]

---

[23] 341 U.S. 123 (1951).

[24] *Id.* at 138–139. This section focuses on the government's own disclosures, but similar concerns about likely third-party retaliation against nongovernmental speakers explain why government orders that a nongovernmental speaker disclose certain sensitive information sometimes run afoul of the First Amendment. *See* NAACP v. Alabama, 357 U.S. 449, 462–463 (1958) ("Petitioner has made an uncontroverted showing that on past occasions revelation of its rank-and-file members has exposed these members to economic reprisal, loss of employment, threat of physical coercion, and other manifestations of public hostility. Under these circumstances, we think it apparent that compelled disclosure of petitioner's Alabama membership is likely to affect adversely the ability of petitioner and its members to pursue their collective effort to foster beliefs which they admittedly have the right to advocate, in that it may induce members to withdraw from the Association and dissuade others from joining it because of fear of exposure of their beliefs shown through their associations and of the consequences of this exposure.").

[25] *McGrath,* 341 U.S. at 142 (Black, J., concurring).

Legal scholar Seth Kreimer emphasizes the coercive power of these sorts of disclosures and designations, describing the government's speech as "informational sanctions:"

> I argue that courts should neither doubt the impact of informational sanctions, nor the constitutional relevance of those impacts. Although the precise effects of disclosure will vary with context, our liberties are at risk when our constitutional law ignores the power of information as speech. . . . [T]he striking thing about the enterprise which Senator McCarthy embodied was that it achieved, strictly through the use of information, a substantial impact on citizens' lives, the discourse of the republic, and the exercise of the First Amendment rights of speech, belief, and association.[26]

Of course, accurate disclosures often offer substantial informational value to the public. Just as we must distinguish the government's legitimate power to criticize speech with which it disagrees from its threats and lies that impermissibly coerce its targets' silence, so too must we distinguish the government's disclosures that inform the public from those that muzzle dissent.[27] This, in turn, requires us to attend to asymmetries of information and power: transparency can expose the powerful to the weak, while privacy can protect the weak from the powerful. Distinguish, for example, a target's interest in keeping certain personal matters secret because she is vulnerable to abuse by power from a target's interest in keeping that information secret to better wield her own power. Law professor Yochai Benkler has characterized the difference between the two as informed by "a theory of asymmetric power . . . . The core of the argument is that privacy is at risk when there are powerful observers and vulnerable subjects. Transparency, by contrast, involves disclosure of information about powerful parties that weaker parties can use to check that power of its abuse. When we say that an act of information disclosure 'threatens privacy' or 'promises transparency' we are making a judgment about who has power and who is susceptible to it and how that power ought to be limited."[28]

In thinking about the Free Speech Clause implications of the government's disclosures or designations, we should thus assess not only their informational value to the public (whether they involve a matter of public concern as opposed to intimate or other private matters) but also their potential to

---

[26] Seth Kreimer, *Sunlight, Secrets and Scarlet Letters: The Tension between Privacy and Disclosure in Constitutional Law*, 140 U. Pa. L. Rev. 1, 12, 28–29 (1991).

[27] *Id.* at 27–28.

[28] Yochai Benkler, *The Real Significance of Wikileaks*, The American Prospect, May 10, 2011.

suppress vulnerable targets' speech.[29] The latter requires us to consider the likelihood of third-party retaliation against the government's targets. As Kreimer notes, "Where the relations between the subject of disclosure and the recipient of the disclosed information are already charged with violent potential, disclosure is a virtual invitation [for violence]."[30] The Supreme Court recognized this in *McGrath*, with its clear-eyed view of how the government's derogatory designations of its targets' speech could spark third-party retaliation against those targets.[31]

The time and place of the government's disclosures and designations also shape their capacity for punishing their targets' expression. Recall *Anderson v. Martin* (discussed in Chapter 3), where the Court found that Louisiana's racially identifying ballot speech invited voters' discrimination and thus violated the Equal Protection Clause; in so holding, the Court underscored the government's expressive intervention "at the most crucial stage in the electoral process – the instant before the vote is cast."[32] In a similar vein, some Justices have suggested that the government's ballot speech about candidates' protected expression can punish those candidates for their political views in violation of the Constitution. In *Cook v. Gralike*, the Court upheld a challenge to a Missouri law that required the state's ballots to note congressional candidates' failure to support term limits.[33] Quoting from its decision in *Anderson*, the Court explained that Missouri's ballot designations disadvantaged the targeted candidates, thus exceeding the state's constitutional power to regulate elections :

> "[B]y directing the citizen's attention to the single consideration" of the candidates' fidelity to term limits, the labels imply that the issue "is an important—perhaps paramount—consideration in the citizen's choice, which may decisively influence the citizen to cast his ballot" against candidates branded as unfaithful.... While the precise damage the labels may exact on candidates is disputed between the parties, the labels surely place

---

[29] The Court has defined speech on a matter of public concern as speech that addresses "a subject of legitimate news interest – that is, a subject of general interest and of value and concern to the public at the time of publication." City of San Diego v. Roe, 543 U.S. 77, 83–84 (2004) (per curiam).

[30] Seth Kreimer, *Sunlight, Secrets and Scarlet Letters: The Tension between Privacy and Disclosure in Constitutional Law*, 140 U. PA. L. REV. 1, 40 (1991); *see also id.* at 60 ("The message that 'we can't get them, but you can' seems less likely to evoke measured reflection than to provoke witch hunts, vigilantes, and fervent calls for more active government participation.").

[31] *McGrath*, 341 at 138–139; *id.* at 142 (Black, J., concurring).   [32] 375 U.S. 399, 402–403 (1964).

[33] Cook v. Gralike, 531 U.S. 510 (2001).

their targets at a political disadvantage to unmarked candidates for congressional office.[34]

Concurring Justices Rehnquist and O'Connor interpreted the First Amendment, more specifically, to protect the "right of a political candidate, once lawfully on the ballot, to have his name appear unaccompanied by pejorative language required by the State," and concluded that the government's ballot speech injured its targets in violation of the Free Speech Clause:

> [O]nly those candidates who fail to conform to the State's position receive derogatory labels. The result is that the State injects itself into the election process at an absolutely critical point—the composition of the ballot, which is the last thing the voter sees before he makes his choice—and does so in a way that is not neutral as to issues or candidates. The candidates who are thus singled out have no means of replying to their designation which would be equally effective with the voter .... [T]he State itself may not skew the ballot listings in this way without violating the First Amendment.[35]

To be sure, we can expect hard causal questions and accompanying disagreements about whether and when the government's disclosures or designations impermissibly silence or punish their targets' protected expression. In *Meese* v. *Keene*, for instance, the Supreme Court grappled with several related issues: whether the government's designation of certain speech as "propaganda" conveyed a negative message, whether the designation would change reasonable listeners' expressive choices, and (if so) whether the government's speech that influences but does not necessarily coerce listeners' expressive choices violates the Free Speech Clause.[36]

Some background may be helpful. Spurred by the circulation of "anonymous anti-American vitriol" in the years leading up to World War II,[37] Congress enacted the Foreign Agents Registration Act in 1938 to require agents of foreign principals who distribute certain materials to ensure their materials' conspicuous labelling as "political propaganda."[38] Decades later, a public official who sought to exhibit Canadian films on acid rain and nuclear

---

[34] *Id.* at 525.   [35] *Id.* at 532.   [36] Meese v. Keene, 481 U.S. 465, 472 (1987).

[37] H.R. Rep. No. 1381, at 2 (identifying the statute's purpose as ensuring "that the American people may know those who are engaged in this country by foreign agencies to spread doctrine salient to our democratic form of government, or propaganda for the purpose of influencing American public opinion on a political question.... We believe that the spotlight of pitiless publicity will serve as a deterrent to the spread of pernicious propaganda. We feel that our people are entitled to know the sources of any such efforts ....").

[38] 22 U.S.C. § 611(j) (1982).

war – films that triggered the Act's labeling requirements – challenged the statute on First Amendment grounds, arguing that the labels' pejorative connotation deterred him from exhibiting the films for fear of damaging his reputation, and would deter others from watching it. A divided Court ultimately concluded that the government's label communicated no derogatory message about the films, and thus would not reasonably deter people from exhibiting or watching them.[39]

Dissenting Justice Blackmun urged, in contrast, that we ask not whether the government's speech *compels* a reasonable person to alter his expressive choices but instead whether the government's speech *influenced* a reasonable person's choices; he then concluded that the government's designation of material as "propaganda" would deter reasonable persons from displaying or watching the film:

> In deciding whether or not to show a film, individuals and institutions are bound to calculate the risk of being associated with materials officially classified as propaganda. Many, such as appellee, reasonably will decline to assume the necessary risk. That risk is particularly high for those who are accountable to the public, among them librarians and elected officials, to cite obvious examples. In addition, the official designation taints the message of a classified film by lessening its credence with viewers. For the film to carry its full force and meaning an exhibitor must attempt to dispel skepticism flowing from the notion that the film is laced with lies and distortions. These burdens are too great and too real in practical terms to be ignored simply because they are imposed by way of public reaction rather than through a direct restriction on speech. . . . For that Governmental action does more than simply provide additional information. It places the power of the Federal Government, with its authority, presumed neutrality, and assumed access to all the facts, behind an appellation designed to reduce the effectiveness of the speech in the eyes of the public.[40]

So far we've been looking at the consequences of the government's expressive choices and whether they silence, coerce, or otherwise punish its targets' speech in ways akin to the government's lawmaking or other regulatory action. But the government's speech can inflict expressive harm on its targets even when it does not alter their decisions about whether or how to speak. Might

---

[39] *Meese*, 481 U.S. at 469. Congress amended the statute in 1995 to replace the term "political propaganda" with "informational materials." Act of Dec. 19, 1995, Pub. L. No. 104-95, 109 Stat. 700 (codified at 22 U.S.C. §§ 611, 614, 616, 618, 621 (2006)).

[40] *Meese*, 481 U.S. at 492–493 (Blackmun, J., dissenting).

the government's speech that disparages or humiliates its expressive adversaries, without more, violate the Free Speech Clause? The next section considers that question.

FOCUSING ON GOVERNMENT EXPRESSION'S EFFECTS: EXPRESSIVE HARM

In earlier chapters, we examined the possibility that the government's speech that inflicts expressive harm may violate specific constitutional protections even when it does not coerce or otherwise change its targets' choices. Expressive harm describes the dignitary injury inflicted by the government's speech that treats its targets as outsiders to the community, in other words, that fails to treat them with some baseline level of respect and concern. Recall that a nonendorsement approach to the Establishment Clause interprets that Clause to bar the government from communicating the message that certain individuals are outsiders to the community because of their religion or nonreligion. An emphasis on expressive harm in the Free Speech Clause context might treat the government's humiliating disclosures about, or disparaging designations of, targets based on their protected expression as inflicting a constitutional wrong regardless of any coercive effect on their targets' expressive choices.

Legal scholar Nelson Tebbe speaks to this possibility when he suggests that we understand free speech theory to require the government's "concern for what I am calling full citizenship—for meaningful participation in political and social life;" he posits that "just as government disfavor can constitute citizens as unequal, so too government disrespect can mark speakers as disregarded or disabled."[41] He proposes that we interpret the Free Speech Clause to protect us from the government's speech that degrades us for our speech, because "people whose speech is rendered inconsequential by a state are made something less than *full* citizens."[42] Under his approach, the Free Speech Clause requires the government to refrain from disparaging speakers because of who they are, but it does not demand that the government refrain from criticizing speakers' ideas and policy positions. "There is a meaningful difference between saying, in a public school setting, that intelligent design does not count as science, despite claims to the contrary by some evangelicals," Tebbe explains, "and

---

[41] Nelson Tebbe, *Government Nonendorsement*, 98 MINN. L. REV. 648, 667–668 (2013).
[42] *Id.* at 686.

teaching children that evangelicals themselves are unworthy of respect as contributors to public discourse."[43]

If the suggestion that the government refrain from personal attacks even as a matter of policy (much less constitutional law) seems naïve today, recall that governments have made different expressive choices over time. Lincoln, for instance, often exemplified expressive deliberation, reflection, and a reluctance to attack others' motives, character, and loyalty. And although FDR "left no doubt about how he felt regarding opponents to his policies in general and the New Deal in particular, [he] did not engage in rhetoric designed to undermine the legitimacy of his opposition. He thought they were wrong, but he seldom indicated that they were unpatriotic (the wartime experience is a limited exception to this rule)."[44] As another illustration,

> Eisenhower put and kept his party in power by deliberately and consistently eschewing partisan rhetoric. Eisenhower may have deliberately underplayed partisan politics because he realized that it would not be an effective strategy for a member of a minority party ... and he realized that divisiveness was not a good marketing device. Whatever his reasoning, Eisenhower's public speech is dominated by two tactics: It is never negative, and it is never divisive or partisan.[45]

Yet again, an expressive harm approach seeks to enforce an intuition that the Constitution requires the government to speak to and about us with a certain baseline of concern and respect. And yet again, an expressive harm analysis triggers indeterminacy concerns, as we struggle to determine when the government's criticism of its targets crosses the line to impermissible humiliation. These sorts of qualms may be at their peak in the Free Speech Clause context where counterspeech is the preferred response to the speech that we dislike, where we generally presume that speech, even the coarsest of speech, is the constitutionally favored means of communicating that some ideas are less worthy than others. But because the government's speech has unusual power to disrespect, to humiliate, precisely because of its governmental source, we might expect more self-restraint from the government than we do from other speakers. Whether those expectations are constitutionally enforceable, however, is a separate, and harder, question.

[43] *Id.*   [44] Mary E. Stuckey, The President as Interpreter-in-Chief 33 (1991).
[45] *Id.* at 54.

FOCUSING ON THE GOVERNMENT'S PURPOSE WHEN SPEAKING: THE GOVERNMENT'S INTENT TO SILENCE

So far we've discussed whether and when the Free Speech Clause constrains the government's speech that inflicts certain harms. When we look at the consequences of the government's speech, we look at whether the targets of the government's speech suffered harm, whether we should hold the government responsible for causing that harm, and whether the relevant constitutional provision bars the government from causing those particular harms. We turn now from the effects of the government's speech on its listeners to the government's reasons for speaking.

A purpose-based approach to the Free Speech Clause understands it to prohibit the government's speech and other choices when motivated by its intent to silence or punish protected speech to which it objects. Again, a purpose-based inquiry brings its own challenges, as many doubt whether we can meaningfully identify the motives underlying the government's exercise of its harder powers, much less those that motivate its expressive choices. Nevertheless, the difficulties inherent in the effects-based inquiries discussed earlier in this chapter – like the challenges in identifying the requisite causal connection between the government's speech and its targets' expression, or in distinguishing constitutionally impermissible disrespect or humiliation (that is, expressive harm) from the everyday sting of criticism – might invite a turn to the purposes underlying the government's expressive choices.

We can see a purpose-based approach at work in some of the Court's decisions resolving Free Speech Clause challenges to the government's exercise of its lawmaking or other regulatory power. In *Heffernan* v. *City of Paterson*, for instance, the Court emphasized the government's improper purpose in finding that the government's exercise of its coercive power, its hard law, violated the Free Speech Clause.[46] In that case, police department leaders demoted an officer whom they mistakenly believed to be supporting a disfavored mayoral candidate. Even though the target had not actually engaged in the speech imputed to him, the Court found the government nonetheless constitutionally liable because it *intended* to punish him for his speech.

The government's censorial motive, its culpable intent, may be relevant to Free Speech Clause analysis for both moral and instrumental reasons. The more the government intends to silence speech, the more likely it will be

---

[46] 136 S. Ct. 1412 (2016).

successful in doing so. And as (now a Supreme Court Justice, then a Professor) Elena Kagan also noted, the government's censorial motive offends nonconsequential values "relating to the stance or attitude we expect the government to adopt in relation to its citizens."[47] As Kagan explained, the government's choices informed by wrongful motives "express different values and have different meanings. This contrast, I think, is what Holmes meant to highlight when he distinguished between stumbling over and kicking a dog. The former may suggest a lack of optimal care, but the latter suggests contempt or hatred."[48] If we understand the Free Speech Clause to deny the government the power to *act* for the purpose of censoring speech, Kagan noted (without elaborating), under certain circumstances we can also understand it to deny the government the power to *speak* for that purpose.[49]

Along these lines, some federal judges have interpreted the First Amendment to bar the government's deliberately false speech about its target intended to discourage its target's protected speech.[50] And another federal court relied on the Free Speech Clause to enjoin a government printer from distributing a government report intended to silence and punish others' speech, a report that referred to selected targets as "pied pipers of pernicious propaganda:"

---

[47] Elena Kagan, *Private Speech, Public Purpose: The Role of Governmental Motive in First Amendment Doctrine*, 63 U. CHI. L. REV. 413, 426 (1996); *see also id.* at 414 ("[N]otwithstanding the Court's protestations [to the contrary], First Amendment law, as developed by the Supreme Court over the past several decades, has as its primary, though unstated, object the discovery of improper government motives. The doctrine comprises a series of tools to flush out illicit motives and to invalidate actions infected with them. Or, to put the point another way, the application of First Amendment law is best understood and most readily explained as a kind of motive-hunting.").

[48] *Id.* at 510.

[49] *Id.* at 431–433 (1996); *see also* Ted Finman & Stewart Macauley, *Freedom to Dissent: The Vietnam Protests and the Words of Public Officials*, 1966 WIS. L. REV. 632, 695 (1966) ("Thus the first rule for evaluating governmental comment on the Vietnam protests is that statements issued for the purpose of provoking resort to private sanctions [such as job loss and physical violence] are improper.").

[50] *See Penthouse Int'l, Ltd. v. Meese*, 939 F.2d 1011, 1020 (D.C. Cir. 1991), *cert. denied*, 503 U.S. 950 (1992) (Randolph, J., concurring) ("I believe the First Amendment may well prohibit government officials from spreading false, derogatory information in order to interfere with a publisher's distribution of protected material. While this might require an inquiry into the official's motive, it is not unusual for a First Amendment violation to turn on whether governmental conduct was undertaken for the purpose of infringing on someone's speech."); *see also Trudeau v. FTC*, 456 F.3d 178 (D.C. Cir. 2006) (considering the possibility that false government press release issued in retaliation for First Amendment activity may violate the First Amendment, but concluding that the contested government press release was not false).

The conclusion is inescapable that the Report neither serves nor was intended to serve any purpose but the one explicitly indicated in the Report: to inhibit further speech on college campuses by those listed individuals and others whose political persuasion is not in accord with that of members of the Committee. If a report has no relationship to any existing or future legislative purpose and is issued solely for sake of exposure or intimidation, then it exceeds the legislative function of Congress; and where the publication will inhibit free speech and assembly, publication and distribution in official form at government expense may be enjoined.[51]

In sum, we can choose to understand the Free Speech Clause to take some means of governmental expression off the constitutional table: these include its threats, lies, and shaming disclosures or designations that inflict certain effects like silencing its targets' speech or humiliating them for their speech. We can also (or instead) choose to interpret the Free Speech Clause to take some governmental ends, or objectives, off the constitutional table, like the government's intent to censor speech with which it disagrees. To illuminate the three approaches' various strengths and limitations, let's again apply them to some specific problems.

COMPARING AND CONTRASTING THE THREE APPROACHES IN ACTION

Recall the hypothetical that opened this chapter: a state agency that retaliates against a governmental critic by falsely asserting, to the target's employer, that the target is a thief and drug abuser – falsehoods that result in the target's firing. This hypothetical is based on the Mississippi State Sovereignty Commission's speech, as described by a federal appellate court decades after the fact:

The Mississippi State Sovereignty Commission ("Commission") gathered personal information about Mississippi citizens from 1957 to 1977, with the purpose of thwarting desegregation and other civil rights work. The Commission's records included information, some of which was not true, about individuals' sexual preferences and activities, financial dealings, political and religious beliefs and affiliations, and drug and alcohol use. This information was disseminated by the Commission to law enforcement agencies, employers, and others prior to 1977. . . . We echo the district court in stating that the

---

[51] Hentoff v. Ichord, 318 F. Supp. 1175, 1182 (D.D.C. 1970); *see also* Note, *Blacklisting through the Official Publication of Congressional Reports*, 81 YALE L.J. 188 (1971) (explaining the subsequent history and implications of the *Hentoff* decision).

thwarting of constitutional imperatives is not a legitimate and proper concern. The Commission compiled personal information on suspected civil rights activists largely for the purpose of suppressing speech contrary in viewpoint to the beliefs of the Commission and with the primary goal of preventing any encroachment upon Mississippi's segregated educational system despite existing federal court orders declaring its demise. . . .[52]

The agency's speech as described here likely infringes the Free Speech Clause under any of the three approaches. If we focus on speech-silencing harm to the target's choices and opportunities, the government's speech violates the Free Speech Clause because it was reasonably likely to, and in fact did, cause the target's firing. If we focus on expressive harm, the agency's speech violates the Free Speech Clause if it humiliates or disparages its target based on protected expression – a likely result given the types of lies at issue. Finally, if we turn instead to the government's reasons for speaking, the government's speech violates the Free Speech Clause if intended to stifle protected speech – also the case here.

But we can imagine more difficult second-stage government speech problems under the Free Speech Clause. For a more recent illustration of these complexities, let's turn to the twenty-first-century example of President Trump and his speech about National Football League (NFL) players who chose to kneel during the pregame national anthem to protest ongoing racial injustice in America - protests that the Constitution protects from the government's punishment. At a political rally, Trump said: "Wouldn't you love to see one of those N.F.L. owners, when somebody disrespects our flag, to say, 'Get that son of a bitch off the field right now, he's fired.'"[53] In the days that followed, Trump tweeted: "If a player wants the privilege of making millions of dollars in the NFL, or other leagues, he or she should not be allowed to disrespect our Great American Flag (or Country) and should stand for the National Anthem. If not, YOU'RE FIRED. Find something else to do!"[54] His many other related tweets included: "If NFL fans refuse to go to games until players stop

---

[52]   ACLU v. Fordice, 84 F.3d 784 (5th Cir 1996), *cert. denied*, 519 U.S. 992 (1996).

[53]   Ken Belson and Julie Hirschfeld Davis, *Trump Attacks Warriors' Curry. LeBron James's Retort: "U Bum."* N.Y. TIMES (Sept. 23, 2017), https://www.nytimes.com/2017/09/23/sports/football/trump-nfl-kaepernick.html [https://perma.cc/ETD5-ZUVA].

[54]   Donald J. Trump (@realDonaldTrump), TWITTER (Sept. 23, 2017, 11:11 AM), https://twitter.com/realdonaldtrump/status/911654184918880260?lang=en;   Donald   J.   Trump (@realDonaldTrump), TWITTER (Sept. 23, 2017, 11:18 AM), https://twitter.com/realDonaldTrump/status/911655987857281024.

disrespecting our Flag & Country, you will see change take place fast. Fire or suspend!"[55] The NFL's response was mixed – at times supportive of and at times antagonistic to the players. Some of the protesting players struggled to find teams willing to offer them contracts and filed collusion grievances against the NFL, alleging that the league organized efforts to deny them employment in retaliation for their protests; these grievances were ultimately resolved in confidential settlements with the NFL.[56]

Did President Trump's speech punish the protesting players' speech in violation of the Free Speech Clause? This problem requires us to determine when the government's speech itself simply criticizes, or instead threatens, others' protected speech. From a free speech perspective, remember that the constitutional constraints, if any, on the president's expression here should be the same if he had instead targeted those displaying a "Heil Hitler" salute to support white supremacy.

If we focus on speech-silencing harm to the players' choices and opportunities, Trump's speech could violate the Free Speech Clause if its targets reasonably understood it as threatening to deploy the government's coercive power against them, or as significantly encouraging others to retaliate against them for their speech.[57] Was Trump just criticizing the protestors? Or was he threatening their jobs? Factors to consider include the governmental speaker's authority over its listeners, whether the government expressly invokes that power, and the point in listeners' decision-making at which the government interjects its speech. Here we can identify factors that cut in both directions. The president is among the most powerful of government speakers. It's one thing for a president to criticize a speaker's ideas, and quite another for a president to urge the speaker's firing. And the speech and tweets were made by a president whose administration showed its willingness to take punitive action against its critics, for example, by revoking security clearances and press passes.[58] On the other hand, that the NFL is a private employer subject to market pressures complicates the causal connection between Trump's speech

---

[55] Donald J. Trump (@realDonaldTrump), TWITTER (Sept. 24, 2017, 3:44 AM), https://twitter .com/realDonaldTrump/status/911904261553950720.

[56] *See* Mark Maske, *Colin Kaepernick, Eric Reid Settle Collusion Grievances against NFL and Teams*, WASH. POST (Feb. 15, 2019) http://www.washingtonpost.com/sports/2019/ 02/15/colin-kaepernick-eric-reid-settle-collusion-grievances-against-nfl-teams/ [https://perma.cc/ 7N2S-MZZZ].

[57] *See* Blum v. Yaretsky, 457 U.S. 991, 1004 (1982).

[58] *See* Julie Hirschfield Davis & Michael Shear, *Trump Revokes ex-C.I.A. Director John Brennan's Security Clearance*, N.Y. TIMES (Aug. 15, 2018); Peter Baker, *Trump Bars CNN's Jim Acosta From White House*, N.Y. TIMES (Nov. 7, 2018).

and any adverse actions it takes against the players: if the league refuses to employ protesting players, does it do so because of Trump's speech, or instead for other reasons, like fans' objections?

If we focus on expressive harm, Trump's speech could violate the Free Speech Clause if it communicates that the protesting players "are unworthy of respect as contributors to public discourse."[59] Does calling Colin Kaepernick, the quarterback who initiated the protests, a "son of a bitch" deliver that message? Or repeatedly urging that protesting players be fired for their speech?

Finally, if we turn to the government's purposes for speaking, Trump's speech could violate the Free Speech Clause if he intended to silence protected speech. And maybe he did. On the other hand, Trump might argue that he sought only to criticize and not to silence; he might argue that he sought to rally support among his partisan supporters rather than to change his targets' expressive choices; he might even argue that he *wanted* the protests to continue because they inspired political action from his own base.

I don't claim that the framework I've suggested here – in which we interrogate the effects of, and the motivations underlying, the government's speech about speech – will make hard second-stage government speech problems easy. And I expect that good, kind, and reasonable people will disagree about how to answer those questions as applied to specific problems. But the exercise of asking and trying to answer these questions itself helps illuminate what makes hard problems hard and easy problems easy – and that's an important step toward principled problem-solving.

WHEN, IF EVER, DOES THE GOVERNMENT'S SPEECH "ABRIDGE THE FREEDOM OF THE PRESS"?

The targets of the government's expressive attacks include not only the individuals and organizations discussed earlier in the chapter, but also the press. Of course, the government and the press have had a contentious relationship from the founding – perhaps inevitably so, given the press's role as government watchdog. For example, animosity toward the press fueled the enactment of the Alien and Sedition Acts in the 1790s, when "[o]ver the course of the debate, Federalists more clearly defined the threat they believed newspapers posed. It was the mediating influence that newspapers had between the people and their representatives in government."[60] Franklin

---

[59] *See* Nelson Tebbe, *Government Nonendorsement*, 98 MINN. L. REV. 648, 686 (2013).
[60] TERRI DIANE HALPERIN, THE ALIEN AND SEDITION ACTS OF 1798: TESTING THE CONSTITUTION 66 (2016).

Roosevelt, as president, "publicly characterized the press as unswervingly opposed to him, and rarely mentioned the press except to criticize it."[61] More recently, during the Watergate crisis, "[President Nixon] accused the now iconic Woodward and Bernstein of 'shabby journalism,' 'character assassinations,' and 'a vicious abuse of the journalistic process.' He charged their employer, the [Washington] Post, with a 'political effort' to 'discredit this administration and individuals within it.'"[62] Journalist David Wise summarized the Nixon administration's expressive approach to the press:

> To the extent that the public could be persuaded, through such attacks, to doubt the credibility, accuracy, and impartiality of the American press, attention would, of course, be diverted from the question of the administration's own credibility. If the viewer can be goaded to kick the tube when Walter Cronkite appears, he may be less likely to vent his anger at Richard Nixon. This, at any rate, was the administration's theory, and it had a remarkable degree of short-range success. Doubt was cast on the credibility of the press, and latent hostility toward the television networks and the news media in general was crystallized and exploited.[63]

The Trump administration has intensified these attacks, with expressive choices that repeatedly seek to undermine the credibility of the press in an apparent effort to sap it of its power to hold him accountable for his own performance. Trump branded the press not only "the enemy of the American people" but also as incorrigibly dishonest; he stated that "[t]he press has become so dishonest that if we don't talk about [sic], we are doing a tremendous disservice to the American people. . . . We have to talk to find out what's going on, because the press honestly is out of control. The level of dishonesty is out of control."[64] He accused the press of being "among the most dishonest human beings on Earth."[65] He has repeatedly described negative press coverage of his administration as inevitably false: "Any negative polls are fake news,

[61] MARY E. STUCKEY, THE PRESIDENT AS INTERPRETER-IN-CHIEF 32 (1991).

[62] ALLAN J. LICHTMAN, THE CASE FOR IMPEACHMENT 27 (2017).

[63] DAVID WISE, THE POLITICS OF LYING: GOVERNMENT DECEPTION, SECRECY, AND POWER 17 (1973).

[64] Jenna Johnson & Matea Gold, *Trump Calls the Media "the Enemy of the American People,"* WASH. POST (Feb. 17, 2017) [https://perma.cc/7JVY-PXH6]; *see also* RonNell Andersen Jones & Lisa Grow Sun, *Enemy Construction and the Press*, 49 ARIZ. ST. L.J. 1301 (2018).

[65] Julie Hirschfeld Davis & Matthew Rosenberg, *With False Claims, Trump Attacks Media on Turnout and Intelligence Rift*, N.Y. TIMES (Jan. 21, 2017) [https://perma.cc/FG9U-7NRU].

just like the CNN, ABC, NBC polls in the election. Sorry, people want border security and extreme vetting."[66]

In contrast to the self-governance, autonomy, and enlightenment interests underlying the Free Speech Clause, courts and commentators commonly identify the values animating the First Amendment's Press Clause as exposing (and thus checking) government misconduct and informing public opinion about a range of matters. The Press Clause protects these watchdog and educator functions from governmental interference for instrumental reasons; in other words, not for the press's own sake, but instead because they ultimately serve the public's interest.[67] Thinking about whether and when the government's speech violates the Press Clause requires us to grapple with two foundational questions about the meaning of the Press Clause: whether the Clause does (or should do) any work other than that already accomplished by the Free Speech Clause and, if so, what specifically that distinct work should include.

A number of commentators have proposed that we interpret the Press Clause to provide the press with a special right to access information under the government's control and to engage in related newsgathering activities.[68] The Supreme Court, however, has yet to interpret the Press Clause to provide the press with rights distinct from those available to all speakers under the Free Speech Clause; its reluctance to date has rested in large part on the perceived difficulties in identifying the "press" that would be entitled to those distinct rights.[69] But some have proposed solutions to this line-drawing problem. Legal scholar Sonja West, for example, urges a functional understanding of the press

---

[66] Glenn Kessler & Michelle Ye Hee Lee, *Fact-Checking President Trump's News Conference*, WASH. POST (Feb. 16, 2017), https://www.washingtonpost.com/news/fact-checker/wp/2017/02/16/fact-checking-president-trumps-news-conference/ [https://perma.cc/T8WQ-H9C6]; *see also* President Donald Trump, Rally in Harrisburg, Pennsylvania (Apr. 29, 2017) (transcript available at http://www.shallownation.com/2017/04/23/video-president-donald-trump-rally-in-harrisburg-pennsylvania-saturday-april-29-2017) [https://perma.cc/EK3L-N2QH] ("Media outlets like CNN and MSNBC are fake news. Fake news… .They're incompetent, dishonest people who, after an election had to apologize because they covered it, us, me, but all of us—they covered it so badly that they felt they were forced to apologize because their predictions were so bad.").

[67] *See* Vincent Blasi, *The Checking Value in First Amendment Theory*, 2 AM. B. FOUND. RES. J. 521, 552 (1977).

[68] STEVEN SHIFFRIN, WHAT IS WRONG WITH THE FIRST AMENDMENT 126 (2017).

[69] *E.g.*, Pell v. Procunier, 417 U.S. 817, 834 (1974) (declining to find an affirmative governmental duty "to make available to journalists sources of information not available to members of the public generally"); Branzburg v. Hayes, 408 U.S. 665, 682–684 (1972) ("The First Amendment does not guarantee the press a constitutional right of special access to information not available to the public generally."); Citizens United v. Fed. Elec. Comm'n, 558 U.S. 310, 352 (2010) ("With the advent of the Internet and the decline of print and broadcast media, moreover, the

that attends to its actual ability and commitment to gather news and disseminate it to the public in ways that serve as "a check on the government and the powerful people;" as she points out, although today almost any of us can be publishers, relatively few of us have the training, capacity, or dedication to be newsgatherers.[70] Some entities already engage in this sort of functional line-drawing exercise to determine who is and is not the press: many states recognize a reporter's privilege that requires them to identify those entitled to protect the confidentiality of their sources from the government's compelled disclosure, and other governmental institutions (like the Supreme Court itself) must similarly decide to whom to issue a limited number of press passes.

If we assume, for purposes of this discussion, that "the press" can be meaningfully identified in ways that permit us to understand the Press Clause to protect rights distinct from those protected by the Free Speech Clause, how might the Press Clause apply to the government's speech?

Just as the government's threats against individual and organizational speakers may coerce or silence their speech in violation of the Free Speech Clause, so too can the government's threats of criminal or economic punishment impermissibly coerce the press in violation of the Press Clause. Nixon, for example, threatened the networks with antitrust lawsuits unless they gave conservatives more air time.[71]

Under some circumstances, we can also understand the Press Clause to prohibit the government's lies that interfere with the press's checking functions. Imagine, for instance, the government's lies to the press about the time and place of key government meetings: these lies deny access to those meetings as effectively as the government's locking of the pressroom's doors.

Other press-related lies and misrepresentations by the government can undercut the press's truth-seeking functions in less direct ways. Sometimes the government misappropriates the identity of the press – in other words, it pretends to be the press in a way that undermines the press's institutional credibility and effectiveness in checking the government and informing public opinion. Consider the following example: in 2010 the FBI impersonated the Associated Press (AP) while investigating bomb threats at a high

---

line between the media and others who wish to comment on political and social issues becomes far more blurred.").

[70] Sonja West, *Press Exceptionalism*, 127 HARV. L. REV. 2434, 2443–2444 (2014).

[71] *See* HELEN THOMAS, WATCHDOGS OF DEMOCRACY? THE WANING WASHINGTON PRESS CORPS AND HOW IT HAS FAILED THE PUBLIC 75 (2006) ("[A] White House aide, acting under instructions from [President Nixon], alerted the television networks that they faced the possibility of antitrust lawsuits if they did not let more conservatives on the networks.").

school in Washington state.[72] FBI agents created fake news stories about the bomb threats and sent them to a suspect under an AP byline, posing as an AP reporter with a request that the suspect review the drafts for accuracy – their hope was to try to get the suspect to make damaging admissions.[73] When the impersonation was revealed, the AP protested that this practice undermined the "most fundamental component of a free press – its independence."[74] As the AP noted, "the individual could easily have reposted this story to social networks, distributing to thousands of people, under AP's name, what was essentially a piece of government disinformation."[75] The AP also worried that this practice could harm AP employees who work in war zones because it makes "suspect [the AP's] claim to operate separately and freely from the U.S. government."[76] The Department of Justice responded by announcing plans to review its policies governing whether and when federal law enforcement agents might claim to be the press.[77]

Sometimes the government produces or commissions material for publication by the press as news or journalists' opinion without identifying itself as the author. In so doing, the government seeks to manipulate the public's attitudes toward its views by deliberately concealing its identity as a message's source, instead pretending that its views are really those of other speakers perceived as less self-interested. Examples include the Reagan administration's payments "to journalists and academics to prepare op-ed columns critical of the Nicaraguan government's arms buildup" that did not disclose their governmental source; the Clinton administration's deals with television networks to run government-approved antidrug messages without attribution to the

---

[72] For detailed discussion of this incident, see Andy T. Wang, *Stealing Press Credentials: Law Enforcement Identity Misappropriation of the Press in the Cyber Area*, 6 U. MIAMI NAT'L SEC. & ARMED CONFL. L. REV. 25, 35 (2015–2016).

[73] Complaint at 3, RCFP, et al v. FBI et al, No. 1:15-cv-01392 (Aug. 27, 2015); Martin Kaste, *FBI Spoofs News Story to Send Spyware to Suspect*, NPR: THE TWO-WAY (Oct. 28, 2014), http://www.npr.org/sections/thetwo-way/2014/10/28/359655386/fbi-uses-newspapers-name-to-send-spyware.

[74] Letter from Karen Kaiser, Gen. Counsel, Associated Press, to Att'y Gen., U.S. Dep't of Justice Eric Holder (Oct. 30, 2014), https://corpcommap.files.wordpress.com/2014/10/letter_103014.pdf

[75] *Id.*

[76] Letter from Gary Pruitt, President and CEO, Associated Press, to Eric H. Holder, Att'y Gen. of the United States, U.S. Dep't of Jusice and James B. Comey, Dir. Fed. Bureau of Investigations (Nov. 10, 2014), https://corpcommap.files.wordpress.com/2014/11/holdercomeyletter.pdf.

[77] James B. Comey, Letter to the Editor, *To Catch a Crook: The F.B.I.'s Use of Deception*, N.Y. TIMES (Nov. 6, 2014), http://www.nytimes.com/2014/11/07/opinion/to-catch-a-crook-the-fbis-use-of-deception.html?_r=0; *see also* OFFICE OF THE INSPECTOR GEN., U.S. DEP'T OF JUSTICE, A REVIEW OF THE FBI'S IMPERSONATION OF A JOURNALIST IN A CRIMINAL INVESTIGATION, https://oig.justice.gov/reports/2016/01607.pdf (last revised Sept. 2016).

government, and the Bush administration's contracts with newspaper columnists to produce op-eds supporting its "No Child Left Behind" policy that failed to reveal the administration's sponsorship.[78] These sorts of misrepresentations may well increase with the development of new technologies that further obscure expression's source: think of "deep fake" technologies in which machine-learning algorithms enable the manipulation of audio or video speech to look like it comes from someone other than the actual speaker.[79]

When the government conceals its authorship of these columns, videos, news releases, and other materials published by the press, it threatens harm to the public as well as to the press as an institution. These misrepresentations mislead the public about the government's actual values and potentially distort public discourse in that the government's messages may carry greater persuasive force than they would otherwise enjoy if the public realized that those messages were the government's. These misrepresentations also undermine the integrity and independence of the press, and thus its effectiveness in performing its checking function, by compromising the media's editorial independence and impairing its ability to hold the government accountable for wrongdoing.

We might understand the Press Clause to bar these sorts of governmental lies that undermine the press's watchdog and educator functions. For example, governmental lies of misappropriation – that is, its lies about being the press – can blur the line between the government and the press in the public's mind in ways that undermine public trust in the independence of the press and thus damage the effectiveness of its news-gathering functions. The government's lies of misattribution – i.e., its lies about not being the press – can similarly interfere with Press Clause functions by misleading the public about the source of press publications in ways that not only threaten to skew the public's decision-making, but also breach the public's trust in the press. In short, if we understand the Press Clause to protect collective public values distinct from those protected by the Free Speech Clause (and there are good reasons why we should), then under some circumstances the government's press-related lies and misrepresentations frustrate those values.

But a more muscular view of the Press Clause rests little on the Court's current doctrine, relying instead on purpose-based, pragmatic, and historical

---

[78] *See* Jodie Morse, *Managing the News: The History and Constitutionality of the Government Spin Machine*, 81 N.Y.U. L. REV. 843, 854 (2006).

[79] *See* Bobby Chesney & Danielle Keats Citron, *Deep Fakes: A Looming Challenge for Privacy, Democracy, and National Security*, 107 CAL. L. REV. (forthcoming 2019).

perspectives. And the operational barriers to recognizing a more robust approach to Press Clause protections to prohibit certain government lies include not only the definitional challenges described earlier but also concerns about courts' institutional competence to decide such matters, partisan (rather than substantive) attacks on the government's speech, and the chilling of important government expression. As we've seen, the government's lies and other expressive choices that inflict more diffuse harms are less amenable to constraint through constitutional litigation than those that pose "concrete and particularized" harms. Together, these concerns invite a turn to the sorts of statutory and other nonconstitutional constraints described in Chapter 7, like statutes that bar the government's lies of misappropriation and misattribution with respect to the press. In any event, identifying and cataloguing the threats to Press Clause values posed by the government's press-related lies and misrepresentations can help us resist ongoing attacks on the press's constitutionally protected functions.

6

The Government's Speech and Political Contests

Suppose that a state's department of education posts materials on its website explaining its support for a pending state ballot initiative that would require the state to make public funds available for parents to pay their children's private school tuition. Suppose too that a state taxpayer who disagrees with the board's position challenges the government's speech in court, alleging that it violates the Constitution. Does the Constitution bar the government from seeking to persuade voters to adopt its preferred position on a matter subject to vote by the people themselves, or by their elected representatives?

The last chapter considered some second-stage government speech problems that require us to distinguish the government's permissible efforts to *convince* its targets from its unconstitutional efforts to *coerce* them. This chapter examines whether the Constitution bars the government's effort simply to *convince* the public on certain matters, investigating long-standing unease about the government's speech that seeks to influence the public's views about specific political contests. When does the government's expressive participation in contested public policy debates valuably aid voters' and legislators' understanding of key issues – and when does the government's speech instead impermissibly interfere with those debates? When, if ever, does the government's speech sufficiently differ from that of other participants in the political marketplace of ideas to require the government's exclusion from that market?

The government expresses its views on contested issues subject to vote by the public or their elected representatives in a variety of ways. Examples include government officials' and agencies' statements, press releases, reports, and analyses critical or supportive of pending ballot or legislative measures, as well as flyers, pamphlets, newsletter articles, online postings, and print and broadcast advertisements communicating their views. Long before the Supreme Court developed a constitutional vocabulary that included the term "government speech," the government's expression on these matters prompted a range of political and legal controversies. These controversies have largely, but not completely, disappeared in recent years for reasons discussed later in the chapter. But unearthing these debates offers another opportunity to think about whether and when the government's speech endangers constitutional protections.

Constitutional objections to the government's political advocacy often emphasize either or both of two arguments. Central to both is the notion that the government's efforts to persuade the public on certain contested political matters pose threats of totalitarianism, of the government's thought control.

The first of these argument posits that the government's voice – with its advantages of resources and power – will inevitably drown out dissent, thus distorting public discourse and altering political outcomes in ways that are fundamentally unfair to those who disagree. Rooted in worries about the consequences of the government's speech, the concern that the government's speech may overwhelm others' voices describes a harmful effect distinct from the threats to individual liberty posed by the government's speech that coerces its targets' choices. (In this chapter we thus put aside the possibility that the government's voice sometimes *coerces* its targets' choices – a harmful effect explored at length in earlier chapters but one rarely alleged in the debates detailed here.)

Rooted in concerns about the purposes for the government's speech, the second argument contends that the government's role as sovereign requires it to refrain from seeking to advance its preferences in certain political contests. Just as some assert that the Establishment Clause requires the government to remain neutral about religious matters, so too do some feel that the Constitution requires the government to remain neutral on certain contested policy matters.[1] Under this view, the government's abandonment of neutrality in these debates is an insult, an affront, to those on the other side regardless of whether the government's persuasive efforts are successful.

---

[1] *See* Robert D. Kamenshine, *The First Amendment's Implied Political Establishment Clause,* 67 Cal. L. Rev. 1104, 1106–1137 (1979)(proposing that courts should read the First Amendment to require "an implied prohibition against political establishment" and arguing that "participation by the government in the dissemination of political ideas poses a threat to open public debate that is distinct from government impairment of individual expression"); Edward H. Ziegler, Jr., *Government Speech and the Constitution: The Limits of Official Partisanship,* 21 B.C. L. Rev. 578, 579 (1979–1980)(objecting to the government's "official partisanship" that includes government speech on pending referenda, constitutional amendments, and legislative proposals).

When we quarrel about the government's speech, we're often quarrelling about what sorts of objectives government may legitimately seek to accomplish. "What a government can properly say depends on what the proper and essential role or function of the government is," law professor Steven D. Smith notes. "And issues of government speech are difficult – intractable, maybe – because there is no agreement about what government is or isn't supposed to be for. In this respect, controversies about government speech are merely symptoms of a deeper disagreement about the proper domain and role of government."[2]

The government speaks for myriad purposes, some more contested than others. "[G]overnment is more than army, police court, and law-maker," Joseph Tussman reminds us. "It is the friendly mailman, the fireman, the social worker. It heals in its hospitals, and above all, I think, it is the public-school teacher. It is foolish to insist that government is really only a coercer and that everything else it seems to do is only a fraudulent attempt to disguise its essential nature."[3] Perhaps least controversially, the government speaks to administer or implement existing policy – as it does, for instance, when it communicates the April 15 deadline for tax filing, or explains how to apply for Social Security benefits. The more the government does, the more it must communicate. For this reason, as political scientist James McCamy explained, the New Deal's expansion of the administrative state "brought an attendant need for more explanation of the [government's new] program and more attention to the possible public reaction to administrative practices. Likewise, as more of the public became involved in any way with the new program, more demands for information were created."[4]

The government speaks not just to administer existing policy, but also to justify its policy choices both large and small. Along these lines, Lincoln continually sought, through his speech, to explain and thus legitimate the federal government's Civil War aims. Recall, for instance, his response to critics of the Emancipation Proclamation in which he described the wartime rationale for his decision:

> You say you will not fight to free negroes. Some of them seem willing to fight for you; but, no matter. Fight you, then, exclusively to save the Union. I issued the proclamation on purpose to aid you in saving the Union.

[2] Steven D. Smith, *Why Is Government Speech Problematic? the Unnecessary Problem, the Unnoticed Problem, and the Big Problem*, 87 DENV. U. L. REV. 945, 968 (2010).

[3] JOSEPH TUSSMAN, GOVERNMENT AND THE MIND 138 (1977).

[4] JAMES C. MCCAMY, GOVERNMENT PUBLICITY: ITS PRACTICE IN FEDERAL ADMINISTRATION 227 (1939).

Whenever you shall have conquered all resistance to the Union, if I shall urge you to continue fighting, it will be an apt time, then, for you to declare you will not fight to free negroes. I thought that in your struggle for the Union, to whatever extent the negroes should cease helping the enemy, to that extent it weakened the enemy in his resistance to you. Do you think differently? I thought that whatever negroes can be got to do as soldiers, leaves just so much less for white soldiers to do, in saving the Union. Does it appear otherwise to you? But negroes, like other people, act upon motives. Why should they do any thing for us, if we will do nothing for them? If they stake their lives for us, they must be prompted by the strongest motive—even the promise of freedom. And the promise being made, must be kept.[5]

Not surprisingly, governments speak not only to administer and justify existing law and policy, but also to change it. Although many see the government's speech for these purposes as inevitable and often valuable, others – at least for a time – found the government's expressive move from administration and explanation to advocacy a step too far, one that threatens to manipulate the public's preferences rather than implement them. "Government has an affirmative obligation to promote individual choice and autonomy by expanding the individual's knowledge, and yet, in a negative sense, it should be constrained from programming the citizen to make preconceived choices," legal scholar Mark Yudof observed. "In a democratic polity, it is one thing to employ mass communications to implement decisions that in some loose sense represent the majority will. It is quite another thing to attempt to fashion a majority though uncontrolled indoctrination activities. The line is a blurred one."[6]

In the rest of this chapter, I squint at that blurry line. I start by explaining the constitutional objections to the government's speech that endorses or opposes specific candidates or parties. I then consider whether those objections still hold when applied to the government's advocacy in ballot and legislative campaigns. The answer is likely no, under the Court's contemporary government speech doctrine (and I agree that the answer should be no), but I close the chapter by identifying certain conditions that exacerbate or diminish the constitutional dangers posed by that speech.

5   Letter from Abraham Lincoln to James C. Conkling (Aug. 26, 1863), *in* 6 COLLECTED WORKS OF ABRAHAM LINCOLN 406, 409 (1953) (footnotes omitted), http://quod.lib.umich.edu/cgi/t/text/text-idx?c=lincoln;cc=lincoln;type=simple;rgn=div1;q1=August%2026%2C%201863; view=text;subview=detail;sort=occur;idno=lincoln6;node=lincoln6%3A849 [https://perma.cc/6978-8H4S].

6   MARK G. YUDOF, WHEN GOVERNMENT SPEAKS: POLITICS, LAW, AND GOVERNMENT EXPRESSION IN AMERICA 15 (1983).

THE GOVERNMENT'S SPEECH THAT TAKES SIDES
IN CANDIDATE CAMPAIGNS

A wide range of federal, state, and local statutes forbid government officials from using the public's resources to endorse or oppose specific candidates or parties.[7] These laws require, among other things, that elected officials who campaign for their own (or others') reelection must do so on their own time and with nongovernmental funds.

Of course, the government's speech is often – perhaps unavoidably – motivated both by public-minded and self-interested purposes. As one of many examples both large and small, consider a controversy over federal highway signs that noted that a federal stimulus package had funded certain construction projects. Critics charged that the signs amounted to "political boosterism," while the federal government as speaker emphasized the signs' informational function so "that taxpayers should know how stimulus dollars are being spent."[8] As law professor Zechariah Chafee explained more generally:

> Some of these quandaries seem to me unavoidable if we are to have any sort of adequate information service. Effective presentations of any recent achievement of the government, no matter how completely it is accepted by everybody, cannot help benefiting the party and the officials who made that achievement possible. . . . In spite of the risks that men who know exactly what they want and are acquainted with the latest techniques for manipulating public opinion will dispose of large sums for their personal or departmental advantage, we may be wise to run those risks for the sake of the values of public information ... in enabling citizens to govern themselves intelligently.[9]

To deal with these quandaries, the statutes that bar the government's campaign speech generally try to draw a bright line, targeting only the government's speech that expressly supports or opposes identified candidates or parties. To be sure, government officials speak about candidate campaigns all the time. But they're supposed to do so on their own time and their own dime.

---

[7] *E.g.*, 5 U.S.C. § 7323 (2018) (forbidding government workers from using their governmental authority to affect "the result of an election").

[8] *See Colorado to Keep Stimulus Highway Signs*, Boulder Daily Camera (Sept. 27, 2009).

[9] Zechariah Chafee, Jr., Government and Mass Communications 764–765 (1965).

Courts and commentators widely share the intuition that the Constitution, regardless of any statutory constraints, also forbids the government's speech supporting or opposing candidates and parties to perpetuate its political power. As law professor Thomas Emerson observed:

> The government's right of expression does not extend to any sphere that is outside the governmental function. This might not seem to be much of a limitation; the governmental function certainly covers an extensive area. Nevertheless the principle does impose some limits. Thus the government would not be empowered to engage in expression in direct support of a particular candidate for office. It is not the function of the government to get itself reelected.[10]

The California Supreme Court took a similar view:

> A fundamental precept of this nation's democratic electoral process is that the government may not "take sides" in election contests or bestow an unfair advantage on one of several competing factions. A principal danger feared by our country's founders lay in the possibility that the holders of governmental authority would use official power improperly to perpetuate themselves, or their allies, in office; the selective use of public funds in election campaigns, of course, raises the specter of just such an improper distortion of the democratic electoral process.[11]

The precise constitutional source of this bar on the government's self-entrenchment, through its speech, remains unclear.[12] Some suggest the Free Speech Clause. Under this view, the government's self-perpetuating speech impermissibly interferes with the public's free participation in democratic self-governance, the value at the core of the First Amendment. As legal scholar Steven Shiffrin contends, "[t]he integrity of the democratic process could rightly be questioned if government officially intervened in the political process to favor particular candidates. Whether or not the intervention was

---

[10] THOMAS EMERSON, THE SYSTEM OF FREE EXPRESSION 713 (1970).

[11] Stanson v. Mott, 17 Cal. 3d 206, 217 (1976).

[12] Justice Scalia, for example, shared this intuition without identifying its constitutional source. *See* National Endowment for the Arts v. Finley, 524 U.S. 569, 599 n.3 (Scalia, J., concurring) ("I suppose it would be unconstitutional for the government to give money to an organization devoted to the promotion of candidates nominated by the Republican Party—but it would be just as unconstitutional for the government itself to promote candidates nominated by the Republican Party, and I do not think that that unconstitutionality has anything to do with the First Amendment.").

powerful, it would ipso facto disturb the first amendment equality principle."[13] Other commentators point instead to equal protection principles as explaining why the Constitution requires the government's evenhandedness in its election-related speech. "[T]he equal protection clause of the fourteenth amendment is violated if the government acts to aid only the incumbent," Dean Erwin Chemerinsky posits. "Those who support challengers have their votes diluted by abuse of incumbency in exactly the same way the malapportionment or stuffing of the ballot box lessens the effectiveness of an individual's vote."[14] Whatever the constitutional locus, most agree that the Constitution forbids the government's speech that involves using the public's resources to endorse or oppose specific candidates or political parties.

What about the government's speech advocating a position not on contested candidate elections, but instead on issue campaigns and other policy contests, like ballot initiatives and referenda subject to vote by the people themselves?[15] Or legislative measures subject to vote by the people's elected representatives? The next section examines those questions.

THE GOVERNMENT'S SPEECH THAT TAKES SIDES IN OTHER POLITICAL CONTESTS

This section starts by sampling some of the political arguments offered to challenge the government's political advocacy, and later turns to related legal arguments as played out in litigation. I excavate these controversies to identify recurring points of discomfort with the government's speech on matters up for vote by the public or their elected representatives. Rather than provide a comprehensive history, I offer some illustrative examples to show why the

---

[13] *See* Steven Shiffrin, *Government Speech*, 27 UCLA L. REV. 565, 602 (1980); *see also id.* ("Citizens are entitled to a government that is neutral in the process of selecting candidates. Whether or not the concept of self-government is 'central' to the first amendment, it is undeniably a first amendment value … ."); *see also* Nelson Tebbe, *Government Nonendorsement*, 98 MINN. L. REV. 648, 706 (2013) ("When the government campaigns against a political party, or against particular candidates, it thwarts their speech, participation, and association—it renders them debilitated as citizens.").

[14] *See* Erwin Chemerinsky, *Protecting the Democratic Process: Voter Standing to Challenge Abuses of Incumbency*, 49 OHIO ST. L.J. 773, 777–778 (1988); *see also* Abner Greene, *Government of the Good*, 53 VAND. L. REV. 1, 38 (2000) ("[Efforts to entrench incumbents and thwart challengers] thus violate [] one of the two key principles of the famous footnote four in *Carolene Products*, and should be deemed invalid.").

[15] A referendum generally enables citizens to enact or reject statutes or constitutional amendments proposed by a legislature, while an initiative enables citizens to draft proposals themselves and submit them to directly to the populace for a vote. Ethan J. Lieb, *Can Direct Democracy Be Made Deliberate?*, 54 BUFF. L. REV. 903, 904 (2006).

government's political speech provokes fear and resentment in some and to illuminate the role of constitutional arguments in fueling or dispelling these fears. As a matter of democratic and constitutional theory, our view on these debates should not turn on whether we agree or disagree, as a partisan matter, with the government's speech in any particular case. But, as is so often the case, partisan and principled interests can be difficult to untangle.

A Sampling of these Debates Outside the Courts

Recall how Teddy Roosevelt and Woodrow Wilson transformed the norms for presidential speech, a development that delighted some and disturbed others. "The president's function has moved from being one of administration to one of legitimation as the spoken word comes to dominate written text and as electioneering and governing move ever close together," communications scholar Mary Stuckey reminds us. "The stark contrast between George Washington's strictly administrative role and Wilson's legitimating role is clear and powerful. As the legitimating function begins to dominate, the spoken word takes precedence over the written, and the distinctions between electioneering and governance become increasingly blurred."[16]

Executive branch agencies quickly internalized these new norms of governmental discourse, provoking the ire of some legislators. The many policy battles over the government's potentially self-serving expression included the 1913 congressional debate over a Department of Agriculture job advertisement seeking a "publicity expert." Unhappy with the agency's investment in self-promoting speech, Congress enacted an appropriations rider forbidding the use of any appropriated funds "for the compensation of any publicity expert unless specifically appropriated for that purpose."[17] The debate illustrates some policymakers' view that the government's neutral (and valuable) "news" or "information" both can and should be distinguished from its self-interested (and dangerous) "publicity," while others doubted the possibility, much less the wisdom, of drawing a line between the two.[18] We'll see recurring versions of this controversy in the decades that followed.

Upon America's entrance into World War I just a few years later, the federal government established the Committee on Public Information (CPI), the

---

[16] Mary E. Stuckey, The President as Interpreter-in-Chief 10, 28 (1991).

[17] Today's successor to this appropriations rider continues to bar agencies from using appropriated funds to hire publicity experts unless specifically appropriated for that purpose. *See* 5 U.S.C. § 3107 (2018).

[18] 63 Cong. Rec. 4409-11 (Sep. 6, 1913) (statements of Reps. Gillett, Fitzgerald & Lever).

agency dedicated not only to explaining the government's war efforts but also to mobilizing the public's support for those efforts. Some regarded the CPI's efforts, led by George Creel, as laudatory in both their ends and their means:

> The mass of messages the CPI delivered were not intended to seduce, deceive, or hypnotize but to educate Americans and others in the gospel of Wilsonian democracy. Brainwashing molds belief by overcoming, even nullifying consciousness. Creel's propaganda, in contrast, was aimed at heightening consciousness for the purpose of creating a set of ideologically based beliefs, individual by individual, yet with perfect uniformity... The result was a torrent of news and other information, but it was not brainwashing. It was reasoned, rational exposition and argument made overwhelmingly powerful by dint of sheer volume, repetition, and ubiquity.[19]

Others, in contrast, worried that the government's speech drowned out all others through its unprecedented volume and variety.[20] Creel himself identified "his primary mission as flooding the nation with news from a single government source;" "[n]ewspapers were not forced to print CPI material, but, in the case of almost all war stories, it was the only source available."[21]

Concerns about the quantity and diversity of the government's speech are less pressing when other sources of information remain available, and when other voices are not muted. But through the CPI, the government invested huge resources in speech to Americans about the war at a time when it not only held a near-monopoly on war-related information, but also prosecuted thousands of dissenters for their speech through the Espionage and Sedition Acts. The government's crackdown on dissent, in turn, led to lawyers' and judges' awakening understanding of the need for robust free speech protections; the Supreme Court's contemporary First Amendment doctrine is in part a response to the government's suppression of speech during World War I.

The CPI's expressive blitz also fueled the public's cynicism about the government's speech more generally. As historian Allan Winkler explains, "Creel's penchant for overstatement and acrimonious argument left some ill feelings. But the propaganda itself was viewed as too boisterous, too exuberant for a world that had hardly been made safe for democracy. Creel had oversold

---

[19] ALAN AXELROD, SELLING THE GREAT WAR: THE MAKING OF AMERICAN PROPAGANDA 82–83 (2009).

[20] The agency's many divisions illustrate its range of activities, divisions that included the "Foreign Language Newspaper Division, Picture Division, Films Division, Bureau of War Expositions, Bureau of State Fair Exhibits, Bureau of Cartoons, [and] Foreign Section." *Id.* at 83.

[21] *Id.* at 112, 114.

his product. Propaganda became a scapegoat in the postwar period of disillusion."[22]

By no means limited to war-related matters, the public's suspicions about the government's speech lingered through the New Deal. "At present the most noticeable attitude toward [government publicity] is a prevailing suspicion that the practice of publicity is an insidious effort to 'put something over' on Congress and the electorate and that the administrative branch of government has no moral right to employ experts in purposeful information," James McCamy wrote in 1939 as he documented the growth of government "publicity" – that is, the government's speech about itself and its programs. "Administrative publicity particularly is suspected as a trend toward thought-control by government: the harmless character it may present now is visualized as a possible evil under some future political party that would frown on free expression."[23]

Related tensions in World War II included those involving the government's federal Office of War Information (OWI), the agency charged by President Franklin Roosevelt with explaining to the public the "status and progress of the war effort and of the war policies, activities, and aims of the Government."[24] Allan Winkler exposes the cleavages within the government itself about whether the government can meaningfully separate its informational and persuasive functions:

> Should [OWI], for example, work on its own to interpret the fundamental issues of war and peace for the public at home? Or should it follow the administration's lead in interpreting the war, if indeed there was a lead to be followed? Should it play a manipulative role in trying to arouse a lethargic people to support a war deemed necessary by the nation's leaders? Or should it simply serve as an information channel, a glorified press bureau whose releases had as little embellishment as possible? There were no easy answers to those questions, for there were disagreements at all levels of government, both outside the organization as well as within.[25]

On one hand, OWI head Elmer Davis (a respected journalist whose reputation for independence and fairness led Roosevelt to recruit him to take

---

[22] ALLAN M. WINKLER, THE POLITICS OF PROPAGANDA: THE OFFICE OF WAR INFORMATION 1942–1945 3 (1978).
[23] JAMES C. McCAMY, GOVERNMENT PUBLICITY: ITS PRACTICE IN FEDERAL ADMINISTRATION 246, 252–253 (1939).
[24] Exec. Order No. 9182, 7 Fed. Reg. 4468 (June 13, 1942).
[25] ALLAN M. WINKLER, THE POLITICS OF PROPAGANDA: THE OFFICE OF WAR INFORMATION 1942–1945 39 (1978).

the agency's helm) identified the agency as engaging in a "strategy of truth."
"This is a people's war, and to win it the people should know as much about it
as they can," Davis averred. "This office will do its best to tell the truth and
nothing but the truth, both at home and abroad. Military information that will
aid the enemy must be withheld; but within that limitation we shall try to give
the people a clear, complete, and accurate picture."[26] But not everyone in the
government shared the ideals of Davis and the writers he employed: "[w]here
the writers sought to inform a public that they considered intelligent enough
to use good judgment if only properly informed, the marketing executives
recruited to work for the government saw the American people as hesitant
consumers who had to be persuaded by gut-level appeals."[27] Meanwhile, the
administration's critics in Congress charged OWI with inappropriately push-
ing self-serving political propaganda rather than simply providing the public
with war-related information: "Southern Democrats condemned 'Negroes and
the War,' a pamphlet written to counteract Japanese propaganda questioning
the stake of the Negro in American society. A pamphlet on taxation and a
primer on inflation ... also came under fire for praising Roosevelt and the
New Deal."[28] Again, controversy raged over whether and when the government's informational speech crosses the line to self-serving or manipulative
speech.[29]

Ultimately the OWI's writers quit in protest. "The crisis peaked over a
pamphlet dealing with the food question. Prepared in January, the pamphlet
drew on Department of Agriculture statistics and concluded with a grim
assessment of the food supply," historian Winkler recounts.[30] When highers-
up pressed for a more optimistic spin, the writers refused and resigned as a

---

[26] HERBERT BRUCKER, FREEDOM OF INFORMATION 105 (1949).
[27] ALLAN M. WINKLER, THE POLITICS OF PROPAGANDA: THE OFFICE OF WAR INFORMATION
1942–1945 62 (1978). Many sought deliberately to distance American governments' expressive
choices from those of contemporary Nazi Germany. As Winkler explains, Goebbels "directed
that all German propaganda appeal to the instincts and emotions, and not to the rational
processes, of the people he was trying to reach. He also followed his master's example by using
the credible lie, which by continuous repetition in time took on the force of fact. The truth, for
Goebbels, was not important, for propaganda, he declared, had 'nothing at all to do with truth.'
Rather, the real aim was success." *Id.* at 19.
[28] Sydney Weinberg, *What to Tell America: The Writers' Quarrel in the Office of War Information*,
55 J. AM. HIST. 73, 83 (1968).
[29] The government's fluctuating expressive choices also reveal its views of the public it seeks to
persuade: from our government's expressive choices, for example, we can learn whether it
thinks we're idealistic, dumb, fearful, selfish, ambitious, or brave.
[30] ALLAN M. WINKLER, THE POLITICS OF PROPAGANDA: THE OFFICE OF WAR INFORMATION
1942–1945 64 (1978).

group, issuing a remarkable public statement that explained their views of the government speech they had been hired to write:

> There is only one issue – the deep and fundamental one of the honest presentation of war information. We are leaving because of our conviction that it is impossible for us, under those who now control our output, to tell the full truth. No one denies that promotional techniques have a proper and powerful function in telling the story of the war. But as we see it, the activities of OWI on the home front are now dominated by high-pressure promoters who prefer slick salesmanship to honest information.[31]

Related disputes reappeared in the decade following World War II, when Congress debated the propriety of executive branch officials' and agencies' advocacy to the public in support of pending legislation.[32] The controversy began when Oscar Ewing, the head of the U.S. Federal Security Administration (precursor to today's Department of Health and Human Services) delivered a series of speeches and reports to generate public support for the Truman administration's proposed health care legislation. "I have reached the considered conclusion that more extensive and efficient Nation-wide planning is the only effective way to accomplish a significant betterment in national health," Ewing asserted. "I am compelled to urge, as strongly as I know how, that the Congress enact, as President Truman has recommended, a system of Government prepayment health insurance."[33]

In response, some members of Congress described Ewing's speech as potentially totalitarian and sought to shut down the executive branch's "propaganda," which they defined to mean its speech "intended to sway debate on those matters which have not had the support or the approval of the Congress."[34] Representative Meacham, for instance, urged that proposed

---

[31] *See* Sydney Weinberg, *What to Tell America: The Writers' Quarrel in the Office of War Information*, 55 J. AM. HIST. 73 (1968).

[32] Recall that Article II of the Constitution, which lists the president's powers and duties, commands that the president "shall from time to time give to the Congress Information of the State of the Union, and recommend to their Consideration such Measures as he shall judge necessary and expedient." U.S. CONST. art. II, § 3.

[33] *See, e.g.*, U.S. FEDERAL SECURITY ADMINISTRATOR OSCAR R. EWING, THE NATION'S HEALTH: A REPORT TO THE PRESIDENT 12–13, 18 (1948).

[34] 97 Cong. Rec. 4098 (1951) (statement of Mr. Phillips); *see also* Hearings on Legislative Activities of Executive Agencies Before the H. Select Comm. on Lobbying Activities 338–339 (disparaging Ewing's efforts in "sell[ing]" that particular piece of legislation" as "mak[ing] speeches and spread[ing] the philosophy of socialism and Government dictatorship"). Powerful private interests like the American Medical Association were unhappy as well. *See* 67 CALIFORNIA MEDICINE 269 (1947) (characterizing Congress as inquiring into "so-called health workshops arranged throughout the country during the last two years, to mobilize pressure

restrictions on the executive's speech were "necessary to strengthen the Congress in the interest of formulating national policy by the people themselves. It is a corollary to that principle that public opinion ought not to be subjected to influence and direction by the executive agencies, the administrative branch of the Government, in the manner that it is today. In a democracy, where public opinion rules in the long run, the media of communication: the press, the radio, and the printed word, are very potent weapons in the control of the affairs of this country."[35]

On the other hand, those opposing the restrictions objected that they would interfere with the government's responsibility to inform the public about its programs. Representative Yates, for example, wondered whether "the effect of the gentleman's amendment in using the word 'propaganda' would jeopardize publication by the Children's Bureau of pamphlets pertaining to the training of children?"[36]

The administration's critics prevailed, and in 1951 enacted an appropriations rider that barred federal agencies from unauthorized expenditures to engage in "publicity or propaganda."[37] That rider has remained in place for the many decades since.[38] But the ban has more bark than bite, as executive branch agencies and officials today, of course, continue to speak to the public extensively about a wide variety of matters, legislative and otherwise. Congress has never defined what it means by prohibited "publicity or propaganda," and the office charged with monitoring the ban's enforcement – the Government Accountability Office (GAO) – has interpreted the ban narrowly, identifying violations very rarely. The GAO has explained its reluctance to interfere with executive branch speech by underscoring the value of the government's persuasive speech:

groups in behalf of a national program for what certain witnesses and authors of propaganda refer to as socialized medicine"); 85 AM. J. PUB. HEALTH 109, 112–113 (1991) (describing the American Medical Association's hostility toward Ewing and his efforts).

[35] 97 Cong. Rec. 4098 (1951) (statement of Mr. Meacham).

[36] *Id.* at 4098 (statement of Mr. Yates); *see also id.* at 4099 (statement of Mr. Fogarty) ("We do not even know what the gentleman calls propaganda. We do not know what he calls the right type of publicity or the wrong type of publicity. That is the fault I find with this amendment."); *id.* at 4100 (Mr. Fogarty) ("Here you are limiting the amount of publicity and propaganda which may be issued by any agency of government in this bill and yet you do not define in the amendment what propaganda is or what publicity is.").

[37] *See* Jodie Morse, *Managing the News: The History and Constitutionality of the Government Spin Machine,* 81 N.Y.U. L. REV. 843, 852 (2006) ("Referred to as the Appropriations 'Propaganda Rider,' a nearly verbatim provision has appeared in every appropriations omnibus bill since 1951.").

[38] *E.g.,* Consolidated Appropriations Act, Pub. L. No. 115-141 (Mar. 23, 2018).

Our decisions reflect societal values in favor of a robust exchange of information between the government and the public it serves. This includes the right to disseminate information in defense of an administration's point of view on policy matters. Accordingly, as part of our efforts to strike the right balance, we have historically afforded agencies wide discretion in their informational activities.[39]

For this reason, the GAO has declined to characterize government's expressive activities as prohibited propaganda as long as they are "reasonably related to the agency's duty to inform the public of agency actions, programs, and policies, or justify and rebut attacks upon its policies."[40] To date, the GAO has intervened only in a few cases involving agencies' "covert propaganda," defined by the GAO to mean agencies' speech on contested policy matters that does not identify its governmental source.[41]

Suspicions about the government's persuasive speech at times extended to the government's efforts to shape the public's choices on matters other than elections or legislative votes. Today we take for granted the notion that the government's top doctor will speak out on public health issues like the dangers of tobacco. But in the early 1960s the Secretary of Health, Education, and Welfare rebuffed calls for the government's study of these issues with the retort, "[I]t is not the proper role of the federal government to tell citizens to stop smoking."[42]

To offer a twenty-first-century illustration, President Obama's use of social media triggered related controversies about whether his administration's reliance on emerging expressive platforms exemplified responsible government outreach and transparency or instead inappropriately sought to manipulate the public. Some commentators expressed alarm at Obama's use of social media to guide reporting and shape news cycles: journalist Juliet Eilperin, for example, described Obama's online presence as enabling the White House to become "its own media production company," one that sometimes

---

[39] Gov. Accountability Office, *Dep't of Health and Human Services–Video News Releases*, B-302710 at 13 (May 19, 2004).

[40] Gov. Accountability Office, *Dep't of Defense–Retired Military Officers as Media Analysts*, B-316443 at 8 (July 21, 2009).

[41] E.g., Government Accounting Office, Letter to Chairman James M. Inhofe (Dec. 14, 2015) (concluding that the Environmental Protection Agency (EPA) had engaged in prohibited "covert propaganda" through a social media campaign supporting its clean water initiative that failed to consistently identify the EPA as the source of the communication).

[42] *See* Mike Stobbe, Surgeon General's Warning: How Politics Crippled the Nation's Doctor 121–122 (2014).

resembled a "state-run news distribution service."[43] Concerns of this type may explain at least some of the initial controversy when, shortly after his inauguration, President Obama announced plans to deliver a speech to be broadcast to all public schools – controversy that largely evaporated upon disclosure of the speech's apolitical content.[44]

In the debates described so far, critics of the government's political advocacy generally expressed their concerns in moral or political rather than constitutional terms, objecting that the government's efforts to persuade the public about certain contested political matters are unfair and sometimes dangerous. But some unhappy with the government's political advocacy sought to enforce their intuitions through legal challenges. The next section explores these arguments as they played out in the litigation setting.

A Sampling of These Debates Inside the Courts

Even in their heyday, legal challenges to the government's political advocacy did not succeed in generating a coherent body of judicial doctrine, as those state and federal courts that upheld plaintiffs' challenges to government's advocacy on contested ballot and legislative campaigns failed to identify a consistent legal source for curbing the government's speech. Many held that state and local governments lacked the power to engage in such speech absent express authorization by state or local law.[45] Others pointed to the Free Speech Clause, the Petition Clause, the Guarantee Clause, and unidentified, perhaps structural, constitutional sources. For example, in 1978 a Colorado

---

[43] Juliet Eilperin, *Here's How the First President of the Social Media Age Has Chosen to Connect with Americans*, WASH. POST (May 26, 2015) https://www.washingtonpost.com/news/politics/wp/2015/05/26/heres-how-the-first-president-of-the-social-media-age-has-chosen-to-connect-with-americans/ [https://perma.cc/6QX9-HT65].

[44] *Obama Urges Students to Work Hard, Stay in School*, CNN.com, Sept. 8, 2009. http://www.cnn.com/2009/POLITICS/09/08/obama.school.speech/index.html

[45] *See, e.g.*, Rees v. Carlisle, 153 P.3d 1131, 1139 (Hawaii 2007) (concluding that a prosecutor's use of public resources to urge voters to support an amendment to Hawaii's Constitution violated state law; prosecutor may offer comments but cannot engage in express advocacy); Citizens to Protect Public Funds v. Board of Ed. of Parsippany-Troy Hills, 13 N.J. 172, 179–182 (N.J. 1953) (concluding that a school board's use of public funds to print a booklet urging voters to "vote yes" on bond referendum was not within the power implied to the board by its express power to operate the schools); Porter v. Tiffany, 11 Or. App. 542 (Or. Ct. App. 1972) (finding no statutory authorization for city water and electric board's expenditure of funds for materials advocating support for ballot measures regarding nuclear power).

federal court invoked both First Amendment[46] and Guarantee Clause concerns in upholding a challenge to a school board's expenditure of public funds to communicate with voters about a pending ballot measure:

> When residents within a state seek to participate in this process by proposing an amendment to the state constitution, the expenditure of public funds in opposition to that effort violates a basic precept of this nation's democratic process. Indeed, it would seem so contrary to the root philosophy of a republican form of government as might cause this Court to resort to the guaranty clause in Article IV, section 4 of the United States Constitution.[47]

And the California Supreme Court suggested more than once that public agencies' expenditures to advocate for or against pending ballot measures "raise potentially serious constitutional questions," without identifying the constitutional source of those questions.[48]

Among the earliest[49] – and subsequently most influential – objections to the government's advocacy on contested ballot measures was that offered by U.S. Supreme Court Justice-to-be William Brennan while he served on the New

---

[46] Mountain States Legal Foundation v. Denver Sch. Dist #1, 459 F. Supp. 357, 360 (D. Colo. 1978) ("[A] grant of express authority for a partisan use of public funds in an election of this type would violate the First Amendment to the United States Constitution.").

[47] *Id.* at 360–362. The Constitution's Guarantee Clause provides that "The United States shall guarantee to every State in the Union a Republican Form of Government . . . ." U.S. CONST. ART IV, § 2. The Supreme Court has long held that Guarantee Clause claims are non-justiciable political questions. *E.g.*, Luther v. Borden, 48 U.S. (7 How.) 1 (1849).

[48] Vargas v. City of Salinas, 46 Cal. 4th 1, 31–32 (Cal. 2009) (considering a challenge to a city's pamphlet, newsletter articles, and website postings that included a critical analysis of the effects of a pending ballot measure to repeal the local utility tax); Stanson v. Mott, 17 Cal. 3d 206, 218 (Cal. 1976) (considering a challenge to the state parks department's expenditure of $5000 to develop promotional materials urging voters to support a bond referendum). Note, however, that the court ultimately decided both cases on statutory, rather than constitutional, grounds. *Vargas*, 46 Cal. 4th at 8–9; *Stanson*, 17 Cal. 3d at 219–220.

[49] But by no means the earliest. *See, e.g.*, Mines v. R.F. Del Valle, 201 Cal. 273 (Cal. 1927) (holding that the express municipal power to operate a public utility did not imply the power to appropriate funding to urge voters to approve a bond referendum to extend the utility); Elsenau v. City of Chicago, 334 Ill. 78, 81 (Ill. 1929) (invalidating as an unauthorized municipal function a city's expenditures for advertisements "that did not purport to be an impartial statement of facts for the information of the voters, but that was an attempt, partisan in nature, to induce the voters to act favorably upon the bond issues submitted in the election"). But some early courts bucked this trend, emphasizing the instrumental value of government's expression on ballot campaigns. *E.g.*, City Affairs Committee of Jersey City v. Bd. of Comm'rs of Jersey City, 41 A.2d 798, 800 (N.J. 1945) ("We think municipalities may, within their discretion and in good faith, present their views for or against proposed legislation or referenda to the people on questions which in their judgment would adversely affect the interests of their residents.").

Jersey Supreme Court.[50] A school board had appropriated a few hundred dollars in public funds to print and disseminate an 18-page booklet that urged voters to support a bond referendum to finance the expansion of several school buildings – an expansion, the board maintained, necessary to ensure adequate educational facilities for the town's children. In dictum[51] that proved persuasive to many later courts, Brennan characterized the government's advocacy as fundamentally unfair to those with different views, and thus not within the board's implied powers:

> [T]he board made use of public funds to advocate one side only of the controversial question without affording the dissenters the opportunity by means of that financed medium to present their side, and thus imperiled the propriety of the entire expenditure. The public funds entrusted to the board belong equally to the proponents and opponents of the proposition, and the use of the funds to finance not the presentation of facts merely but also arguments to persuade the voters that only one side has merit, gives the dissenters just cause for complaint. The expenditure is then not within the implied power and is not lawful in the absence of express authority from the legislature... .
>
> [S]imple fairness and justice to the rights of dissenters require that the use of public bodies of public funds for advocacy be restrained within those limits in the absence of a legislative grant in express terms of the broader power.[52]

Other courts similarly characterized the government's participation in these ballot debates as fundamentally unfair.[53] Concluding that "the appropriate function of government in connection with an issue placed before the

---

[50] Citizens to Protect Public Funds v. Board of Ed. of Parsippany-Troy Hills, 13 N.J. 172 (N.J. 1953).

[51] The court determined the issue to be moot because the election had already occurred. *Id.* at 178 ("Plainly, then, any issues as to both the booklet and the radio broadcast are moot .... Nevertheless, the importance of the question makes appropriate our comment upon the Action taken.").

[52] *Id.* at 180–182.

[53] *E.g., Mines,* 201 Cal. at 287 (characterizing the use of public funds to advocate on ballot measure as "manifestly unfair and unjust" to those with dissenting views); Palm Beach County v. Hudspeth, 540 So. 2d 147, 154 (Fla. App. 4 Dist. 1989) ("If government, with its relatively vast financial resources, access to the media and technical know-how, undertakes a campaign to favor or oppose a measure placed on the ballot, then by so doing government undercuts the very fabric which the constitution weaves to prevent government from stifling the voice of the people."); Anderson v. City of Boston, 376 Mass. 178, 195–196 (Mass. 1978) ("Fairness and the appearance of fairness are assured by a prohibition against using public tax revenues to advocate a position which certain taxpayers oppose.").

electorate is to enlighten, not to proselytize," a Florida state court offered a typical analysis:

> While the county not only may but should allocate tax dollars to educate the electorate on the purpose and essential ramifications of referendum items, it must do so fairly and impartially. Expenditures for that purpose may properly be found to be in the public interest. It is never in the public interest, however, to pick up the gauntlet and enter the fray. The funds collected from taxpayers theoretically belong to proponents and opponents of county action alike. To favor one side of any such issue by expending funds obtained from those who do not favor that issue turns government on its head and is the antithesis of the democratic process.[54]

Many of these cases involved challenges to government's advocacy for or against pending initiatives and referenda involving the financing of public schools and other government services.[55] But agencies' 1970s advocacy in support of ratification of the Equal Rights Amendment (ERA), which proposed to amend the Constitution to expressly prohibit governmental discrimination based on sex, sparked similar challenges. A New York state court, for example, enjoined the state's human rights agency from preparing flyers, pamphlets, and broadcast ads in support of a referendum to amend the state constitution to include the ERA.[56] In so doing, the court again distinguished what it considered the government's permissible efforts to inform the public from its impermissible efforts to persuade, equating the latter with totalitarianism:

> So long as they are an arm of the State government they must maintain a position of neutrality and impartiality. It would be establishing a dangerous and untenable precedent to permit the government or any agency thereof, to use public funds to disseminate propaganda in favor of or against any issue or candidate. This may be done by totalitarian, dictatorial or autocratic

---

[54] *Hudspeth*, 540 So. 2d at 154.

[55] *E.g.*, Campbell v. Joint Dist. 28-J, 704 F.2d 501 (10th Cir. 1983) (concluding that school district's expenditures urging approval of financing proposal were unauthorized under state statute); Coffman v. Colorado Common Cause, 102 P.3d 999 (Colo. 2004) (concluding that secretary of state's press releases opposing statewide ballot initiative concerning school funding violated state statute prohibiting public agencies from using more than $50 in public monies to support or oppose ballot measures); Stanson v. Mott, 17 Cal. 3d 206 (Cal. 1976) (considering challenge to state agency's expenditures to urge support for increased parks funding); Carter v. City of Las Cruces, 121 N.M. 580 (Ct. App. N. Mex. 1996) (considering taxpayer's challenge to city officials' expenditures of public funds to support ballot measure to empower the city to acquire a private electric utility).

[56] Stern v. Kramarsky, 84 Misc. 2d 447 (N.Y. Sup. Ct. Special Term 1975).

governments but cannot be tolerated, directly or indirectly, in these democratic United States of America. This is true even if the position advocated is
believed to be in the best interests of our country. To educate, to inform, to
advocate or to promote voting on any issue may be undertaken, provided it is
not to persuade nor to convey favoritism, partisanship, partiality, approval or
disapproval by a State agency of any issue, worthy as it may be.[57]

While many of these challenges focused specifically on the government's
expenditure of public funds for expressive purposes, others objected to any
governmental deviation from neutrality in these contests, regardless of
whether the expression required the use of public monies.[58] According to
these challengers, the government must not take sides, period, in these
political contests. Others remained sanguine about government entities' advocacy in support of referenda they propose themselves, but objected to the
government's expressive opposition to ballot initiatives proposed instead by
citizens.[59]

But many other courts and commentators saw no legal problem with the
government's advocacy on contested ballot initiatives and legislative proposals.
Justice William Brennan himself later embraced the value of the government's speech in these settings when he sat on the United States Supreme
Court. There – years after repudiating a local government's persuasive efforts
while on New Jersey's state supreme court[60] – he stayed a state court's order
that had stopped the city of Boston from spending public funds to express its
views on a ballot referendum on residential and commercial property tax rates.
His change of heart emerged shortly after the U.S. Supreme Court's ruling in
First National Bank of Boston v. Bellotti.[61] There the Court struck down, on
First Amendment grounds, Massachusetts' campaign finance law that had
limited corporate campaign expenditures on pending ballot campaigns. The
Court's ruling now empowered corporate participation in public debates over
ballot measures, and the corporations' speech, in turn, had triggered Boston's

[57] *Stern*, 84 Misc. 2d at 452.
[58] E.g., Choice-in-Education League v. Los Angeles Unified Sch. District, 17 Cal. App. 4th 415
(Cal. App. 2nd 1993); King County Council v. Public Disclosure Comm'n, 93 Wash. 2d 559
(Wash. 1980).
[59] *See, e.g.*, Alabama Libertarian Party v. City of Birmingham, 694 F. Supp. 814, 817–818 (N.D.
Ala. 1988) ("While defendants might be forbidden to spend funds to support candidates, oppose
initiative proposals, etc., they are not forbidden to publicize and seek public support for their
own governmental proposals.").
[60] Citizens to Protect Public Funds v. Board of Ed. of Parsippany-Troy Hills, 13 N.J. 172
(N.J. 1953).
[61] 435 U.S. 765 (1978).

efforts to rebut their arguments. Emphasizing the value of the government's voice in informing the voters on contested ballot measures – especially in countering powerful private speech – Justice Brennan was among the first (and few) to see the link between the government's speech and campaign finance debates:

> In light of *Bellotti*, corporate industrial and commercial opponents of the referendum are free to finance their opposition. On the other hand, unless the stay is granted, the city is forever denied any opportunity to finance communication to the statewide electorate of its views in support of the referendum as required in the interests of all taxpayers, including residential property owners.[62]

So concerns about a fair fight can cut both for and against the government's advocacy on contested ballot campaigns. Sometimes the government's speech may overwhelm that of less well-financed opponents, but at other times the government can counterbalance the speech of corporations and other powerful speakers, especially in light of the Supreme Court's reluctance to interpret the First Amendment to permit the government to control the volume of political speech from wealthy private interests.[63]

Still more controversies involving the ERA further illustrate competing views about the comparative costs and benefits of the government's speech on ballot measures and other policy contests. Emphasizing both the inevitability and the value of the government's expressive participation in these debates, a California appellate court denied a First Amendment challenge to the state women's commission's promotion of the ERA. In so doing, the court rejected even the possibility, much less the wisdom, of the government's expressive neutrality:

> The root problem with plaintiffs' free speech contention is that it proves too much. They offer no point of distinction between government speech addressing the status of women and government speech on any other topic, save that they deem the topic of women's status "controversial." But controversial or not, it is too late in the day to contend the economic and social status of women is not a legitimate topic of governmental concern. If the government, i.e., the governor and legislative leaders, cannot appoint a commission to speak on the topic without implicating plaintiffs' First

---

[62] City of Boston v. Anderson, 439 U.S. 1389, 1390 (1978) (granting stay) (Brennan, J.).
[63] *See* Citizens United v. Federal Election Comm'n, 558 U.S. 310 (2010).

Amendment rights, it may not address any other "controversial" topic. If the government cannot address controversial topics it cannot govern.[64]

One court even characterized the government as having a *duty* to share its views on such measures with the public:

> The City and its officials not only have the right, but the duty, to determine the needs of its citizens and to provide funds to service those needs... .This court has a serious doubt as to whether government entities should be required to stand silently by while propositions which can impact on their tax structures, funds, services, and programs are voted upon, even if initiated by others, unless participation is statutorily forbidden by an appropriate authority.[65]

In recent years, legal challenges to the government's expressive participation in contested policy campaigns have become increasingly rare – and their success rarer still. Why might this be? I suggest a couple of possible answers. First, the once-sharp distinction between governing and campaigning has now disappeared. For a range of reasons that include changes in the norms of governmental discourse, the emergence of new expressive technologies, and the largely unfettered role of money in politics, it's increasingly hard to separate the government's speech that implements existing policy from its speech that advocates for its policy preferences.

Second, and perhaps relatedly, the Supreme Court's first-stage government speech doctrine recognizes both the inevitability and the value of the government's speech on a wide range of matters. Recall, as discussed in Chapter 1, that the Court has rejected arguments that the First Amendment bars the government from taxing individuals to support the government's speech with which they disagree; holding that objecting taxpayers' remedy is at the polling place rather than the courthouse.[66] As the Court made clear, the government cannot compel us to endorse or deliver, its views but it can tax us to support all sorts of government activities, including its speech. In other words, the Supreme Court's contemporary government speech doctrine rejects expectations of the government's expressive neutrality.

---

[64] Miller v. Cal. Commission on the Status of Women, 151 Cal. App. 3d 693, 701 (Cal. Ct. App. 1984).

[65] Alabama Libertarian Party v. City of Birmingham, 694 F. Supp. 814, 817–818 (N.D. Ala. 1988).

[66] E.g., Johanns v. Livestock Marketing Ass'n, 544 U.S. 550 (2005).

Even so, the Court has yet to engage a challenge to the government's advocacy on a contested ballot or legislative matter. But the few lower courts that have since considered constitutional challenges to the government's participation in those debates have applied the Court's government speech doctrine to deny those claims. For example, this chapter's opening hypothetical is based on a case where one federal appellate court considered, and rejected, a First Amendment challenge to a local school board's speech in opposition to pending school voucher legislation.[67] Among other things, the plaintiff there objected to the school board's voter-directed speech on pending legislation, arguing for First Amendment limits on a government body's advocacy to voters on a matter to be decided by the state legislature.[68] The court disagreed, concluding that political accountability rather than First Amendment litigation remains the appropriate remedy for those unhappy with their government's position on pending legislation.[69]

Another federal appellate court considered a First Amendment challenge to a city's expenditure of public funds to express its views on various initiatives related to the restructuring and funding of the town's fire department. A divided panel rejected the challenge: "To hold that [the city's] advocacy converts its treasury to a public forum would severely limit the town's ability to self-regulate and would be tantamount to a heckler's veto, where the government could not speak for fear of opening its treasury to the public."[70] But demonstrating that these debates are not entirely dead, the panel's dissenting judge contended that the Constitution requires the government's expressive neutrality in contests to be decided by the people's vote: "I believe that the Constitution properly prohibits the government from having a horse in the race when it comes to elections. When government advocates on one side of an issue, the ultimate source of governing power is shifted away from the people and the threat of official doctrine exists."[71]

---

[67] Page v. Lexington County Sch. Dist. No. One, 531 F.3d 275, 287 (4th Cir. 2008).

[68] *Id.* at 287–288. [69] *Id.*

[70] Kidwell v. City of Union, 462 F.3d 620, 624 (6th Cir. 2006), *cert. denied*, 550 U.S. 935 (2007).

[71] *Id.* at 634 (Martin, J., dissenting); *see also id.* at 635–636 ("[O]rdinary democratic controls are insufficient as a remedy in situations where governmental influence threatens to undermine the independent political process. Governmental advocacy and campaign expenditures could arguably threaten to undermine free and fair elections, could be coercive, and could reasonably undermine the reliability and outcome of elections where the government acts as a participant.... Perhaps it is time for the Supreme Court to reconsider its Guarantee Clause jurisprudence.").

The Constitutional Value (and Danger) of the Government's Advocacy in Contested Policy Campaigns

Earlier chapters explored the potential value of the government's speech, often – and perhaps especially – on contested political matters. The government's speech – so long as we know that it's the government's speech – generally enhances political accountability by informing voters of their government's priorities and preferences. The government's speech adds to the marketplace of available ideas and arguments, especially (but not only) as a counter to less accountable and nontransparent expression from powerful private sources. And the government's expression sometimes provides a helpful heuristic, or cognitive shortcut, for those who do not have the time or inclination to evaluate competing arguments for themselves.

To elaborate, the government's voice can add additional perspectives to the ideas and arguments available for voters' consideration.[72] Because many initiatives and referenda directly implicate government services and their financing, affected governmental bodies may have valuable expertise to offer on the merits of those measures. Consider, as just one example, a series of three 2010 Colorado ballot measures generated by private parties that proposed to cut at least a billion dollars annually in state taxes, and thus government funding.[73] Supporters characterized the measure as "forc[ing] the government to operate more efficiently and cut bloated spending."[74] In response, the state's governor urged voters to reject the measures, arguing that they could have a devastating effect on the state economy that "would set Colorado back a generation." More specifically, "[Governor] Ritter pledged to rally against the three ballot measures at every speech he gives until the vote in November,"[75] "call[ing] them 'three of the most backward-thinking ballot measures

---

[72] See THOMAS EMERSON, THE SYSTEM OF FREE EXPRESSION 697–698 (1970) ("Participation by the government in the system of freedom of expression is an essential feature of any democratic society. It enables the government to inform, explain, and persuade – measures especially crucial in a society that attempts to govern itself with a minimum use of force. Government participation also greatly enriches the system; it provides the facts, ideas, and expertise not available from other sources.").

[73] See Steve Raabe, Ritter Says Tax-Cutting Ballot Initiatives Would Cripple Colorado, DENVER POST, May 14, 2010, available at http://www.denverpost.com/ci_15083169.

[74] Id.

[75] Aldo Svaldi, Political Rivals in Colorado Seek Alliance against Three Ballot Initiatives, DENVER POST (May 24, 2010). https://www.denverpost.com/2010/05/23/political-rivals-in-colorado-seek-alliance-against-three-ballot-initiatives/ [https://perma.cc/H397-WULJ].

this state has ever seen.'"[76] My point here is not that the government's views are necessarily correct, much less disinterested, but instead that they can provide value to voters by revealing the views of those who would be charged with implementing the measure if enacted.

And at its best (but of course government is not always at its best), the government's voice on contested policy issues can respond to speech by powerful and well-financed private parties that might not otherwise face effective rebuttal. Take, as an example, the California Real Estate Association's 1964 proposed ballot measure to repeal the state's fair housing law that prohibited racial discrimination in the sale or lease of property.[77] Resisting any "open housing" laws[78] on the grounds that "people give property its value" and that "majorities as well as minorities have rights,"[79] the real estate association started with $100,000 in "seed money," a substantial sum at the time.[80] Opponents of the measure included not only a wide variety of civil rights and other private groups,[81] but also California Governor Pat Brown[82] and Senator Pierre Salinger.[83]

Of course, government speakers are not monolithic in their views on race or any other issue. Three decades later, California Governor Pete Wilson and University of California Regent Ward Connerly were among the governmental speakers that supported Proposition 209, a ballot proposition that amended the state constitution to prohibit state and local governments' affirmative action programs in California.[84] Again, the government's voice adds to those available to voters collecting information about pending ballot measures.

The government's speech on ballot issues may prove especially valuable to voters by responding to private power that sometimes operates in nontransparent ways.[85] Not only are ballot measures often the subject of campaign speech by powerful and well-financed private parties, but the identity of such

---

[76] Editorial, *Candidates Weigh in on Right Side of Ballot Items*, DENVER POST (Feb. 25, 2010) https://www.denverpost.com/2010/02/25/candidates-weigh-in-on-right-side-of-ballot-items/ [https://perma.cc/X3PM-BUQQ].

[77] *California: Proposition 14*, TIME, Sept. 25, 1964.   [78] *Id.*

[79] KURT SCHUPARRA, TRIUMPH OF THE RIGHT 105 (1998).

[80] Totton J. Anderson & Eugene C. Lee, *The 1964 Election in California*, 18 WESTERN POLITICAL Q. 2, 470 (1965).

[81] *Id.* at 124.   [82] *Id.* at 471   [83] *California: Proposition 14*, TIME, Sept. 25, 1964.

[84] Pete Wilson, Ward Connerly & Pamela Lewis, *Arguments in Favor of Proposition 209*, http://vigarchive.sos.ca.gov/1996/general/pamphlet/209yesarg.htm [https://perma.cc/KN5E-TU9J].

[85] *See, e.g.*, DAVID MICHAELS, DOUBT IS THEIR PRODUCT: HOW INDUSTRY'S ASSAULT ON SCIENCE THREATENS YOUR HEALTH 90, 201 (2008) (documenting efforts by tobacco companies to contest medical evidence about cigarettes' health hazards, and by oil companies to cast doubt on scientists' findings about the role of fossil fuels in contributing to climate change).

powerful private parties may not be clear, obscuring the public's efforts to assess such speakers' self-interest and credibility:

> Interest groups strategically obscure their involvement when they believe identification would hurt their campaigns. Many industry groups form political committees to conduct campaign activities under non-descriptive names like "Californians for Paycheck Protection" (religious conservatives supporting limitations on labor union political activity), "Alliance to Revitalize California" (Silicon Valley executives supporting a tort reform measure), and "Californians for Affordable and Reliable Electrical Service" (industry opponents of utility regulation).[86]

Similarly, advocates for statewide initiatives seeking to ban all forms of affirmative action named themselves the "American Civil Rights Institute," an identifier that at least some voters found confusing.[87] For these reasons, voters often cannot be sure of the source of private parties' campaign speech and are thus deprived of a key cue to the expression's credibility. The government's counterspeech, so long as it is transparently governmental in source, can serve a valuable checking function.

To be sure, public entities and officials often have considerable self-interest in the outcome of contested ballot measures and legislative proposals, and the government's speech extolling its policy successes also serves its officials' reelection interests. But a speaker's self-interested motivation does not necessarily negate the value of that information to the listener. What the listener needs, ideally, is an understanding of the speaker's self-interest when evaluating her speech. This understanding may be more readily available with respect to government as opposed to private speech: so long as we insist on the government's transparency, voters can assess the government speaker's self-interest, and hold her accountable for it.

Of course, the government does not always speak in opposition to powerful private interests – indeed, it is often aligned with them. But the government itself is far from monolithic. Instead, it comprises a large number and range of potential government speakers, both individual and institutional, with various and competing interests. Different branches of government can and do disagree in a way that helps inform voters. These disagreements occur both

[86] Michael S. Kang, *Democratizing Direct Democracy: Restoring Voter Competence through Heuristic Cues and "Disclosure Plus,"* 50 UCLA L. REV. 1141, 1158 (2003).

[87] Christine Chambers Goodman, *(M)Ad Men: Using Persuasion Factors in Media Advertising to Prevent a "Tyranny of the Majority" in Ballot Propositions,* 2 HAST. COMM. & ENT. L.J. 247, 257 (2010).

horizontally (for example, when the executive disagrees with the legislature) as well as vertically (when federal and state governments disagree). That government speech is by no means homogenous both adds to its informational value and detracts from its potential danger.

Transparently governmental speech on contested policy debates also offers a valuable heuristic, or cognitive shortcut, for those with neither the time nor the inclination to analyze the competing policy arguments themselves. Among the most effective of these heuristics are the opinions of trusted – or distrusted – third parties, parties that include experts, community leaders, and the government. The government's views are by no means necessarily wise, popular, or persuasive. Instead, they provide value to voters who know whether their values align with those of the government speaker. Whether the government's views persuade the many voters who rely on the source of speech as a proxy for its credibility depends on whether those voters view the government speaker with trust or distrust. In short, so long as we know that the government is speaking, and so long as other voices and sources of information remain unfettered, the government's speech on pending policy contests furthers voters' self-governance, autonomy, and enlightenment interests.

But the government's speech on these issues becomes more dangerous if accompanied by its suppression of others' speech or by other efforts to control the information available to the public. As legal scholars Randy Bezanson and William Buss observed:

> Like the government press release that is distributed to news organizations but whose publication is left wholly to the news editors' discretion, government speech may be perfectly consistent with the rule of a privately controlled marketplace of ideas so long as distribution is left to the uncoerced and free choices of private market actors. But if government couples its press release with a command that it be distributed, or with the power to override private distribution mechanisms, the marketplace can no longer be deemed privately controlled and the choices made about ideas in the market can no longer be deemed independent of government interference. . . . [T]he principal First Amendment risks presented by government speech lie in the means employed in its production and distribution, not in the ends government seeks to achieve through speech.[88]

We must be alert to these threats, remaining attentive to the government's efforts to coerce or censor others' speech and to monopolize information.

---

[88] Randall P. Bezanson & William G. Buss, *The Many Faces of Government Speech*, 86 IOWA L. REV. 1377, 1507, 1510 (2001).

Earlier chapters considered some of these dangers, like the government's threats, lies, disclosures, and other expressive effects that have the effect or intent of silencing or punishing other sources of speech. Here I flag a few more.

Ideally, a democratic government shares information and encourages dialogue, debate, and other forms of counterspeech. But at times the government instead stifles rebuttal by stripping the public of access to key information. As legal scholar Mark Yudof observed, "government expression and secrecy can sometimes" be the functional equivalent of censorship.[89]

Along these lines, the government can control information by abandoning efforts to collect or report data. In 2004, for instance, the Bureau of Labor Statistics "became involved in a controversy related to what some interpreted as a deliberate attempt by George W. Bush's administration to conceal information of which it disapproved. Specifically, the Bureau announced its plan to make major changes in the Current Employment Statistics (CES) survey" and to stop collecting separate data by sex in major industries.[90] More recent examples include the Trump administration's decision to remove scientific information about climate change from federal agencies' websites such that some estimate that it cut available public data sets by 25 percent.[91] Legislatures, like executive branch actors, sometimes also halt the collection of data that could threaten a preferred factual narrative; for example, "[a]t the request of the National Rifle Association, Congress forbade the Centers for Disease Control and Prevention from gathering statistics on gun violence."[92]

And the government sometimes resists oversight that might otherwise produce information that challenges the government's preferred narrative. It can do so by refusing to engage in dialogue with other government speakers,[93] or

---

[89] Mark G. Yudof, When Government Speaks: Politics, Law, and Government Expression in America 138 (1983).

[90] Robert Lopresti, When Women Didn't Count: The Chronic Mismeasure and Marginalization of American Women in Federal Statistics 102 (2017); *id.* at 252 ("This book contains multiple examples, over many decades, of government authors expressing astonishment that so many women were working for a living.").

[91] See Juliet Eilperin, *Under Trump, Inconvenient Data Is Being Sidelined*, Wash. Post (May 14, 2017), https://www.washingtonpost.com/politics/under-trump-inconvenient-data-is-being-sidelined/2017/05/14/3ae22c28-3106-11e7-8674-437ddb6e813e_story.html [https://perma.cc/7H44-HN3F].

[92] Robert Lopresti, When Women Didn't Count: The Chronic Mismeasure and Marginalization of American Women in Federal Statistics 3–4 (2017).

[93] See Burgess Everett & Josh Dawsey, *White House Orders Agencies to Ignore Democrats' Oversight Requests*, Politico, (June 2, 2017), http://www.politico.com/story/2017/06/02/federal-agencies-oversight-requests-democrats-white-house-239034 [https://perma.cc/H5QU-

by limiting the public's access to the results of such oversight. Journalists Mark Mazzetti and Matthew Rosenberg, as an illustration, reported in 2017 that the Trump administration had begun returning to Congress copies of a 6,700-page Senate report on the CIA's interrogation methods, methods that included waterboarding, sleep deprivation, and more: "[t]he ... move raises the possibility that most of the copies could be locked in Senate vaults indefinitely or even destroyed — and increases the risk that future government officials, unable to read the report, will never learn its lessons."[94]

Newer expressive technologies may exacerbate these concerns by empowering the government, like other powerful speakers, to reach its listeners immediately and without intermediation from the press or other skeptical third parties.[95] Law professor Rick Hasen, for example, observes that "[c]heap speech has dramatically lowered costs for those who want to draw on people's fears and rile them up for violent purposes."[96] Legal scholar Julie Cohen uses the term "infoglut" to describe this era of cheap and plentiful speech fueled by technology, along with its attendant and often unanticipated dysfunctions: "Information abundance also enables new types of power asymmetries that revolve around differential access to data and to the ability to capture, store, and process it on a massive scale."[97] And as law professor Tim Wu explains:

> [I]t is no longer speech itself that is scarce, but the attention of listeners. Emerging threats to public discourse take advantage of this change.... The low costs of speaking have, paradoxically, made it easier to weaponize speech as a tool of speech control. The unfortunate truth is that cheap speech may be used to attack, harass, and silence as much as it is used to illuminate or debate.[98]

4NNA] ("The idea, Republicans said, is to choke off the Democratic congressional minorities from gaining new information that could be used to attack the president.").

[94] Mark Mazzetti, Matthew Rosenberg & Charlie Savage, *Trump Administration Returns Copies of C.I.A. Torture Report to Congress*, (June 2, 2017), https://www.nytimes.com/2017/06/02/us/politics/cia-torture-report-trump.html [https://perma.cc/S69N-Y4ED].

[95] And, as discussed in Chapter 1, some expressive technologies mask the government's authorship of, and thus its political accountability for, various messages.

[96] Richard Hasen, *Cheap Speech and What It Has Done (to American Democracy)*, 16 FIRST AM. L. REV. 200, 216 (2018).

[97] Julie E. Cohen, *The Regulatory State in the Information Age*, 17 THEO. INQ. IN L. 369, 384 (2016); *see also id.* ("Under conditions of infoglut, the problem is not scarcity but rather the need for new ways of cutting through the clutter, and the re-siting of power within platforms, databases, and algorithms means that meaning is easily manipulated.").

[98] TIM WU, KNIGHT FIRST AMENDMENT INST., IS THE FIRST AMENDMENT OBSOLETE? 1, 3 (2017).

Other governments have deployed these weapons against other countries as well as against their own citizens.[99] Wu points to China to show how the government can exploit cheap and abundant speech to threaten its listeners' interests: "What [researchers] have discovered is a regime less intent on stamping out forbidden content, but instead focused on distraction, cheerleading, and preventing meaningful collective action."[100]

Constitutional law can address some, but not all, of these dangers. The next chapter considers a range of possible means, both constitutional and nonconstitutional, for countering and influencing the government's destructive expressive choices.

---

[99] *See* Nathaniel Persily, *Can Democracy Survive the Internet?*, 28 J. OF DEM. 63, 70 (2017) (discussing how Russian bots targeted the American electorate as part of a campaign to influence and manipulate the 2016 elections).

[100] TIM WU, KNIGHT FIRST AMENDMENT INST., IS THE FIRST AMENDMENT OBSOLETE? 10 (2017).

7

Responding to The Government's Destructive Speech

This book has focused primarily on how we might *think* about the constitutional questions sparked by the government's speech. Now it turns to available responses, in other words, what we might *do* about the government's destructive expressive choices. Because this book centers on the constitutional implications of the government's speech, this chapter starts by discussing the remedies available through constitutional litigation. Because those remedies, while valuable, are also limited and imperfect, the chapter then turns to other possible constraints on the government's speech that do not rely on constitutional litigation.

CONSTITUTIONAL REMEDIES

There's no point in filing a constitutional challenge to the government's speech unless meaningful remedies are available to cure a violation, if found. Legal scholar Mark Yudof was among the first to recognize the harms threatened by the government's speech; he was also among the first to realize the barriers to the judiciary's ability to redress these dangers. In Yudof's view, "[t]he difficulties in fashioning remedies are so substantial that they corroborate the wisdom of courts in general in avoiding the attempt to delimit the boundaries of unconstitutional government expression."[1] He doubted the value of injunctions – that is, courts' orders that the government stop doing or saying something – because he worried that those remedies raised separation of powers concerns and threatened to chill valuable government speech (although he acknowledged their value in addressing certain outrageous cases in which the government would otherwise be likely to repeat its misconduct).

---

[1] Mark G. Yudof, When Government Speaks: Politics, Law, and Government Expression in America 205–207 (1983).

He noted the possibility of declaratory relief – that is, a court's declaration that the government's choices violated the Constitution – but wondered about its utility. And he saw at best a very limited role for monetary damages, primarily in cases involving discrete harms like defamation or invasion of privacy.

To be sure, the search for constitutional remedies for the government's harmful expression can be challenging. But, as we'll see, it is far from futile. A search for remedies is also increasingly important at a time when the government's expressive powers continue to grow – along with the government's willingness to use these powers for disturbing purposes and with troubling consequences. As a long-standing body of precedent reveals, the tools available for naming, and stopping, the government's speech that inflicts constitutional injuries include injunctive relief, declaratory relief, and damages.

Injunctive Relief

Plaintiffs often challenge state and local governments' expressive (and other) choices under 42 U.S.C. section 1983, "the broadest federal civil rights statute and among the most consequential [, which] provides a private cause of action against any person who, 'under color' of state law, causes the deprivation of rights secured by the 'Constitution and laws' of the United States."[2] Injunctive relief is available under section 1983 to put a stop to state and local governments' speech found in violation of the Constitution (and attorney's fees also may be available for prevailing plaintiffs).[3] Think, for example, of the government's religious speech held to violate the Establishment Clause. As Chapter 2 explained, the Supreme Court itself has granted injunctive and declaratory relief in numerous cases involving successful Establishment Clause challenges to the government's religious speech, and lower courts also frequently order the government to cease, take down, or excise its religious speech found to violate the Establishment Clause.[4]

As yet another illustration, recall *Anderson* v. *Martin* (discussed in more detail in Chapter 3), where the Supreme Court enjoined the government's

---

[2] Stephen B. Burbank & Sean Farhang, Rights and Retrenchment: The Counterrevolution against Federal Litigation 30 (2017).

[3] 42 U.S.C. § 1988(b).

[4] *E.g.*, McCreary Cnty. v. ACLU, 545 U.S. 844 (2005); Santa Fe Indep. Sch. Dist. v. Doe, 530 U.S. 290 (2000); Lee v. Weisman, 505 U.S. 577, 592 (1992); Cnty. of Allegheny v. ACLU, 492 US 573 (1989); Joyner v. Forsyth County, 653 F.3d 341 (4th Cir. 2011); Robinson v. City of Edmond, 68 F.3d 1226 (10th Cir. 1995); Summers v. Adams, 669 F. Supp. 2d 637 (D.S.C. 2009).

speech that encouraged voters to discriminate based on race in violation of the Equal Protection Clause. There the plaintiffs filed a successful action under section 1983 to put a stop to Louisiana's state law that required the government to state each candidate's race on all ballots.[5]

Injunctive relief is similarly available against speech by the federal government and its officials for claims brought directly under the First (for alleged Free Speech, Free Press, and Establishment Clause violations) or Fifth (for alleged due process and equal protection violations) Amendments. Think of *Joint Anti-Fascist Refugee Committee* v. *McGrath* (discussed in more detail in Chapter 5), where several organizations sought declaratory and injunctive relief from the Attorney General's statement characterizing them as Communist front organizations. Reversing the lower court's dismissal of the claim, the Court identified injunctive and declaratory relief as available remedies:

> These complaints do not raise the question of the personal liability of public officials for money damages caused by their ultra vires acts. They ask only for declaratory and injunctive relief striking the names of the designated organizations from the Attorney General's published list and, as far as practicable, correcting the public records. The respondents are not immune from such a proceeding.[6]

As another example, recall that the Court also ordered injunctive relief to stop the government's threatening speech that silenced its targets' expression in violation of the Free Speech Clause in *Bantam Books, Inc.* v. *Sullivan* (discussed in Chapter 5).[7] Lower courts have similarly enjoined the government's expressive choices that are sufficiently coercive of its targets' speech to violate the First (or, with respect to state and local governments, Fourteenth) Amendment.[8]

In short, courts not uncommonly enjoin, and thus put a stop to, the government's speech that infringes specific constitutional protections. And courts are not necessarily limited to traditional forms of injunctive relief that simply require the government to stop or remove its constitutionally harmful speech: as legal scholar Tracy Thomas explains more generally, courts can

---

[5] 375 U.S. 399, 402 (1964).   [6] 341 U.S. 123, 140–141 (1951).   [7] 372 U.S. 58 (1963).

[8] E.g., Backpage.com v. Dart, 807 F.3d 229, 234–235 (7th Cir. 2015); Playboy Enterprises, Inc. v. Meese, 639 F. Supp. 581, 587–588 (D.D.C. 1986).

also issue prophylactic injunctions to require training, monitoring, and other actions to ensure the government's compliance with the Constitution.[9]

Declaratory Relief

In cases where injunctive relief is unavailable (as can be the case, for example, where the government is unlikely to repeat its expressive choices that have infringed upon its targets' constitutional rights[10]), declaratory relief generally remains available to "call out" governmental speech that violates specific constitutional protections.[11] Unlike injunctive relief, declaratory relief involves neither a command to the defendant nor a sanction for noncompliance; instead we can understand it as a form of "soft law" that nevertheless performs important expressive and deterrent functions.[12] As one federal district court explained, "A declaratory judgment [that a government official has violated the Constitution] should be sufficient, as no government official—including the President—is above the law, and all government officials are presumed to follow the law as has been declared."[13] Declaratory relief also leaves open the possibility of further relief that can take the form of injunctions or damages.[14]

Damages

Sometimes the government's speech inflicts injury of the sort that the law has traditionally treated as quantifiable, and thus amenable to monetary damages.

---

9   Tracy A. Thomas, *The Prophylactic Remedy: Normative Principles and Definitional Parameters of Broad Injunctive Relief*, 52 BUFF. L. REV. 301, 309 (2004).
10 *See* City of Los Angeles v. Lyons, 461 U.S. 95 (1983) (holding that the plaintiff did not have standing to seek an injunction against the police department's allegedly unconstitutional use of chokeholds when the plaintiff could not show that he would likely again suffer from such a chokehold).
11 *See* 28 U.S.C. § 2201. For examples of successful claims for declaratory relief for the government's unconstitutional speech, see Helen Norton, *Remedies and the Government's Constitutionally Harmful Speech*, 9 CONLAWNOW 49 (2018).
12 *See* Samuel L. Bray, *The Myth of the Mild Declaratory Judgment*, 63 DUKE L.J. 1091, 1124 (2014) ("The central difference between the declaratory judgment and the injunction in contemporary American law is *management*, in the sense of continuing judicial direction and oversight of the parties. The injunction enables a high degree of management. The declaratory judgment does not. As a result, the decision to grant one or the other of these remedies should chiefly be a decision about the degree of direction and oversight that the relationship of the parties requires of the court.").
13 Knight First Am. Inst. v. Trump, 302 F. Supp. 3d 541, 549 (S.D.N.Y. 2018).
14 28 U.S.C.A. § 2202 ("Further necessary or proper relief based on a declaratory judgment or decree may be granted, after reasonable notice and hearing, against any adverse party whose rights have been determined by such judgment.").

Think of a governmental employer's racially or sexually harassing speech that creates a hostile work environment, discussed in Chapter 3.[15] Or a law enforcement officer's threats, discussed in Chapter 4, to tell 18-year-old Marcus Wayman's grandfather that Marcus was gay, a threat that led the young man to commit suicide.[16] Think too of the government's threatening speech that leads to its target's job loss. As an illustration (discussed in more detail in Chapter 5), a federal appellate court refused to dismiss a Section 1983 claim for damages by a plaintiff who alleged that the government had retaliated against her constitutionally protected speech with its false and coercive speech to her employer that led to her firing.[17]

Even when the constitutional injuries inflicted by government speech can be difficult to quantify in monetary terms, nominal damages can serve both expressive and deterrent functions. Nominal damages are a "trifling sum awarded when a legal injury is suffered but there is no substantial loss or injury to be compensated" and serve as a declaration that the plaintiff's legal rights have been violated.[18] This can be the case, for example, when the government's speech silences its targets, or causes them to refrain from exercising a protected right or from seeking a certain opportunity. Indeed, the Court has emphasized the value of nominal damages more generally in section 1983 cases where constitutional injuries are hard to quantify in monetary terms:

> By making the deprivation of such rights actionable for nominal damages without proof of actual injury, the law recognizes the importance to organized society that those rights be scrupulously observed; but at the same time, it remains true to the principle that substantial damages should be awarded only to compensate actual injury or, in the case of exemplary or punitive damages, to deter or punish malicious deprivations of rights.[19]

[15] E.g., Kopman v. City of Centerville, 871 F. Supp. 2d 875 (S.D.S.D. 2012) (denying defendants' motion for summary judgment on a section 1983 claim for compensatory and punitive damages where the government official's harassing workplace speech "permeated and poisoned [the plaintiffs] work environment").

[16] E.g., Sterling v. Borough of Minersville, 232 F.3d 190 (3rd Cir. 2000) (denying defendants' motion for summary judgment on a section 1983 claim for damages for police officers' threat to disclose young man's sexual orientation).

[17] Paige v. Coyner, 614 F.3d 273, 276–283 (6th Cir. 2010).

[18] See BLACK'S LAW DICTIONARY 396 (7th ed. 1999). In contrast, a declaratory judgment is "a binding adjudication that establishes the rights and other legal relations of the parties without providing for or ordering enforcement." Id. at 846.

[19] Carey v. Piphus, 435 U.S. 247, 266 (1978); see also Memphis Community Sch. Dist. v. Stachura, 477 U.S. 299, 308 n.11 (1986) ("Our discussion of that issue makes clear that nominal damages, and not damages based on some undefinable "value" of infringed rights, are

The award of nominal damages can thus establish the unconstitutionality of the government's actions. And, by putting government officials on notice of such action's unconstitutionality, the award of nominal damages may eliminate the availability of qualified immunity from money damages in future cases. Relatedly, the possibility of nominal damages enables "the court to reach the constitutional issue in a world of legal uncertainty without confronting the officer with a threat of personal liability."[20]

Note that the government and its officials enjoy immunity from damages in certain contexts. As the Court has explained:

> To the extent that the threat of liability encourages [government] officials to carry out their duties in a lawful and appropriate manner, and to pay their victims when they do not, it accomplishes exactly what it should. By its nature, however, the threat of liability can create perverse incentives that operate to *inhibit* officials in the proper performance of their duties. In many contexts, government officials are expected to make decisions that are impartial or imaginative, and that above all are informed by considerations other than the personal interests of the decisionmaker. Because government officials are engaged by definition in governing, their decisions will often have adverse effects on other persons. When officials are threatened with personal liability for acts taken pursuant to their official duties, they may well be induced to act with an excess of caution or otherwise to skew their decisions in ways that result in less than full fidelity to the objective and independent criteria that ought to guide their conduct. In this way, exposing government officials to the same legal hazards faced by other citizens may detract from the rule of law instead of contributing to it.[21]

For these reasons, the Court has held that governmental actors enjoy absolute immunity from money damages when engaged in certain essential governmental functions,[22] and the president is absolutely immune from

---

the appropriate means of "vindicating" rights whose deprivation has not caused actual, provable injury.").

[20] JAMES PFANDER, CONSTITUTIONAL TORTS AND THE WAR ON TERROR xviii (2017). Because the award of nominal damages materially alters the legal relationship of the parties, it sometimes also permits the award of attorney's fees to the plaintiff. Farrar v. Hobby, 506 U.S. 103, 121 (1992) (discussing 42 U.S.C. § 1988).

[21] Forrester v. White, 484 U.S. 219, 223 (1988).

[22] *See id.* at 227–229 (discussing judges' absolute immunity from damages when performing certain judicial functions, while concluding that state court judge did not have absolute immunity from damages under section 1983 for his alleged sex-based demotion of a probation officer).

monetary damages for injuries caused by his official acts as president.[23] And
government actors found to have violated the Constitution when engaged in
functions that do not trigger absolute immunity often still enjoy "qualified
immunity" from money damages so long as they did not violate law that was
clearly established at the time and of which a reasonable person would have
been aware.[24] Statutes also sometimes immunize government actors from
liability in certain situations: for example, the Federal Tort Claims Act does
not permit defamation suits against federal government speakers.[25] But governmental immunities often operate to bar only suits for money damages and
not suits seeking injunctive or declaratory relief, and in certain circumstances
immunities from damages may be limited, waived, or otherwise overcome to
achieve important public purposes.[26]

The Constitution's Speech or Debate Clause specifically provides federal
legislators with immunity against liability, both criminal and civil, for their
legislative speech, like their speech on the floor of Congress or in committee
reports. (As the Court has made clear, not all of a federal legislator's speech is
legislative speech protected by the Clause.[27]). The Clause seeks to protect the

[23] Nixon v. Fitzgerald, 457 U.S. 731 (1982). But the president is not immune from damages for his
actions before becoming president. *See* Clinton v. Jones, 520 U.S. 681 (1997). For an excellent
discussion of the possibilities for, and barriers to, constitutional litigation challenging the
president's speech, *see* Sonja R. West, *Suing the President for First Amendment Violations*, 71
OKLA. L. REV. 321 (2018).

[24] *See* Harlow v. Fitzgerald, 457 U.S. 800, 818 (1982).   [25] 28 U.S.C. § 2680(h).

[26] *E.g.*, Buckley v. Fitzsimmons, 509 U.S. 259 (1993) (declining to find that a prosecutor's
allegedly false statements made when announcing a defendant's indictment fell within the
zone of prosecutorial functions that are absolutely immune from damages liability); Forrester
v. White, 484 U.S. 219, 227–229 (1988) (concluding that state court judge did not have absolute
immunity from damages under section 1983 for his alleged sex-based demotion of a probation
officer); Sterling v. Borough of Minersville, 232 F.3d 190 (3rd Cir. 2000) (denying defendants'
qualified immunity claim in a section 1983 action for damages for police officer's threat to
disclose young man's sexual orientation); Kopman v. City of Centerville, 871 F. Supp. 2d 875
(S.D.S.D. 2012) (rejecting defendants' claim of qualified immunity in a section 1983 action for
compensatory and punitive damages for harassing workplace speech).

[27] *E.g.*, Hutchinson v. Proxmire, 443 U.S. 111, 133 (1979) ("Newsletters and press releases, by
contrast [to voting and preparing committee reports], are primarily means of informing those
outside the legislative forum; they represent the views and will of a single Member. It does not
disparage either their value or their importance to hold that they are not entitled to the
protection of the Speech or Debate Clause."); Doe v. McMillan, 412 U.S. 306, 313–314
(1973) ("Members of Congress may frequently be in touch with and seek to influence the
Executive Branch of Government, but this conduct 'though generally done, is not protected
legislative activity.' Nor does the Speech or Debate Clause protect a private republication of
documents introduced and made public at a committee hearing, although the hearing was
unquestionably part of the legislative process.") (quoting Gravel v. United States, 408 U.S. 606,
625 (1972)).

federal legislative function from interference; indeed, at times the Clause has enabled crucial disclosures by members of Congress to confront and expose executive branch secrecy and lies. For example, when the Nixon administration sought to enjoin newspapers' publication of the Pentagon Papers, Senator Mike Gravel read excerpts of the Papers on the Senate floor, protected from the President's interference by the Speech or Debate Clause.[28] As a more recent example, Senators Ron Wyden and Mark Udall "announced on the Senate floor that the Obama administration had adopted a secret, implausible interpretation" of federal domestic surveillance law; this disclosure, in turn, led to further investigations and further disclosures by public and private actors alike.[29]

But the Speech or Debate Clause also protects, and thus enables, pernicious legislative speech like that of Joseph McCarthy and his Senate committee. As an illustration, the day after Senator Gravel read the Pentagon Papers into the Congressional record, "Nixon discussed as his next move recruiting 'another Senator McCarthy' – some right-wing exuberant to crush the conspiracy as only someone with congressional immunity against libel and slander could do."[30]

＊ ＊

Rather than provide an exhaustive treatise on remedies, my purpose here is simply to flag an extensive body of precedent that identifies the constitutional remedies available to stop or redress the government's speech that violates specific constitutional protections. Constitutional litigation and attendant remedies are especially vital when meaningful political remedies are unavailable; this can be the case, for example, when the government lies, obscures its messages' governmental source, or otherwise speaks in ways that frustrate the public's ability to hold the government politically accountable for its speech. This can also be the case when the government's hurtful speech is politically popular, for example, when the government's speech targets minority groups or vulnerable individuals who cannot protect themselves politically.[31]

---

[28] *See* JOSH CHAFETZ, CONGRESS'S CONSTITUTION 216 (2017).   [29] *Id.* at 221.
[30] RICK PERLSTEIN, NIXONLAND: THE RISE OF A PRESIDENT AND THE FRACTURING OF AMERICA 581 (2008).
[31] *See* United States v. Carolene Products Co., 304 U.S. 144, 153 n.4 (1938) (suggesting that "prejudice against discrete and insular minorities may be a special condition, which tends seriously to curtail the operation of those political processes ordinarily to be relied upon to protect minorities, and which may call for a correspondingly more searching judicial inquiry"); JOHN HART ELY, DEMOCRACY AND DISTRUST: A THEORY OF JUDICIAL REVIEW (1980) (advocating judicial review as a means of protection for minorities who are unable to protect themselves from majorities through the political process).

But constitutional litigation is no panacea, and we should consider, and at times prefer, nonconstitutional options. As Thomas Emerson (who was among the first to notice both the ubiquity of and the dangers potentially posed by the government's speech) observed, "[T]he judicial structure is not capable, by itself, of fully protecting in practice the theoretical rights guaranteed under our system of freedom of expression. Full realization of those rights must depend ultimately upon attitudes ingrained in the public mind and support extended by the body politic as a whole."[32] The next section considers those additional possibilities.

BEYOND CONSTITUTIONAL LITIGATION: NONCONSTITUTIONAL REMEDIES

The remainder of this chapter outlines a range of (often overlapping) statutory, political, structural, and expressive strategies for influencing the government's expressive choices, strategies available to a variety of actors that include legislatures, courts and lawyers, other government actors, the press, and the people themselves.[33]

Legislatures

Although this book focuses on the Constitution, statutes – laws enacted by legislatures – can also constrain the government's speech. As legal scholar Mark Yudof observed in his groundbreaking work, "The greatest threat of government domination and distortion of majoritarian processes emanates from executive bodies and officers. The greatest hope of restraining that power lies with the legislative branches of government."[34] Statutes offer a particularly attractive alternative because they can be carefully tailored to address specific contexts that threaten especially grave harms, permitting legislatures to choose a scalpel over a bludgeon when addressing the government's abuse of its expressive powers.

More specifically, legislatures can enact statutes that target, and check, the government's injurious speech to certain audiences, on certain topics, by

---

[32] Thomas Emerson, *Freedom of Expression in Wartime*, 116 U. Pa. L. Rev. 975, 1007 (1968).

[33] Although I focus on law and politics, there are still other possibilities. In other words, we need to think about law, but not only about law. *See* Lawrence Lessig, *The New Chicago School*, 27 J. Legal Stud. 661, 662–664 (1998) (describing how law, social norms, markets, and architecture (or code) all can regulate human behavior in different ways).

[34] Mark G. Yudof, When Government Speaks: Politics, Law, and Government Expression in America 47 (1983).

certain speakers, or in other settings that threaten serious harm. Through statutes, legislatures can enact laws that require the government's transparency, its deliberation, and its accuracy. Through statutes, legislatures can limit the government's speech on certain matters or for certain purposes. Through statutes, legislatures can also encourage counterspeech, for example, by protecting whistleblowers and other speakers.

Statutes That Require the Government's Transparency

Legislatures can enact statutes to require government officials to disclose certain facts by requiring, for example, that they disclose their tax returns or their receipts of various emoluments, as legal scholars Laurence Tribe and Joshua Matz suggest.[35] Through statutes, legislatures can also require government actors to disclose available legal protections to ensure that vulnerable listeners are aware of their legal rights or other key information. Some states, for example, require law enforcement officers to notify minors of additional protections available under state law, like the right to have a parent or other adult present during interrogation.[36] And through statutes, legislatures can require the government to maintain records of its speech.[37]

Statutes That Require the Government's Speech to Be Truthful

While transparency-enhancing statutes *require* certain government speech, statutes can also *prohibit* the government's damaging speech, like its lies. For example, statutes can prohibit the government's speech that obscures transparency, such as the government's lies that it is the press as well as its lies that it is not the press (what I call lies of misappropriation and misattribution, discussed in more detail in chapter 5). More specifically, legislatures can prohibit law enforcement officers from pretending to be the press, and they can prohibit government speakers from concealing themselves as the authors of material prepared for publication or broadcast by the press.

Some statutes already prohibit certain lies in certain settings by speakers generally, including but not limited to government speakers. Perjury law exemplifies this setting-specific approach, as it targets lies under oath (by

---

[35] *See* LAURENCE TRIBE & JOSHUA MATZ, TO END A PRESIDENCY 67 (2018).

[36] JUSTIN DRIVER, THE SCHOOLHOUSE GATE: PUBLIC EDUCATION, THE SUPREME COURT, AND THE BATTLE FOR THE AMERICAN MIND 233–234 (2018) (discussing related protections under North Carolina law).

[37] *E.g.*, 5 U.S.C. § 552 (requiring government to accurately maintain and disclose certain records).

governmental and nongovernmental speakers alike) that are material to certain high-stakes decisions. Other examples include laws that prohibit lies (and other misconduct) that interfere with law enforcement investigations and related matters, like statutes that prohibit the obstruction of justice.

Other statutes target lies made to certain audiences. Consider the Federal False Statements Act, which prohibits lies to federal government officials – including but not limited to those made by other government speakers – that are "predictably capable of affecting" government decision-making.[38] The lies prohibited by the Act include not only lies that may affect the government's decisions to grant certain benefits or contracts but also the government's decisions about whether and how to deploy the government's investigative energies.[39] The statute thus reaches lies that pose collective harm to the public by depleting or diverting public resources.

In certain circumstances, private law remedies like tort law can constrain the government's lies and other destructive expressive choices. Consider, for example, defamation law, which takes a harm-specific approach by targeting lies that damage their individual targets' reputation. Although legislatures currently shield many government actors from monetary liability for their defamatory lies through a variety of immunities, they need not do so. Some states, for example, choose to permit defamation actions against state or local government speakers,[40] and some commentators like legal scholar Aziz Huq urge the amendment of the Federal Tort Claims Act to permit similar actions against federal government speakers.[41]

Other nonconstitutional constraints prohibit lies by certain government speakers. As an illustration, the Model Code of Judicial Conduct and the Model Rules of Professional Conduct impose an explicit duty of truthfulness

---

[38] 18 U.S.C. § 1001(a) (2012) ("[W]hoever, in any matter within the jurisdiction of the executive, legislative, or judicial branch of the Government of the United States, knowingly and willfully ... makes any materially false, fictitious, or fraudulent statement or representation ... shall be fined under this title, imprisoned not more than 5 years ... or both."); *see also* Kungys v. United States, 485 U.S. 759, 771 (1988) (explaining that a statement is "material" if "predictably capable of affecting" a government decision).

[39] *See* United States v. Gilliland, 312 U.S. 86, 93 (1941) ("The amendment indicated the congressional intent to protect the authorized functions of governmental departments and agencies from the perversion which might result from the deceptive practices described.").

[40] *See* Nadel v. Regents of Univ. of Cal., 34 Cal. Rptr. 2d 188, 190 (Cal. Ct. App. 1994).

[41] *See* Aziz Huq, *When Government Defames*, N.Y. TIMES, Aug. 10, 2017 ("Congress should enact a judicial remedy for any person defamed by an official of the federal government speaking or writing to the public;" Huq proposes that remedies be limited to "a declaratory judgment finding the statement false and defamatory.").

on judges and on government actors (and others) who are also members of the bar.[42] For example, Arkansas suspended former President Clinton's state bar license for five years[43] based on a federal court's conclusion that he had given "false, misleading, and evasive answers that were designed to obstruct the judicial process" in civil litigation alleging that he had engaged in sexual harassment while governor of Arkansas.[44] As is the case with perjury prohibitions, these constraints seek to remedy not only the potential harms of deception to individual parties, but also harms to the public's trust in the administration of justice more broadly.

Some speaker-specific approaches target damaging speech only by certain government speakers. For example, the Model Rules of Professional Conduct impose heightened requirements of truthfulness on prosecutors as a particular type of government speaker,[45] again to prevent harm both to individual litigants as well as to the public's collective trust in the criminal justice system.

And, as a comparative matter, the United Kingdom's Ministerial Code outlines expectations of ethical conduct for ministers who lead government departments, including expectations for their speech.[46] Section 1.1 of the Code states that "Ministers of the Crown are expected to behave in a way that upholds the highest standards of propriety,"[47] and section 1.2(c) describes this expectation more specifically to prohibit lies to Parliament: "It is of paramount

---

[42] MODEL CODE OF JUDICIAL CONDUCT R. 4.1(A)(11) (2007) (prohibiting judges and judicial candidates from "knowingly, or with reckless disregard for the truth, mak[ing] any false or misleading statement"); MODEL RULES OF PROF'L CONDUCT R. 3.3(a)(1) (2014) ("A lawyer shall not knowingly[] make a false statement of fact or law to a tribunal ... ."); MODEL RULES OF PROF'L CONDUCT R. 4.1(a) (2014) ("In the course of representing a client a lawyer shall not knowingly[] make a false statement of material fact or law to a third person[.]"); MODEL RULES OF PROF'L CONDUCT R. 8.4(c) (2014) ("It is professional misconduct for a lawyer to[] engage in conduct involving dishonesty, fraud, deceit or misrepresentation[.]"). Although many disciplinary actions under these rules punish lies like fraud or perjury that violate other legal constraints, some hold lawyers and judges to higher standards of truthfulness by punishing lies that would likely not be punishable if uttered by nonattorneys. *See In re* Pautler, 47 P.3d 1175 (Colo. 2002); *In re* Carpenter, 95 P.3d 203 (Or. 2004).

[43] Neal v. Clinton, No. CIV 2000-5677, 2001 WL 34355768, at *3 (Ark. Cir. Ct. Jan. 19, 2001). The State also assessed a fine of $25,000. *Id.*

[44] Jones v. Clinton, 36 F. Supp. 2d 1118, 1127 (E.D. Ark. 1999).

[45] *See* MODEL RULES OF PROF'L CONDUCT R. 3.8 (2014) (requiring prosecutors not only to refrain from lying but also to make affirmative disclosures in some circumstances).

[46] CABINET OFFICE, MAY 2010 MINISTERIAL CODE, 2009–2010, H.C. DEP. 2010-1253 (U.K.), *available at* https://www.gov.uk/government/uploads/system/uploads/attachment_data/file/61402/ministerial-code-may-2010.pdf [http://perma.cc/EY2A-3C79].

[47] *Id.* § 1.1; *see also* Lesley Dingle & Bradley Miller, *A Summary of Recent Constitutional Reform in the United Kingdom*, 33 INT'L J. LEGAL INFO. 71, 88–89, 96 (2005) (describing the expectations generated by these nonlegal norms); Rt. Hon. Lord Goldsmith QC, *Keynote Address*, 59 STAN. L. REV. 1155, 1156–1158 (2007) (same).

importance that Ministers give accurate and truthful information to Parliament, correcting any inadvertent error at the earliest opportunity. Ministers who knowingly mislead Parliament will be expected to offer their resignation to the Prime Minister."[48]

Statutes That Limit the Government's Speech for Certain Purposes or on Certain Topics

Through statutes, legislatures can cap, or ban altogether, expenditures for the government's speech on certain topics or in certain settings. For example, through statutes legislatures can address concerns that the government's speech will drown out others' speech. Along these lines, many states prohibit state employees or officers from using state facilities or funds in "the promotion of or opposition to a ballot proposition."[49] As another example, consider policymakers' concerns about efforts by the George W. Bush administration's White House Office of Political Affairs to use government resources to fund expression to reelect incumbents. In response, a House Committee recommended elimination of that office as well as amendments to federal law to create more meaningful penalties for the government's electioneering speech.[50]

Recall too the long-standing debates over the government's expressive display of the Confederate flag (discussed in Chapter 3). California chose to end this debate within its borders by enacting a statute that forbade the state from displaying the logo: "[T]he State of California may not sell or display the Battle Flag of the Confederacy, also referred to as the Stars and Bars, or any similar image, or tangible personal property, inscribed with such an image unless the image appears in a book, digital medium, or state museum that serves an educational or historical purpose."[51]

---

[48] MAY 2010 MINISTERIAL CODE § 1.2(c).

[49] *See* Okla. Sta. Ann. § 16-119 (2010) (prohibiting state officials from "direct[ing] or authoriz[ing] the expenditure of any public funds under his care, except as specifically authorized by law, in support of or opposition to any measure which is being referred to a vote of the people by means of initiative or referendum, or which citizens are attempting to put to initiative or referendum"); Rev. Code of Wash. Ann. 42.52.180 (2010) ("No state officer or state employee may use or authorize the use of facilities of an agency, directly or indirectly for the purpose of ... the promotion of or opposition to a ballot proposition.").

[50] U.S. House of Representatives Committee on Oversight and Government Reform, Draft Committee Report, The Activities of the White House Office of Political Affairs ii (October 2008).

[51] CAL GOV'T CODE § 8195.

Statutes That Require the Government's Deliberation and Consultation

Recall that certain constitutional provisions require government actors to talk to the public or with each other – like the requirement that the president deliver her assessment of the State of the Union to Congress, and that she explain her reasons for vetoing a bill.[52] Through statutes, legislatures can, and sometimes do, accomplish similar goals. Think, for instance, of the Administrative Procedure Act (APA), which requires government agencies to solicit and consider public comments on their proposed rules and regulations, and then to explain and support their response in their final rulemaking. Some commentators have urged courts to interpret, or Congress to amend, the APA to invalidate any final agency action as arbitrary and capricious when the agency seeks to support it with inaccurate assertions. Along these lines, some courts have interpreted the National Environmental Protection Act (NEPA) to prohibit agencies from issuing environmental impact statements based on false, inaccurate, or misleading assertions.[53]

Statutes That Protect Counterspeech That Challenges and Exposes the Government's Destructive Speech

Through statutes, legislatures can provide legal protections for those who counter the government's destructive speech with speech of their own. These include whistleblowers who expose governmental lies and other misconduct, like FBI Deputy Director Mark Felt (Watergate's "Deep Throat") and Sergeant Joseph Darby (who exposed the mistreatment of prisoners at Abu Ghraib). Recall from Chapter 1 that the Supreme Court's decision in *Garcetti* v. *Ceballos* held that the First Amendment does not protect public employees' speech pursuant to their jobs, but tried to downplay the decision's impact by inviting legislatures to enact statutory protections for those workers' whistle-blowing speech. But available statutory protections remain patchwork and incomplete, and legislatures can and should take action to strengthen them.

Legislatures' Counterspeech

Legislatures can also respond to other governmental actors' destructive expressive choices through public pressure and pushback. Examples include

---

[52] U.S. CONST. art. II, § 2, cl. 1; *id.* at art. II, § 3.
[53] *See* Nat. Res. Def. Council v. U.S. Forest Serv., 421 F.3d 797, 811–813 (9th Cir. 2005) (finding that the agency's use of inflated, inaccurate, and misleading data violated NEPA).

engaging in vigorous legislative oversight of the executive's alleged lies and other speech, requiring relevant officials to testify about those expressive choices under oath, and denying funding to government agencies engaged in lying or other harmful expression.

Legislatures can also create what some call "internal separation of powers" checks on the executive branch. At the federal level, more specifically, Congress has statutorily created inspectors general ("IGs") charged with monitoring various agencies for misconduct, including its lies. As an illustration, the Veterans' Administration's Office of Inspector General documented a variety of misrepresentations by the agency with respect to clinic waiting times and other matters related to patient care.[54] Along these lines, legal scholar James O'Reilly has proposed the statutory creation of agency ombuds charged with responding to complaints about false and inaccurate agency speech (presumably including complaints about alleged agency lies). The United Kingdom has adopted a similar approach, creating an independent government watchdog agency specifically charged with assessing and publicizing the (in)accuracy of the government's speech.[55]

Legislatures' counterspeech includes censure resolutions.[56] As Laurence Tribe and Joshua Matz explain, a legislature's "resolution of censure is merely an expression of opinion rather than an individualized punishment by the legislature."[57] Recall the Senate's nineteenth-century censure of President Andrew Jackson. A century later, the Senate censured Joe McCarthy for his expressive abuse of his Senate colleagues.[58]

Even so, the Senate's expressive choice to censure McCarthy took a long time coming, and the conspicuous lack of resistance by other government speakers enabled McCarthy to thrive for as long as he did. As one of many examples, President Dwight D. Eisenhower abandoned plans to defend General George Marshall from McCarthy's verbal assaults; Eisenhower's silence

---

[54] VA. OFFICE OF INSPECTOR GEN., DEP'T OF VETERANS AFFAIRS, REPORT NO. 14-02603-267, VETERANS HEALTH ADMINISTRATION: REVIEW OF ALLEGED PATIENT DEATHS, PATIENT WAIT TIMES, AND SCHEDULING PRACTICES AT THE PHOENIX VA HEALTH CARE SYSTEM iii (2014).

[55] *See* Carl Bialik, *This U.K. Sheriff Cites Officials for Serious Statistical Violations*, WALL ST. J. (June 3, 2009, 11:59 PM).

[56] MICHAEL J. GERHARDT, IMPEACHMENT: WHAT EVERYONE NEEDS TO KNOW 113 (2018) ("Censure is a declaration of misconduct made by the House or the Senate. It takes the form of a simple resolution, which each chamber has the power to approve by a simple majority vote.").

[57] LAURENCE TRIBE & JOSHUA MATZ, TO END A PRESIDENCY 85 (2018). Of course, as Tribe and Matz further observe, "[t]he trick is ascertaining what effect, if any, a censure will have." *Id.*

[58] 100 CONG. REC. 16, 392–393 (1954).

only encouraged McCarthy's attacks.[59] For years, Republicans in Congress similarly declined to challenge their fellow party member because they found that his fearmongering worked to their political advantage. Only after Senate oversight hearings finally exposed his overreaching did McCarthy's popularity drop sufficiently to embolden the Senate to vote to censure him for what they found to be his "contemptuous" and "reprehensible" conduct.[60]

Impeachment

Legislatures' response to certain government officials' lies and other misconduct can include impeachment, and thus removal from office. On the federal level, the U.S. Constitution empowers Congress to impeach and convict federal judges and certain civil officers for "Treason, Bribery, or other high Crimes and Misdemeanors."[61] As legal scholar Michael Gerhardt explains, Congress has interpreted "civil officers" to mean "executive and judicial officials who wield substantial authority," and has interpreted impeachable offenses to "encompass serious abuses of power, breaches of trust and serious injuries to the Republic."[62] Impeachment thus offers a remedy for government officials' speech that inflicts more diffuse harms that elude judicial enforcement, like some of the lies about the government's justification for military intervention or its lies to avoid legal and political accountability (discussed in Chapter 4).

Andrew Johnson faced, but survived, impeachment charges that included those rebuking him for his allegedly intemperate speech. Richard Nixon faced impeachment for, among other things, his speech alleged to obstruct justice – but resigned before the full House could consider the charges. Bill Clinton also faced, but survived, impeachment charges for his speech alleged to violate perjury and obstruction of justice laws. In the twenty-first century, Congress impeached and convicted federal judge Thomas Porteous in part for his lies to the president, the FBI, and the Senate about his preconfirmation misconduct that included receiving kickbacks as a state court judge.[63]

---

[59] *See* JAMES B. RESTON, DEADLINE: A MEMOIR (1991) ("[T]he trouble with [Eisenhower's] technique of judicious leaving-alone was that McCarthy destroyed a lot of other people before Eisenhower finally had enough.").

[60] 100 CONG. REC. 16, 392–393 (1954).

[61] U.S. CONST. art. II, § 4 ("The President, Vice President and all civil Officers of the United States, shall be removed from Office on Impeachment for, and Conviction of, Treason, Bribery, or other high Crimes and Misdemeanors.").

[62] MICHAEL J. GERHARDT, *supra* note 56.   [63] *Id.* at 56.

To be sure, whether and when an official's lies or other misconduct justifies impeachment is a matter of considerable controversy. As Tribe and Matz observe in considering impeachment's possibilities for, and limitations in, addressing abusive governmental speech:

> There comes a point at which a president can properly be impeached for his statements. Nixon reached that point: the House Judiciary Committee included his public falsehoods in its article of impeachment for obstructing justice. By the same token, Congress may choose to consider Trump's public remarks bearing on the Russia investigation if it opens an impeachment hearing. More generally, a president may be impeached for his public statements when they are intimately connected to – or essential to the execution of – a broader course of corrupt and abusive conduct. But rarely, if ever, will words alone suffice for impeachment. That's true even of offensive statements that target vulnerable minorities and undermine demo-cratic institutions. Impeaching solely on the basis of a president's public remarks would verge dangerously close to accepting maladministration as a removable offense. Politicians frequently make imprecise, hyperbolic, insulting, flattering, and misleading comments. A politician who didn't could never make his way to the White House. Allowing Congress to remove a president on the ground that he has made divisive and incendiary public statement would only invite structural instability.[64]

Note that all of the options available to legislatures – including the enact-ment of statutes, vigorous oversight, and impeachment – require legislatures' political will. And that political will may be lacking when the contested government speech is politically popular, as can be the case of the govern-ment's speech that targets vulnerable individuals and groups. We now turn to the many actors other than legislatures who can help check the government's destructive expressive choices.

Other Governmental Actors' Counterspeech

Judges, of course, adjudicate disputes involving the government's speech, where they can attend to whether and when the government's speech threatens specific constitutional protections. But judges also play an important role in checking the government's destructive speech through their own speech in their concurrences, dissents, and statements off the bench. Recall, for example, federal district Judge Carlton Reeves's lengthy dictum detailing

---

[64] Laurence Tribe & Joshua Matz, To End a Presidency 65 (2018).

governments' longstanding display of the Confederate flag to communicate white supremacy (discussed in Chapter 3). More recently, Chief Justice John Roberts issued a public statement in response to President Trump's criticism of a federal judge who had issued a temporary injunction blocking the administration's new limits on political asylum appeals. A frustrated Trump told reporters, "This was an Obama judge. I'll tell you what, it's not going to happen like this anymore." Shortly afterward, Roberts asserted: "We do not have Obama judges or Trump judges, Bush judges or Clinton judges. What we have is an extraordinary group of dedicated judges doing their level best to do equal right to those who appear before them. That independent judiciary is something we should all be thankful for."[65]

Federalism principles – which divide power vertically among federal, state, and local governments – also offer structural means for other governmental actors to influence the government's expressive choices. These efforts include litigation, public pressure, and counterspeech. State attorneys general have often performed this function, for example, by challenging the federal government's choices that threaten constitutional protections.

Government speakers' own self-restraint provides yet another option, one upon which we have long relied. In other words, government officials can and should choose not to engage in lies, misrepresentations, and other expressive choices that undermine key constitutional values.[66] The more powerful the government actors involved, the more they should choose their words carefully.[67]

The government's own workforce is another precious source of counterspeech that challenges the government's destructive expressive choices. Sometimes this counterspeech takes the form of government workers' public protests, sometimes their internal resistance, and sometimes their more innovative forms of counterspeech. For example, in response to the Trump

---

[65] *See* Robert Barnes, *Rebuking Trump's Criticism of "Obama Judge," Chief Justice Roberts Defends Judiciary as "Independent,"* WASH. POST (Nov. 21, 2018) [https://perma.cc/2SYK-AJ8K].

[66] *See* Ted Finman & Stewart Macauley, *Freedom to Dissent: The Vietnam Protests and the Words of Public Officials,* 1966 WIS. L. REV. 632, 696–697 (1966) (urging government speakers who criticize private parties' protest to "behave in a manner calculated to promote rationality rather than error," exercise "more than ordinary care" to avoid misstatements, and couple "criticism of dissent with a reminder that protest and dissent are a vital part of the American tradition").

[67] As political scientist and legal scholar Corey Brettschneider counsels, for example, the government should "reject hate speech while still protecting it ... use your bully pulpit to explain that hateful viewpoints, though constitutionally protected, should be rejected outright by the people." COREY BRETTSCHNEIDER, THE OATH AND THE OFFICE 129 (2018).

administration's removal of climate change data from federal agencies' web-sites,[68] some National Park Service employees created a new Twitter feed to repost key information.[69]

Government officials can resist the government's destructive expressive choices not only through their voice, their counterspeech, but also through their exit – in other words, through their noisy resignation.[70] Memorable examples include the group resignation of the writers and journalists who staffed the federal government's Office of War Information (OWI) during World War II, protesting what they felt were the government's efforts to mislead the public (discussed in more detail in Chapter 6). Senator Daniel Patrick Moynihan resigned from the Senate Select Committee on Intelligence in response to then-CIA Director William Casey's lies about the government's mining of Nicaraguan harbors during the Iran-Contra affair; Moynihan returned to the Committee when Casey apologized.[71] And Gerald Ford's press secretary Jerry terHorst resigned because he thought the President had lied to him about his plans to pardon Nixon.[72]

The Press

Of course, the press itself is a source of counterspeech and pushback. At its best, the press challenges the accuracy of government's factual assertions at the time they're made, thus promoting public discussion and governmental self-reflection. As one of many examples, prodding by the press helped inspire the Surgeon General's report on the dangers of tobacco: when a journalist asked President Kennedy about the hazards of cigarettes at a press conference, the president had no answer and punted the matter to the Surgeon General.[73]

---

[68] See Juliet Eilperin, *Under Trump, Inconvenient Data Is Being Sidelined*, WASH. POST (May 14, 2017), https://www.washingtonpost.com/politics/under-trump-inconvenient-data-is-being-sidelined/2017/05/14/3ae22c28-3106-11e7-8674-437ddb6e813e_story.html [https://perma.cc/7H44-HN3F].

[69] See Abby Ohlheiser, *A Running List of All the Possible Subtweets of President Trump from Government Twitter Accounts*, WASH. POST (Jan. 27, 2017) [https://perma.cc/W9ZK-PR8A].

[70] See ALBERT O. HIRSCHMAN, EXIT, VOICE, AND LOYALTY: RESPONSES TO DECLINE IN FIRMS, ORGANIZATIONS, AND STATES (1970) (explaining that individuals can change organizational behavior through voice (i.e., counterspeech objecting to the group's behavior) or exit (i.e., demonstrating their unhappiness by leaving the group altogether).

[71] See Richard G. Powers, *Introduction* to DANIEL PATRICK MOYNIHAN, SECRECY: THE AMERICAN EXPERIENCE 3 (1998).

[72] See MARY E. STUCKEY, THE PRESIDENT AS INTERPRETER-IN-CHIEF 97 (1991).

[73] See MIKE STOBBE, SURGEON GENERAL'S WARNING: HOW POLITICS CRIPPLED THE NATION'S DOCTOR 121–122 (2014).

Of course, the press is not always at its best. Journalist James Reston, for example, chronicled the press's years-long failure to challenge Joseph McCarthy's expressive attacks:

> [M]ost news going to the papers and to the radio and television stations was comparatively free of analysis or even explanation. It was a sound enough theory and took into account everything but the arts of political deception. For example, putting quotation marks around McCarthy's false charges did not relieve us of complicity in McCarthy's campaign. Many newspapers condemned him on their editorial pages but gave him plenty of space on the front pages, which had more effect on public opinion. . . .[74]

The People Themselves: Politics and Protest

The people themselves have an important role to play in confronting and countering the government's destructive speech. Our political remedies include voting, campaigning, lobbying, petitioning, and protesting. And we the people can seek to cultivate habits of mind as both speakers and listeners to help influence our leaders' expressive choices. For example, we can be both more skeptical of our leaders' speech and simultaneously more open to the possibility that we ourselves (and our trusted proxies) may be vulnerable to mistake and error. We can recognize and challenge patterns in the government's destructive choices when they occur. For instance, because vulnerable individuals and groups pay a steep price when the government chooses its targets based on stereotypes and falsehoods, the public should remain skeptical of such claims and insist on evidence for the government's assertions.

These responses can seem especially limited at a time when expressive choices involving generosity, nuance, and humility rarely reap political rewards. But as puny as these efforts to challenge the government's destructive speech sometimes feel, the alternative – doing nothing – is doomed to failure. McCarthy – to name a particularly notorious government speaker – defied the norms of governmental discourse of his time, yet lasted nearly six years, at least in part due to the acquiescence of governmental and nongovernmental speakers alike. As legal scholar Geof Stone recounts, "[d]uring a speech on the [Senate] floor, McCarthy piled hundreds of documents in front of himself, supposedly substantiating charges of Communist infiltration. He defiantly dared any senator to inspect them." When Senator Herbert Lehman "walked to McCarthy's desk and held out his hand for the documents . . . [h]is fellow

---

[74] James B. Reston, Deadline: A Memoir 216–217 (1991).

senators lowered their eyes or looked away. McCarthy snarled under his breath, 'Go back to your seat, old man.'"[75]

As communications scholar Kathleen Hall Jamieson observes, "[t]he demise of Joe McCarthy demonstrates that a sustained form of rebuttal is required to dispel an entrenched form of guilt by association."[76] We can find no substitute for persistent pushback, on all fronts, to the government's speech that threatens our constitutional commitments.

---

[75] Geoffrey R. Stone, *Free Speech in the Age of McCarthy: A Cautionary Tale*, 93 CALIF. L. REV. 1387, 1398–1399 (2005) (quoting STEWART ALSOP, THE CENTER: PEOPLE AND POWER IN POLITICAL WASHINGTON 8 (1968)).

[76] KATHLEEN HALL JAMIESON, DIRTY POLITICS: DECEPTION, DISTRACTION, AND DEMOCRACY 71 (1992).

Conclusion

At its core, constitutional law addresses the uses and abuses of government power. This includes the use and abuses of the government's expressive powers. This book represents my effort to describe and explore the complexities of the constitutional questions triggered by the government's speech, and to offer a framework for thinking about those questions. My objectives also include highlighting the government's speech in its many manifestations, with its vast array of audiences, topics, means, motives, and consequences. The more we recognize the volume and variety of the government's speech in our lives, the more thoughtfully we can puzzle over its constitutional implications.

We're used to thinking about the constitutional rules that apply to what the government does, rather than what it says. We're used to thinking about speech as something that the Constitution protects, rather than something that itself might violate the Constitution. Thinking about the constitutional rules that apply to the government's speech invites important and challenging questions about both the nature of speech and the nature of government. What value does the government's speech offer, what dangers does the government's speech threaten – and does the Constitution protect us from those dangers?

Speech is complicated and powerful, and so is the government. The government's speech has unusual capacity for both value and harm precisely because of its governmental source. We need to empower our government to operate effectively to serve and protect us, even while we need to constrain its power to harm us. But this is no easy task, requiring care and attention to nuance. Efforts to identify constitutional constraints on the government's speech invite important concerns about the separation of powers, about courts' institutional competence to enforce those constraints, and about the possibility of deterring and dampening valuable government speech. For these reasons, we should often seek nonconstitutional responses to the government's destructive expressive choices. But under some circumstances, the government's speech infringes specific constitutional protections when it causes certain injuries or seeks to accomplish certain illegitimate purposes (even if we disagree about which ones).

The government's speech packs great power. Even – and perhaps especially – in times of grave crisis, the government's speech can be inspiring, humane, and successful in achieving essential public purposes. At times, however, the government's speech instead threatens, bullies, divides, and deceives for self-interested reasons, and sometimes with crushing results. Either way, the government's expressive choices are just that: the government's choices about whether and when to speak, what to say, how to say it, and to whom. This book identifies some of the motivations for and consequences of those choices, as well as the means for constructively influencing those choices that are available to courts, lawyers, other governmental actors, the press – and the rest of us.

Index

9/11 attacks, 2, 95
Abington Sch. Dist. v. *Schempp*, 82
abortion, 32–33, 45, 49–50, 127–150
ACLU v. *Capitol Square Review and Advisory Bd*, 69, 86
ACLU v. *Fordice*, 174
ACLU v. *Mabus*, 100, 163
ACLU v. *Mississippi*, 100, 163
Acosta, Jim, 175
Adams, John Quincy, 21
Adarand Constructors, Inc. v. *Pena*, 105
Addison v. *City of Baker City*, 162
Administrative Procedure Act, 225
affirmative action, 207
agriculture, 12
Agriculture, U.S. Department of, 12, 45, 51, 190, 193
AIDS epidemic, 22, 97
Alabama, 3, 82, 99, 101, 120, 123, 164
Alabama Libertarian Party v. *City of Birmingham*, 201, 203
Alien and Sedition Acts, 13, 176
Am. Commc'n Ass'n v. *Douds*, 159
Anderson v. *City of Boston*, 199
Anderson v. *Martin*, 108, 166, 213
Andrew v. *Clark*, 64
animus, 24, 86, 88, 106, 119–120, 125–126
anticlassification theory, 104, 108, 111, 114–115, 122, 125–126
antisubordination theory, 104, 108, 111, 113, 115, 125–126
Arendt, Hannah, 132
Ariz. Civil Liberties Union v. *Dunham*, 69, 92
Arizona, 69, 118, 143
Arkansas, 83, 97, 223

Arkansas Educational Television Comm'n v. *Forbes*, 28–29
Associated Press, 179
Attorney General, 103, 123, 158, 164, 214
attorney's fees, 213, 217

Backpage.com v. *Dart*, 161, 214
ballot initiatives, 26, 189, 199, 201, 204–205
ballot speech, 108, 146, 166–167
Bantam Books, Inc. v. *Sullivan*, 160, 214
Bartley, Numan, 22, 99, 118
Battle v. *Board of Regents*, 62
Bd. of Ed. of Westside Comm'y Sch. v. *Mergens*, 47
beef, 34–35, 50, 64
Bezanson, Randall, 208
Bible, the, 69, 82, 84, 86, 92
Black, Hugo, 82, 164
Blackmun, Harry, 32, 168
Bloomberg, Michael, 96
Blum v. *Yaretsky*, 109, 175
Board of Regents of Univ. of Wisconsin System v. *Southworth*, 34, 118
Boaty McBoatFace, 48
Bolling v. *Sharpe*, 93
Bormuth v. *County of Jackson*, 75
Bradley v. *Hall*, 146
Branzburg v. *Hayes*, 178
Brennan, John, 175
Brennan, William, 148, 198, 201–202
Brettschneider, Corey, 229
Brewer, Susan, 12, 21, 132
Breyer, Stephen, 128
Brown v. *Board of Education*, 22, 98, 105
Brown, Pat, 206
Bruff, Harold, 14, 17–18

Buckley v. *Fitzsimmons*, 218
Bumper v. *North Carolina*, 138
Bureau of Labor Statistics, 209
Bush v. *Vera*, 115
Bush, George W., 2, 16, 59, 95, 130, 181, 209,
    224, 229
Buss, William, 208

California, 14, 153, 206, 224
Cambodia, 131
Campbell v. *Joint Dist. 28*, 200
Carey v. *Piphus*, 216
Carter v. *City of Las Cruces*, 200
Carter, Jimmy, 100
Caruso v. *Yamhill County*, 146
Casey, William, 230
CBS v. *Democratic National Committee*, 31
censure, 14, 21, 226
Centers for Disease Control and Prevention,
    13, 209
Central Intelligence Agency, 131–132, 175, 210,
    230
Chafee, Zechariah, 187
Chafetz, Josh, 4, 7, 15, 219
Chase, Samuel, 15
Chemerinsky, Erwin, 189
Chi. Bar Ass'n v. *White*, 146
China, 211
Choice-in-Education League v. *Los Angeles
    Unified Sch. District*, 201
Christianity, 70, 74, 78, 86
Christmas, 78, 84
Church of the Lukumi Babalu Aye, Inc. v. *City
    of Hialeah*, 87
Church, Frank, 14
Citizens to Protect Public Funds v. *Board of Ed.
    of Parsippany-Troy Hills*, 197
Citizens United v. *Federal Election Comm'n*,
    178, 202
City Affairs Committee of Jersey City v. *Bd. of
    Comm'rs of Jersey City*, 198
City of Cleburne v. *Cleburne Living Center*, 117
City of Ladue v. *Gilleo*, 46
City of Los Angeles v. *Lyons*, 89, 215
City of Pleasant Grove v. *Summum*, 35–39, 44,
    46
City of San Diego v. *Roe*, 65, 166
Civil War, the, 17, 42, 93, 95, 185
Civilian Conservation Corps, 13
Clapper, James, 130
climate change, 45, 206, 209, 230

Clinton v. *Jones*, 218
Clinton, Bill, 180, 223, 227, 229
Cnty. of Allegheny v. *ACLU*, 47, 69, 75, 77–78,
    80, 88, 213
Cnty. of Sacramento v. *Lewis*, 152–153
Cnty. of Santa Clara v. *Trump*, 87
Coffman v. *Colorado Common Cause*, 200
Colby, Thomas, 152
Cold War, the, 96
Coleman v. *Miller*, 120
Colorado, 87, 117–118, 205
Comey, James, 180
Committee on Public Information, 12, 190
Communism, 32, 90, 158, 164
Confederate flags, 39–40, 119–124
Confederate symbols, 19, 39, 42, 45–46, 51,
    94–95, 99, 122, 224, 229
Congressional committees, 2, 14–15, 18, 48, 101,
    125, 132, 157, 173, 224, 228, 230
Congressional Record, 4
Conn. Dep't of Pub. Safety v. *Doe*, 149
Connerly, Ward, 206
Connick v. *Myers*, 65
Cook v. *Gralike*, 166
Corbin, Caroline Mala, 76
Cornelius v. *NAACP Legal Defense and
    Educational Fund, Inc.*, 36
Coszalter v. *City of Salem*, 162
counterspeech, 14, 100, 209
creation science, 69, 83
creches, 69, 75, 78, 84
Creel, George, 191
Cronkite, Walter, 177
crosses, 69, 75, 86, 95
Cuban missile crisis, 129

damages, 26, 90, 111, 213–218
Daniels v. *Harrison Cnty. Bd.*, 120
Daniels v. *Williams*, 153
Darby, Joseph, 225
Davis v. *Monroe Cnty. Bd. of Educ*, 110
Davis v. *Zant*, 135
Davis, Elmer, 192
Davison v. *Randall*, 57
declaratory relief, 26, 213, 215, 218
deep fake technologies, 55, 181
defamation, 148–149, 213, 218, 222
Defense of Marriage Act, the, 125
desegregation, 22, 97–98, 100, 107, 123, 173
Detainee Treatment Act, 16
Dewey, Thomas, 22

digital expressive technologies, 53, 56
disability, 147
District of Columbia, 1, 21
Doe v. McMillan, 218
Doe v. Silsbee Ind. Sch. Dist., 60
Driver, Justin, 139
Dudziak, Mary, 96

Edwards v. Aguillard, 69, 83
Eisenhower, Dwight D., 21, 69, 97, 129, 170,
    194, 226
Elk Grove Unified Sch. Dist. v. Newdow, 79, 84
Ellsberg, Daniel, 132
Elsenau v. City of Chicago, 198
Emancipation Proclamation, the, 185
Emerson, Thomas, 157, 188, 205, 220
Engel v. Vitale, 68, 81
Epperson v. Arkansas, 69, 83
Equal Rights Amendment, 200
Espionage and Sedition Act, 191
evolution, 69, 83
Ewing, Oscar, 194
Ex parte Tipton, 146

Farrar v. Hobby, 217
Federal Bureau of Investigation, 2, 103, 163,
    179–180, 225, 227
Federal Emergency Management
    Administration, 13
Federal False Statements Act, 222
Federal Reserve Board, 22
Federal Tort Claims Act, 222
federalism, 11, 17, 70, 208, 229
Federalists, 15, 145
Felt, Mark, 225
First National Bank of Boston v. Bellotti, 201
Fish v. Kobach, 145
flags, 19, 42, 45, 47, 52, 89, 94, 99, 121, 174, 224,
    229
Florida, 16, 98
football, 47, 68, 77, 85, 174
Foraker v. Chaffinch, 62
Ford, Gerald, 230
Foreign Agents Registration Act, 167
Forrester v. White, 217–218
Free Exercise Clause, 47, 87
Freedom from Religion Found., Inc. v. Obama, 91

Garcetti v. Ceballos, 61–67, 225
Georgia, 99–100, 120–121, 123
Gerhardt, Michael, 226–227

Gertner, Nancy, 16
Ginsburg, Ruth Bader, 59
Gitlow v. New York, 161
González v. Douglas, 118
Government Accountability Office, 20, 195
Gravel, Mike, 219
Griffin v. Department of Veterans Affairs, 42
Grutter v. Bollinger, 116
Guarantee Clause, 5, 198, 204
guns, 14, 209

harassment law, 110–111, 122, 124, 216
hard power, 7
Harlow v. Fitzgerald, 218
Harper v. Virginia State Bd. of Elections, 145
Harris v. Forklift Systems, Inc., 110, 113
Health and Human Services, U.S. Department
    of, 32
health care legislation, 194
Health, Education, and Welfare, Secretary of,
    196
Heffernan v. City of Paterson, 171
Hein v. Freedom from Religion Found., Inc., 90
Hentoff v. Ichord, 173
heuristics, 44, 146, 205, 208
Hill, Jessie, 143, 150
Holder, Eric, 103
homosexuality. See sexual orientation
House Un-American Activities Committee,
    157–158
Hughes, Charles Evan, 15
Hunt, Lester, 158
Hutchinson v. Proxmire, 218

Illinois, 146
Illinois v. Perkins, 137, 140
immigrants, 101
immunities, governmental, 111–112, 147, 217,
    219, 222
impeachment, 15, 18, 134, 227–229
In God We Trust, 69, 75, 79, 84
injunctive relief, 26, 164, 212, 214
inspectors general, 226
Int'l Refugee Assistance Project v. Trump, 115
Internal Revenue Service, 13, 185
Iran-Contra, 230
Iraq, 12, 21, 130
Islam, 86–88, 90, 95, 103

J.D.B. v. North Carolina, 139
Jackson, Andrew, 14, 17, 226

Jamieson, Kathleen Hall, 232
Japanese-Americans' internment, 1, 95, 102, 135
Jefferson, Thomas, 13, 17, 19, 145
Johanns v. Livestock Marketing Ass'n, 34–35, 37, 39–40, 42, 50, 203
Johnson, Andrew, 18, 98, 114, 227
Johnson, Lyndon B., 2, 94, 130–131
Joint Anti-Fascist Refugee Committee v. McGrath, 90, 164, 214
Jones v. Clinton, 223
Joyner v. Forsyth County, 213
justiciability, 10, 24, 89, 133

Kaepernick, Colin, 175
Kagan, Elena, 78, 172
Kavanaugh, Brett, 91
Keller v. State Bar of California, 31
Kennedy, Anthony, 72–75, 77, 140
Kennedy, John F., 19, 104, 129, 230
Kennedy, Robert F., 123
Keyishian v. Bd. of Regents, 27
Kidwell v. City of Union, 204
King County Council v. Public Disclosure Comm'n, 201
King, Martin Luther, 48, 64, 94
Kitrosser, Heidi, 66
Knight First Am. Inst. v. Trump, 56, 58, 215
Koop, C. Everett, 97
Kopman v. City of Centerville, 110, 216, 218
Korematsu v. United States, 102, 136
Kreimer, Seth, 165–166
Kungys v. United States, 222

Laird v. Tatum, 90
Landrieu, Mitch, 94
Lane v. Cent. Ala. Comm. College, 63
Lane v. Franks, 63
Laos, 131
Latif v. Holder, 136
law enforcement officers' speech, 129, 136–139, 221
Lawrence v. Texas, 101, 125
Lee v. Weisman, 47, 68, 73, 140, 213
Legal Services Corp. v. Velazquez, 29
legislative oversight, 15, 35, 134, 209, 215, 226–227, 229
Lehman, Herbert, 231
Lemon v. Kurtzman, 81
LePage, Paul, 103
Lessig, Lawrence, 44, 220
Lewis v. United States, 136

Liberty & Prosperity 1776, Inc. v. Corzine, 60
license plates, 1, 39, 49, 51–53, 69, 86
Lincoln, Abraham, 17, 170, 185–186
Lippmann, Walter, 12
Lombard v. Louisiana, 107
Louisiana, 83, 94, 107, 109
Lujan v. Defenders of Wildlife, 89
Lund v. Rowan County, 75
Luther v. Borden, 198
Lynch v. Donnelly, 69, 77, 84
Lynumn v. Illinois, 138

Madison, James, 13
Madsen v. Women's Health Ctr., Inc, 141
Marsh v. Chambers, 68, 73
Marshall, George, 226
Marshall, Thurgood, 140
Massaro, Toni, 28, 149, 154, 159
massive resistance, 98, 100, 118, 123–124
Masterpiece Cakeshop, Ltd. v. Colorado Civil Rights Comm'n, 87
Matal v. Tam, 40–41
Matz, Joshua, 221, 226, 228
McCamy, James, 185, 192
McCarthy, Joseph, 101, 157–158, 165, 219, 226, 231
McCreary Cnty. v. ACLU, 69, 80, 213
McNamara, Robert, 7, 11, 131, 156
Meese v. Keene, 90, 167
Memphis Community Sch. Dist. v. Stachura, 216
menorahs, 75, 78
Meritor Savings Bank v. Vinson, 110
Mexico, 130
Miller v. Cal. Commission on the Status of Women, 203
Miller, William Lee, 21
Mines v. R.F. Del Valle, 198
Miranda v. Arizona, 5, 136–137, 139, 221
misappropriation, 181–182, 221
misattribution, 181–182, 221
Mississippi, 2, 98, 100, 121–122, 124, 162, 173
Mississippi State Sovereignty Commission, 100, 162, 173
Missouri, 14, 166
Model Code of Judicial Conduct, 16, 222
Model Rules of Professional Conduct, 16, 222–223
monuments, 19, 36–38, 46, 52, 69, 94, 124
Moore v. Bryant, 121–122, 124
Morales v. Jones, 63

Moran v. Burbine, 140, 153
mottos, government, 1, 7, 52, 69, 75, 79, 86
Mount Healthy City Sch. Dist. v. Doyle, 66
Mountain States Legal Foundation v. Denver Sch. Dist #1, 198
Moynihan, Daniel Patrick, 230
Mueller, Robert, 227
Murphy, Frank, 102, 136
Muslims, 86, 96, 103, 117
Myers v. Thompson, 16

NAACP v. Alabama, 164
NAACP v. Hunt, 120
Nadel v. Regents of Univ. of Cal., 222
Nat. Res. Def. Council v. U.S. Forest Serv., 225
National Endowment for the Arts v. Finley, 188
National Environmental Protection Act, 225
National Football League, 174–175
National Park Service, 230
National Rifle Association, 209
Nativity scenes. *See* creches
Nazis, 21, 133, 193
Neal v. Clinton, 223
New Deal, 13, 170, 185, 192–193
New Hampshire, 7, 52
New York, 81, 96, 103
Newdow v. Roberts, 91
Nicaragua, 180
Nixon v. Fitzgerald, 218
Nixon, Richard M., 1, 7, 18, 130–131, 177, 179, 219, 227–228, 230
North Carolina State Conference of NAACP v. McCrory, 145
Nullification Proclamation, 17

O'Connor, Sandra Day, 76–79, 84, 125, 167
oaths, 4, 63, 75, 99, 221, 226
Obama, Barack, 19–20, 94, 130, 196, 219, 229
obstruction of justice, 227
Office of War Information, 192, 194, 230
Ohio, 15, 69, 86, 189
Oklahoma, 86
Okwedy v. Molinari, 161
Opinion Clause, the, 4

Page v. Lexington County Sch. Dist. No. One, 54, 204
Paige v. Coyner, 162, 216
Palm Beach County v. Hudspeth, 199–200
Papandrea, Mary-Rose, 130

Parents Involved in Cmty. Schs. v. Seattle Sch. Dist. No. 1, 104
Patent and Trademark Office, 40
Paul v. Davis, 148–149
Pearl Harbor, 131
Pell v. Procunier, 178
Pennsylvania, 142
Pentagon Papers, 7, 11, 130, 132, 156, 219
Penthouse Int'l, Ltd. v. Meese, 172
People v. Thomas, 138
perjury, 221, 223, 227
Petition Clause, 197
Pickering v. Board of Education, 65
Planned Parenthood, 32, 49, 143
Planned Parenthood of Southeastern Pennsylvania v. Casey, 141–143, 152, 230
Playboy Enterprises, Inc. v. Meese, 214
Pledge of Allegiance, the, 7, 52, 69, 75, 79
police officers' speech, 55, 129, 137, 139–140
political question doctrine, 133
Polk, James K., 130
Porteous, Thomas, 227
Porter v. Tiffany, 197
postage stamps, 48–49
Powers, Francis Gary, 129
prayer, 8, 24, 47, 68, 73–74, 77, 81–82, 85, 90
privacy, invasion of, 128, 147–148, 165, 213
proclamations, 14, 16, 29, 92
propaganda, 90, 99, 132, 167, 172, 191, 193–196, 200
prosecutors' speech, 135, 138, 148, 160, 223
proselytization, 75
public employees' speech, 23, 30, 52, 60, 63, 65, 229
public forum doctrine, 35, 37, 39, 42, 55, 57, 204

Reagan, Ronald, 95, 130, 180
Rees v. Carlisle, 197
Reeves, Carlton, 124, 228
Rehnquist, William, 167
remedies, 26, 63, 146, 212–215, 219, 222, 231
reproductive rights, 134, 144, 147, 150
resolutions, 13–14, 29, 99, 226
Reston, James, 157, 231
Reynolds v. Sims, 144
Rhode Island, 84
Rice v. Cayetano, 104, 114
Roberts, John, 229
Robinson v. City of Edmond, 86, 213
Rochin v. California, 153–154

Roe v. Wade, 141, 143
Romer v. Evans, 117–118
Roosevelt, Franklin D., 15, 19, 22, 170, 177, 192
Roosevelt, Theodore, 18, 190
Rosenberger v. Rector and Visitors of the University of Virginia, 33
Rumsfeld v. Forum for Academic and Institutional Rights, Inc, 29
Russia, 228
Rust v. Sullivan, 32–34, 37, 49, 61

Santa Fe Indep. Sch. Dist. v. Doe, 47, 68, 77, 85, 213
Scalia, Antonin, 72, 74–75, 126, 188
school vouchers, 1, 54, 64, 204
separation of powers, 11, 17, 89, 133, 208, 212, 226, 233
sexual orientation, 3, 38, 93, 101, 111, 124, 147
Shepard, Matthew, 38
Shiffrin, Steven, 188
Shilts, Randy, 98
shock-the-conscience test, 155
slavery, 21, 98, 124
Slobogin, Christopher, 137
Smith v. Cherry, 146
Smith, Steven, 119, 185
Smokey Bear, 1, 13
Snowden, Edward, 130
social media, 19–20, 53, 55, 57, 196–197
Social Security, 13, 185
soft power, 7
Solicitor General, U.S., 1, 95, 135
Sotomayor, Sonia, 59, 87
source cues, 46, 49, 51, 207
Souter, David, 35, 38, 61, 80, 149
South Carolina, 54, 69, 86, 99
South Dakota, 143
Speech or Debate Clause, 4, 218–219
Spiegla v. Hull, 62
standing, 76, 89–92, 119, 121–124, 133, 215
Stanson v. Mott, 188, 198, 200
State of the Union address, 2, 4, 17, 19, 28, 133, 194, 225
Stephens, Alexander, 124
Sterling v. Borough of Minersville, 147, 216, 218
Stern v. Kramarsky, 200
Stevens, John Paul, 28, 38, 66, 105, 140
Stewart, Potter, 31
Stone v. Graham, 83
Stone, Geoffrey, 101, 163, 231
Stuckey, Mary, 17, 20, 22, 170, 177, 190, 230

Suhre v. Haywood Cty, 91
Summers v. Adams, 69, 86, 213
Surgeon General, 1–2, 7, 28–29, 97, 156, 196, 230
Sylvester, Arthur, 129

Take Care clause, 5
Tam, Simon, 40
Tebbe, Nelson, 150, 169, 176, 189
Ten Commandments, 36, 69, 75, 83
Tennessee, 83
terHorst, Jerry, 230
Texas, 3, 39, 101, 142
Thanksgiving proclamations, 68
Thomas, Clarence, 70, 105
tobacco, 1–2, 7, 28–29, 156, 196, 206, 230
Tonkin Gulf, 131–132
totalitarianism, 184, 200
Town of Greece v. Galloway, 68, 70, 73–74, 77
trademarks, 40
transparency, 6, 23, 30, 43, 53, 64, 208
Tribe, Laurence, 221, 226, 228
Trudeau v. FTC, 172
Truman, Harry, 194
Trump v. Hawaii, 87, 117, 136
Trump, Donald J., 1, 14, 20, 22, 56–59, 86, 145, 153, 174–178, 209–210, 227, 229–230
Tuchman, Barbara, 132
Tuggle v. Mangan, 110, 123
Tulis, Jeffrey, 19
tweets, 20, 58, 174
Twitter, 20, 48, 56, 58–59, 145, 174, 230

U.S. Dep't of Agriculture v. Moreno, 117
Udall, Mark, 219
undue burden, 141–144, 150–151
United Kingdom, 48, 223, 226
United States v. American Library Association, 28
United States v. Anderson, 153
United States v. Black, 154
United States v. Byram, 137
United States v. Carolene Products Co., 219
United States v. Gilliland, 222
United States v. Kalfayan, 135
United States v. Rogers, 138
United States v. Virginia, 107
United States v. Windsor, 114, 116–117, 125
Utah, 36

Vardaman, James, 2, 98
Vargas v. City of Salinas, 198

Vermont, 13
Veterans Administration, 42, 226
Vietnam, 1, 7, 12, 130–132, 158, 172, 229
Village of Arlington Heights v. Metropolitan Housing Corp., 117
Virginia, 13, 22, 99, 145
voter fraud, 145

W.E.B. Dubois Club, 158
Walker v. Texas Div., Sons of Confederate Veterans, 28, 39, 51
Wallace v. Jaffree, 69, 82
Wallace, George, 48, 99, 123
Washington v. Davis, 107, 116
Washington, George, 17, 190
Watergate scandal, 130, 177, 225
Watts v. United States, 160
websites, 1, 53–55
Weise v. Casper, 59–60
West Virginia State Bd. of Education v. Barnette, 10, 52
West, Sonja, 178
Westmoreland, William, 132
Whalen v. Roe, 147

whistleblowers' speech, 63, 134, 221, 229
white supremacy, 3, 98, 114, 118, 123, 175
Whole Woman's Health v. Hellerstedt, 142
WikiLeaks, 12
Wilkinson, J. Harvie, 64
Williams v. Herron, 110, 123
Williams-Yulee v. Fla. Bar, 16
Wilson, Pete, 206
Wilson, Woodrow, 13, 18, 96, 102, 190
Winkler, Allan, 192–193
Wise, David, 131, 157, 177
women's suffrage, 96
Woodlock v. Orange Ulster B.O.C.E.S., 62
Wooley v. Maynard, 7, 52
World War I, 12, 18, 96, 102, 132, 190–191
World War II, 1, 21, 28, 95, 102, 131–132, 135, 167, 192, 230
Wright v. Rolett Cnty, 110
Wyden, Ron, 130, 219
Wyoming, 38

Yudof, Mark, 186, 209, 212, 220

Zablocki v. Redhail, 141

For EU product safety concerns, contact us at Calle de José Abascal, 56–1°,
28003 Madrid, Spain or eugpsr@cambridge.org.

www.ingramcontent.com/pod-product-compliance
Ingram Content Group UK Ltd.
Pitfield, Milton Keynes, MK11 3LW, UK
UKHW020330140625
459647UK00018B/2102